How Hysterical

Religion/Culture/Critique
Series editor: Elizabeth A. Castelli

How Hysterical: Identification and Resistance in the Bible and Film
By Erin Runions
(2003)

HOW HYSTERICAL

IDENTIFICATION AND RESISTANCE IN THE BIBLE AND FILM

ERIN RUNIONS

First published 2003 by
PALGRAVE MACMILLAN™
175 Fifth Avenue, New York, N.Y. 10010 and
Houndmills, Basingstoke, Hampshire, England RG21 6XS.
Companies and representatives throughout the world.

PALGRAVE MACMILLAN is the global academic imprint of the Palgrave Macmillan division of St. Martin's Press, LLC and of Palgrave Macmillan Ltd. Macmillan® is a registered trademark in the United States, United Kingdom and other countries. Palgrave is a registered trademark in the European Union and other countries.

ISBN 0-312-29572-3
ISBN 0-312-29573-1 (pbk.)

Library of Congress Cataloging-in-Publication Data

Runions, Erin.
   How hysterical : identification and resistance in the Bible and film / Erin Runions.
      p. cm. – (Religion/culture/critique 1)
   Includes bibliographical references and index.
      ISBN 0-312-29572-3 – ISBN 0-312-29573-1 (pbk.)
      1. Social problems in motion pictures. 2. Motion pictures—Moral and ethical aspects. 3. Motion pictures—Religious aspects. 4. Sociology, Biblical. I. Title. II. Series.
PN56.S48R86 2003
7891.43'6822–dc21   2002044715

A catalogue record for this book is available from the British Library.

Design by Newgen Imaging Systems (P) Ltd., Chennai, India.

First edition: August 2003
10 9 8 7 6 5 4 3 2 1

Printed in the United States of America.

This book is dedicated to six political comrades, who are good friends and salutary influences:

Adrienne Gibb
Anna Kruzynski
Michael Casey
José Henriquez
Daniel Lang/Levitsky
Meredith Slopen

CONTENTS

SERIES EDITOR'S PREFACE

RELIGION/CULTURE/CRITIQUE is a series devoted to publishing work that addresses religion's centrality to a wide range of settings and debates, both contemporary and historical, and that critically engages the category of "religion" itself. This series is conceived as a place where readers will be invited to explore how "religion"—whether embedded in texts, practices, communities, or ideologies—intersects with social and political interests, institutions, and identities.

How Hysterical: Identification and Resistance in the Bible and Film by Erin Runions not only inaugurates the series but also elegantly embodies the theoretical values around which the series is organized. Runions reads canonical and contemporary theoretical texts with, through, and against biblical texts and Hollywood cinema. The purpose of these readings is first to disrupt the identifications with systems of dominance that the Bible and (both studio-produced and independent) film tend to naturalize and then to imagine alternative points of identification that can serve a wide-ranging politics of resistance. In *How Hysterical,* Runions is not interested in uncovering how "religion" or "the Bible" is represented in cinema, but in how the ideological structures of the biblical text constitute Western culture's "primal scene," a scene that is re-enacted symptomatically in surprising cultural spaces. By creating a theoretically sophisticated set of critical lenses through which her readers might gaze, Runions offers a truly innovative and provocative model for reconceptualizing the relationship between religion and culture.

Elizabeth A. Castelli
RELIGION/CULTURE/CRITIQUE Series Editor

New York City
February 2003

PERMISSIONS

The author and editors gratefully acknowledge the permissions of the following journals and publishers to reprint these essays in their revised form: Sheffield Academic Press for "Hysterical Phalli: Numbers 16, Two Contemporary Parallels, and the Logic of Colonization," in George Aichele, ed., *Culture, Entertainment and the Bible* (2000), pp. 182–205; and also for portions of Erin Runions, *Changing Subjects: Gender, Nation, and Future in Micah*, Playing the Texts 7 (2001); the Society of Biblical Literature for "Zion is Burning: Gender Fuck in Micah," from *Semeia* 82 (1998), pp. 225–46; Trinity International Press for "Why Girls Cry: Gender Melancholia and Sexual Violence in Ezekiel 16 and *Boys Don't Cry*," in George Aichele and Richard Walsh, eds., *Screening Scripture: Intertextual Connections Between Scripture and Film* (2002), pp. 188–214.

ACKNOWLEDGMENTS

Book writing seems so solitary, but in reality it is a collective endeavor. I have many people to thank for their help and support in this particular effort. Let me begin with the people to whom this book is dedicated, those who have given me hope in what seems like an apocalyptic and fascistic time of hopelessness, living in New York City. First, two lifelines and soul mates: Adrienne Gibb, for her sharp insights into politics and culture, for hours of emotional and political processing, and for teaching me a little of her art of creating bodily comfort; and Anna Kruzynski, with whom I have grown up and hope to grow old politically, from whom I have and continue to learn about life and politics, and whose unsurpassed energy, keen analysis, and incredible organizational skills are a constant source of inspiration. Then there is my as-yet-unnamed affinity group to thank: José Henriquez (ad hoc member), whose sarcasm and skeptical enthusiasm have made many hours at demonstrations, meetings, parties, and bars more enjoyable, and who has persistently encouraged me in writing this book, as well as the previous one; Daniel Lang/Levitsky, whose combination of creativity and intellect is truly brilliant and has given rise to endless hilarious and productive conversations; Meredith Slopen, political dynamo and fellow ranter against patriarchy in activism; and Michael Casey, jester, pixie, fellow traveler, whose insights, humor, and creative vision have woken me to new possibilities and have made my life a better place.

I owe a debt of gratitude to those whose friendship and academic mentoring have made it possible for me to continue: Dave Diewert, who first got me interested in careful reading of the Hebrew Bible, and who then encouraged me to make the links to radical politics; Robert Culley, for challenging me to hone those skills and for continuing to offer encouragement and support; and Elizabeth Castelli, who has sponsored me as a postdoctoral fellow at Barnard College, and whose generosity, wit, wisdom, and skill as a scholar make her a phenomenal role model and mentor. During my time at Barnard, I have also been extremely fortunate to have been permitted to audit seminars with Elizabeth Castelli, Gayatri Spivak, Ann Pellegrini, David Eng, Gil Anidjar, and Taylor Carmen, all of whom have challenged me to think harder and differently. I am also grateful to

Fiona Black and Scott Kline, two colleagues whose intellectual friendship has been formative and is ongoing, through and beyond grad school. Both Fiona and Scott have challenged me to be a better scholar through the quality of their own work; and equally important, their friendship keeps me sane. I have also been grateful and proud to have two more senior colleagues, Jennifer Glancy and George Aichele, take an interest in my work; both have become good friends and have been incredibly encouraging and helpful.

In terms of institutional support, I have been most fortunate to have been the beneficiary of le Fonds FCAR for two years of postdoctoral funding, for which Barnard College's Center for Research on Women, and Department of Religion graciously granted me institutional affiliation. Moreover, the programming at the Center for Research on Women, under the direction of Janet Jakobsen, has been extremely thought provoking and has helped to develop my interest in the relationships between identification, emotion, and politics.

In addition to these various forms of support, I must thank those who have read portions of this text and given invaluable feedback: George Aichele, Guy Austrian, Michael Casey, Elizabeth Castelli, Adrienne Gibb, Jennifer Glancy, Scott Kline, Anna Kruzynski, Daniel Lang/Levitsky, Mutaamba Maasha, Loris Mirella, Rosamond Cary Rodman, and Yvonne Sherwood. The arguments made here have been made clearer and stronger because of these careful and insightful readers; any faults that remain are my own. In addition to those to whom I have dedicated the book, I would also acknowledge the influence of Liz Bishop, Guy Austrian, Ayça Çubukçy, Mutaamba Maasha, and Loris Mirella, all of whom have the invaluable quality of depth and nuance in radical political analysis, and whose friendships I appreciate greatly. I am also grateful to Guy Austrian for his most superior skill in making editorial suggestions, copyediting, and helping to prepare the manuscript; and to Michael Casey for helping with the index. And I am much indebted to the folks at Palgrave, especially Amanda Johnson in so adroitly seeing the project through, and Rick Delaney for his excellent editing and editorial comments. Finally, I am, as always, grateful to the various members of my immediate and extended family for their foundational and ongoing support and love.

Erin Runions
October 2002

List of Film Stills

Introduction

Identification and Resistance

This book is concerned with the intersection of two crucial but perhaps overlooked political influences, the Bible and film. As bell hooks suggests, viewers' identifications with images affect how they see themselves and how they act, which can in turn powerfully affect the political constellation in which they find themselves. hooks cites filmmaker Pratibha Parmar, who writes, "Images play a crucial role in defining and controlling the political and social power to which both individuals and marginalized groups have access. The deeply ideological nature of imagery determines not only how other people think about us but how we think about ourselves" (quoted in hooks 1992, 5). The same thing might be said of religion, and perhaps doubly so of images grounded in religion. Religious texts and images, as well as received interpretations of them, hold out points of identification not only for adherents to the faith represented, but also, increasingly, for those who identify as spiritual. The religious images and ideas with which people identify help to mold their actions and political stances.

Indeed, those concerned with political change, social transformation, and the fight against oppression have found it essential to include in the political calculus the influence of images and religion on identity formation. The Bible is, of course, a dominant religious influence in the West, one that persistently finds its way into images in popular culture. This book therefore examines biblical images, themes, and sensibilities in a number of popular films. Specifically, I am interested in the ways that both the Bible—most often here the Hebrew Bible, though at times the Christian New Testament—and popular film are similar with respect to questions of identification with and resistance to hegemonic and oppressive societal norms and ideals. Both the Bible and popular film tend to assume and demand very specific kinds of identifications, but at the same time to open up unlikely spaces for alternate identifications. This book looks at the points of identification held out by the Bible and film for readers and viewers. It explores the way that various points of identification normalize oppressive political and cultural configurations such as colonization, patriarchy, the heterosexual gender binary, wealth, and whiteness.

The method used is one of comparing biblical and filmic texts, by focusing them through theoretical lenses. I use what might broadly be defined as poststructuralist, psychoanalytic, Marxist theory (including feminist, queer, postcolonial, and ideological critical approaches) to discuss the similarities that emerge in each chapter between biblical passage(s) and film. Each chapter uses theory to read a film with and against a similar biblical text, regardless of whether the Bible appears as direct citation in the film. The premise here is that whether or not the Bible is obviously present in a cultural product, it still often acts as a kind of "primal scene," which gets repeated in various ways through popular culture, creating similarities where they may be least expected. In comparing seemingly disparate texts, the similarities and differences can bring to light and critique sites of identification and resistance that might otherwise be obscure. This approach to reading is important because the Bible remains a culturally defining text, and so the world it projects, as part of culture, may be influential on the same level as film. The Bible may also influence film and theory in all sorts of hidden ways. While it is not my intent to set out the points of convergence and divergence in the way that biblical and filmic texts operate within culture, I take as a starting point the notion that they both contribute to, reinforce, and occasionally challenge norms for thinking about race, colonialism, gender, and sexuality, as well as the types of identification that sustain or resist these norms.

If identification determines ideological positioning and subsequent action, as Louis Althusser would have it (see chapter 1), then attending to possibilities for alternative points of identification is crucial in mobilizing resistance. As film theorists have been pointing out, viewers (or readers) do not necessarily only identify with the norms most obviously or formally offered up as points of identification;[1] they also sometimes identify differently, resistantly (Diawara 1988; Glendhill 1988; Hansen 2000 [1986]; Stacey 1994, 1999 [1991]). Thus, I am also interested in the configurations of texts and intertexual relations that might prompt these kinds of alternate identifications. This work is not a study of actual audience identification (e.g., Stacey 1999 [1991]), but rather of emerging possibilities for resistant identification.

Five of the six films chosen here—*Light it Up, Remember the Titans, Three Kings, Paris Is Burning, Boys Don't Cry*, and *Magnolia*—depict, in some way, real-life situations of systemic and individual violence and political struggle. While these films present interpretations of real events, their reality factors make discussions of them translatable to ongoing political struggles. For instance, *Light it Up* directly addresses the question of police brutality in New York City, and it alludes to the particular case of the unarmed young African immigrant, Amadou Diallo, shot forty-one times by four police officers in the Bronx. *Remember the Titans* is the retelling of a high-school football team's struggle in Virginia to integrate black and white players and of their success in uniting the town. Dealing with race in a more brutal fashion, across nations, *Three Kings* is a fanciful depiction and critique of the colonial violence of the U.S. invasion of Iraq in 1991. *Paris Is Burning*—a documentary on drag queens in Harlem—shows the gendered articulation of race and class, in its record of the hopes, struggles, and violence lived by lower-income, transgendered and/or gay, black, and Latina/o people in New York City. *Boys Don't Cry* also addresses the problem of violence against transgendered people, in a retelling of the murder of Brandon Teena in 1995. Although the sixth film, *Magnolia*, does not have clearly signaled real-life references, it addresses the real and present issues of patriarchy and the day-to-day impact of media, in particular of television.

The fact that biblical citations or similarities with biblical texts appear in the retelling of these stories indicates that both movie-makers and the movie-going public may rely more heavily than directly apparent on biblical themes, tropes, and images in understanding and interpreting political issues and events. One might not immediately suppose that biblical passages—such as the prophetic texts of Isaiah, Ezekiel, and Micah, the apocalyptic text of Revelation, or the narrative tales of Cain and Abel, the exodus, Korah's rebellion, and the visit of the Magi to the infant Christ—are at work in the cultural imagination about political conflicts. But it is with and through such texts that these political struggles are projected into culture. Contemporary stories of oppression, struggle, and resistance are often strangely similar to biblical stories and themes, or they are interpreted directly through biblical themes and images. Contemporary retellings of political struggles deploy, resemble, modify, or differ from biblical themes in ways that both reveal a little of how those struggles are already interpreted and influence how they will be interpreted in the future. Moreover, where they occur explicitly, biblical images offer up familiar and perhaps emotionally comfortable points of identification. Such homely points of identification position viewers in very specific ways with respect to the privileges and oppressions arising from colonialism, patriarchy, the heterosexual gender binary, wealth, and whiteness. Even where biblical images are not directly present, similarities to biblical themes and passages might affect on which side of an issue viewers choose to position themselves. If the Bible is thus present in film, and if film is one of the ways by which such events and struggles become available to people and by which people align themselves with or against the oppressed, then the interrogation of the cross-fertilization between the Bible and film may be helpful in strategizing resistance.

My thinking on resistance to various forms of oppression grows out of my own overlapping and changing positions. The readings I offer in this book have been shaped by my social location as a white anti-(neo)colonialist activist, and an academic. The themes in this book have percolated for years in my involvement first in the student movement, and then in anarchist organizing against the military, the prison industry, police brutality, and transnational capital. In this work, it has become increasingly apparent to me that social change can only come through a process whereby people's ideological commitments shift; but effecting such a shift is an extremely complex task. It seems to me that understanding the conscious and unconscious emotional attachments and identifications that are at the heart of these commitments is crucial to understanding how people might begin to identify differently.

During the time I developed my political thinking, I also moved along academically, out of publicly funded education and into the Ivy League. Through political conversation, reflection, and transition, I have learned that I must contend with my own immense privilege and its implication in the structures I critique. During my time in New York City, I have had especially to confront my own embeddedness in the ubiquitous structures of white supremacy. This realization has caused me to step back and reconsider my place within the activist world. Where once I thought I could save the world (like so many liberals-turned-anarchists before me), now I know that I can only begin to join the struggle because others who have experienced oppression more directly have led and continue to lead the way. I write this book as an ally in the struggles against racism, sexism, and neocolonialism. I hope that the study of the Bible and film through a mixture of theory and politics can help, in some small fashion, to break down the cultural processes that hold these oppressions in place.

The Bible, Film, and Theory

Other scholars' analyses of biblical images in film have opened up space for reading the political implications of viewers' identifications with biblically weighted popular films.[2] Three works in particular are foundational to the kind of work I do. First, Bruce Babington and Peter William Evans (1993) argue that earlier Hollywood biblical epics (1920s–1950s) are the secularized dramatizations of the religious bases of U.S. life. As such, these epics depict the political subtexts of the United States versus its (many) enemies in biblical terms (1993, 14, 53–58). Thus, Babington and Evans show that the political use of biblical imagery is part of the Hollywood tradition.

Along slightly different lines, the essays in Alice Bach's edited *Semeia* volume, *Biblical Glamour and Hollywood Glitz* (1996), examine how filmic depictions of biblical stories take on contemporary preoccupations and anxieties, which then get read back onto viewers' understandings of the biblical texts employed. This process strangely modifies the influence of the Bible on culture. In this volume, a number of articles initiate important political discussions, which *How Hysterical* adjoins, regarding the construction of gendered and racial identities through filmic use of biblical and early Christian themes. For instance, Jennifer Glancy (1996) explores how the film *Demetrius and the Gladiators* takes up the "dialectic of slavery and gender" (1996, 143) in a way that reflects the political concerns of the 1950s. She shows how the film's black slave, Glichon, is presented as truly free, thus acting "as a catalyst to self-reflection on the part of the white subject" (1996, 140–41). The black slave's strength of character merely acts as a springboard for the movement into ideal and free masculinity for Demetrius. Though not said in so many words, Glancy's argument suggests that the film thus sets up an ideal, free, white masculine hero as a point of identification for viewers. Judith Weisenfeld (1996) goes one step further when she argues that filmic depictions of African American identity through religious and biblical themes positions African Americans in specific ways with respect to inclusion or exclusion from American national identity. Weisenfeld clearly demonstrates the politically motivated construction of varying points of identification through biblical images. In the case of King Vidor's *Hallelujah*, "the self-contained black world . . . exists merely as a shadow of an absent, yet strongly-implied white world that sets a standard for 'true' religiosity" (Weisenfeld 1996, 162). In contrast to Vidor, Oscar Micheaux "presents African Americans as able to construct a bridge between themselves and sympathetic white Americans through the practice of Christianity" (Weisenfeld 1996, 162).[3]

Similarly, the essays in the volume *Screening Scripture: Intertextual Connections Between Scripture and Film*, edited by George Aichele and Richard Walsh (2002), lays the groundwork for the kind of analysis I do in this book. These essays look at the interplay between the Bible and film, in what the editors call the translation of Scripture into film and the transformation of Scripture in the process (2002, viii–ix). A number of the essays in this volume take up cultural criticism and psychoanalytic theory to aid in their analyses, using theorists such as Jean Baudrillard and Walter Benjamin (Aichele 2002; Pippin 2002), Sigmund Freud and Jacques Lacan (Boer 2002; Kelso 2002), and Antonio Gramsci (Dyck 2002). This kind of theoretical analysis of the Bible and film (see also Aichele 1997; Boer 1998; Glancy 1996; Koosed and Linafelt 1996) sets the stage for the kind of work to which I put theory in this volume.

Building on these readings of the Bible and film, but moving in a slightly different direction, *How Hysterical* has a pointed and political focus. I am less concerned with reading direct citation of Bible in film (though sometimes biblical allusions provide a way into recognizing a larger biblical undercurrent) than I am with analyses of a more hypostatized biblical influence. I am certainly not the first to have read Bible and film (or TV) together without necessarily reading Bible *in* film (e.g., Rowlett 2000; M. E. Donaldson 1997; Aichele 1997; Rosenberg 1998; Boer 1999, 33–52; Pippin 2002; Brabban 2002; Staley 2002; Burnett 2002). What is distinctive about the way that Bible, film, and theory are read here is the persistent turn to contemporary situations, to what Benjamin might call the "time of now." As already indicated, my underlying argument is that the Bible influences culture not only through film, but also through the ways that political events and issues are understood and engaged.[4]

This kind of political reading of the Bible and film falls within the larger category of cultural-studies approaches to biblical studies. Biblical scholars have begun exploring the impact of Bible on culture and vice versa, in works ranging from explorations of the appearance of biblical texts in cultural configurations, to the British-school, political, anticapitalist analysis of culture.[5] Though, as Stephen Moore points out, there is a branch of biblical cultural studies that "seems to have sprung up entirely independently of non-biblical cultural studies" (1998a, 20), there is another branch that has brought a welcome analysis of biblical texts through cultural critics such as Michel Certeau, Homi Bhabha, Stuart Hall, Zygmunt Bauman, Benjamin, Judith Butler, and Slavoj Žižek. And there is yet another type of biblical cultural studies: as Moore points out, Fernando Segovia has used the term "cultural studies" to refer to the increasing attention paid to the cultural positionality of biblical interpreters and critics, and to a critical analysis of all readers of biblical texts and their reading strategies (Segovia 1995; 2000). *How Hysterical* fits into these two latter strands of cultural biblical studies, with their use of theory, attention to ideological processes, and concern with readerly identifications.

Although, as Moore suggests, the work of Louis Althusser has been crucial to the development of cultural studies outside of biblical studies—and there is no doubt that his work plays an important role in this book—I would like to push backward and outward in delineating the intellectual heritage for cultural studies. The questions of identification, resistance, and ideology that come up again and again in these essays are ones that are particularly well addressed by cultural critics, theorists, and philosophers, who, like

Althusser, either make use of the writings of G. W. F. Hegel, Karl Marx, Freud, and Lacan, or who can be read productively with (or against) them. For instance I make use of feminist, queer, poststructural theorists Butler and Lee Quinby; postcolonial theorist Bhabha; ideological critics Benjamin, Althusser, and Žižek; and philosophers Alexandre Kojève, Jacques Derrida, Baudrillard, and Paul de Man. There is, of course, a genealogy here, beginning with Hegel and radiating out through Marx and Freud. In spite of Freud's own disavowal of his philosophical heritage (Derrida 1987 [1980], 259–91), his work is often used in conjunction with Hegel and Marx in contemporary philosophical and psychoanalytic thought. Kojève especially helped make the link between Hegel and psychoanalytic theory for a generation of theorists, especially through his discussion of Hegel's thinking on desire (and in this list, he especially influenced Lacan, positively, and Althusser, negatively). Likewise Derrida, de Man, Lacan, and Althusser have mediated, modified, and deconstructed Hegel, Freud, and Marx for another generation of theorists, influencing Žižek, Butler, Bhabha, Quinby (via Foucault), and Baudrillard.

To be sure, there are significant differences and complex discussions between many of these thinkers, which it is not my purpose to outline here. But I note their common philosophical heritage because their conceptual convergences are not accidental, nor are the similarities in the themes that emerge in this book, in drawing on them. More importantly, these theorists' attention to concepts such as the unconscious, the subject's positioning within language, processes of identification, material determinants for cultural and political formations, and the possibilities for reading differently and for subverting the dominant order has made their writings useful to the kind of ideological critical work I do here. Though at times I read these theorists critically (especially Kojève, Žižek, and Baudrillard), they are all helpful in thinking through the inner workings of the films and texts, as well as the positioning of the reader with respect to these texts. Moreover, these influential and/or resistant philosophical and theoretical rubrics bring into view the particular political stakes of identification with, or resistance to, the films' narratives. So for instance, reading the biblical quotations in *Remember the Titans* through Hegel and Kojève shows how the film sets viewers up to misrecognize contemporary forms of racism in the United States, such as the prison industrial complex (chapter 2). Likewise, reading *Boys Don't Cry* and Ezekiel 16 alongside Butler's description of gender melancholia suggests that the violence in these texts might be the social working-out of heterosexual gender identifications (chapter 5).

A couple of qualifications are in order here. First, evidently, the theory I employ is not primarily film theory, nor am I trying to make a specific intervention into film theory, so much as into biblical studies and cultural studies. Space does not permit me to engage the plethora of film theory that also uses the thinkers engaged here. I am aware, however, that these discussions are taking place, and I try to indicate points of intersection. Second, in laying out these writers' thoughts, I do not pretend to be revealing something undiscovered. This theory has been well read, analyzed, and critiqued by many before me. I read it again because I believe that it enables thinking about the Bible and film together in new ways. I hope that these essays will serve to introduce the theory to those unfamiliar, in a way that moves beyond merely reiterating it, to thinking through it critically. Moreover, there is some repetition of key theoretical points throughout the book, because each chapter is designed to stand on its own, as well as to contribute to the overall argument of the book (which is more synchronic than diachronic). And finally, I would stress that all of the arguments in this book are only *readings* of the Bible and film. In other words, I do not try to lay out the definitive reading of these texts, but rather to offer what I hope are persuasive readings showing the kinds of identifications urged by the Bible and these films, as well as the alternate identifications they might provoke.

Hysteria

Resistance is not the most obvious or usual response to the oppressions established through identification with dominant norms. More frequently, resistance to oppression is met with a set of powerful prohibitions and ingrained responses that bar the way to change and maintain the status quo. Resistance is often met with some kind of disdain, whether violent or simply patronizing. Resistance gets called hysteria. This appellation both codes resistance as effeminate (hysteria being a term largely applied to women) and denigrates women at the same time. Thus, *How Hysterical* explores, in various and sometimes indirect ways, the misogynist trope of hysteria as it relates to identification and resistance.

The connection between hysteria, identification, and resistance is furnished by psychoanalysis. In psychoanalytic terms, hysteria is considered failed identification with the dominant, patriarchal (symbolic) order. Juliet Flower McCannell reads this failure, along with Freud, as the failure to identify with the appropriate gender, so that "the hysteric subject unconsciously demands, 'Am I a man or a woman?'" (2000, 29). David Eng reads this failed identification more broadly, in discussing the failure of clearly defined racial identification (also bound up with the question of masculine identification). In treating narratives about Asian American men, Eng shows the difficulty for Asian Americans in identifying fully with either "Asian" or

"American" (2001, 182). As failed identification, hysteria might be read as what Homi Bhabha calls "liminal identification," that is, identification with a point that is neither here nor there: it is in-between. Hysteria represents a different kind of identification, an identification with difference.

Reading hysteria as a resistant, alternate form of identification, an identification with difference, moves in a slightly different direction from Anne Freidberg's assertion that "identification can only be made through recognition, and all recognition is itself an implicit confirmation of the ideology of *status quo* . . . a compulsion for sameness, which, under patriarchy, demands critique" (1990, 45). The idea here is that an identification can be formed with something or someone not quite recognizable either as self or other.

I would further suggest that these and other kinds of failures in identification—for instance, failure to identify with the capitalist order—are caused by resistance. Indeed, in psychoanalytic terms, hysteria is caused by a resistance to remembering or knowing an earlier traumatic event in the hysteric's life (and for Freud, these were sexual traumas). For Breuer and Freud, hysteria is the excessive and visceral representation of a forgotten traumatic wound. It is the conversion of a trauma onto the body (Breuer and Freud 1955 [1893–1895], 10–11, 206). As Freud puts it, the hysteric puts up resistance to an incompatible idea, "forced out of consciousness and out of memory" (Breuer and Freud 1955 [1893–1895], 269).[6] Not only is hysteria caused by resistance, however; it also enables resistance by revealing the possibility of alternate identification to others. Nonetheless, hysteria, like so many other liminal states and practices, is ambivalent. Thinking of hysteria in this way may open up a different route through the question that feminists have raised as to whether or not hysteria is subversive of authority and patriarchy, or whether it simply gives reasons for them to be perpetuated. As an alternate point of identification, hysteria might be de facto subversive; but then again, it might also be recuperated, pulled from the margins into the center, depending on what incompatible ideas it shuts off (see chapters 2 and 3). Thus I read the designation "hysteria" in its ambiguity, exploring its capacities for resisting as well as for capitulating to dominating norms.[7]

That being said, "hysteria" does not figure in the forefront of all of the chapters. Rather, it often appears through related concepts: excess, trauma, the sublime, apocalypse. All of these concepts have to do in some way with loss, through resistance or blockage, and the remainder of that loss. The hysterical symptom is the excessive remainder of a lost or forgotten trauma; like the sublime, it represents the unrepresentable; like apocalypse, it cryptically makes known things hidden.[8] This is not to say that these concepts are strictly equivalent, but to say that there is a homology between them, a correspondence between their theoretical structures and behavioral properties. The two chapters that deal most explicitly with hysteria are chapters 1 and 3, while the other chapters explore it obliquely.

Chapter 1, "Hysterical Phalli: Numbers 16, Gustafsen Lake, *Light it Up*, and Police Brutality," looks at how resistance to identification with the state and the law produces hysteria where it may be least expected. Here I read Žižek's Lacanian reformulation of Althusser's notion of ideological interpellation to explore the logic of the relation between violence and resistance. I look at three portrayals of violence in response to resistance: the biblical story of the squelching of Korah's rebellion, the filmic story of police violence against youth of color in Queens, and the news accounts of heavy, militaristic police attack on aboriginal traditionalists in northwestern Canada in 1995. In each narrative, agents of the law respond violently to acts of resistance. Althusser's conflation of law and ideology and Žižek's phallocentric description of ideology structured around a volatile, socially grounded antagonism give some clue as to why the phallic law erupts the way it does. Failed identification on the part of protesters does not render them hysterical, so much as it unveils the fundamental social antagonism in a way that sends the law itself—that is, the phallus—into hysterics.

Chapter 2, "Hollywood's Hegel Reads the Bible: *Remember the Titans*, Race Relations, and the Prison Industrial Complex," looks at the sublime character of the Hebrew poetry employed in *Remember the Titans* and its use in building a misrecognition of current forms of racism. On the surface, this chapter is the one least concerned with hysteria. Here I build on the Althusserian framework established in chapter 1 to examine the ideological impact of the Hegelian work to which biblical citations are put in *Remember the Titans*. This film about U.S. race relations—enacted through the story of a football team forced to integrate black and white players—resembles the narrative of Hegel's master–slave dialectic in a way that is particularly pressing to interrogate when thinking about the prison industrial complex as the new form of slavery in the United States. The biblically enhanced Hegelian subtexts of desire, master–slave recognition, and work-as-perfection undermine the seemingly progressive message of the film. Through filmic use of the Bible, the white viewer is positioned as master to misrecognize the situation of the increasingly enslaved U.S. black and Latina/o population. Taking the analysis of biblical quotations one step further, following Paul de Man's suggestion (1983) that Hegel's *Aesthetics* may reveal the Achilles' heel of the Hegelian dialectic, I look at how the biblical quotations found in the *Aesthetics* might inform an analysis of the Hegelian dialectic at work in the film. De Man shows that for Hegel, Hebraic poetry is the sublime, and as such it is external to the dialectic. I suggest that the film's use of sublime Hebrew poetry may be a symptom of what is excluded from the film's treatment of race, that is, the systemic racism that keeps a frighteningly large number of people of color incarcerated and held "in storage" (cf. Breuer and Freud 1955 [1893–1895], 133), like the incompatible idea of racism that has been split off from society's consciousness. Thus it would seem that the biblical text acts as a hysterical symptom in that it enables the forgetting of traumatic, systemic violence.

Chapter 3, "Framing the Golden Fetish: *Three Kings* and the Biblical Exodus Tradition," deals explicitly with hysteria in its ambivalence. In this chapter, I read hysteria as excess and consider why (and how) its potential for subversion is itself subverted. I take up the notion that the hysterical symptom is the leftover, or remainder, of a trauma. Along these lines, I use Baudrillard's notion of the simulacrum as a springboard into a discussion of the postmodern trope of "supplement" as it relates to the hysterical symptom. I notice that Baudrillard's description of the simulacrum as symptom is much like Derrida's discussion of frame as supplement. Because Baudrillard called the media coverage on the war in the Gulf simulacral, likening it to a hysterical symptom, and because the supplement is hailed far and wide as the harbinger of subversion par excellence, I ask why one particular excessive media portrayal of the war in the Gulf, *Three Kings*, does not inspire resistance to the ongoing attack on Iraq by the United States. Turning to the biblical frame, I find that it is enmeshed with several other frames, all of which are peripheral to the film's gold fetish. This elaborate and interlocking set of frames is also implicated in a complex set of relations between sexism, messianism, humanism, commodity fetishism, and colonialism. Ultimately, the film's frames position the viewer to support, rather than resist, U.S. imperialism. Thus in this context, the film's biblical framing takes on the role of a hysterical symptom as a defense against recognition of the trauma of war.

Chapters 4 and 5 pick up the theme of cross-gendered identification that appears in some of Freud's writings on hysteria (1959 [1908]; 1959 [1909], 230).[9] Here I am interested in transgendered identifications as failed identifications with binary gender norms, and also as engendering resistance to those norms. Chapter 4, "Zion is Burning: Genderfuck and Hybridity in Micah and *Paris Is Burning*," treats the transgression of gender codes in Micah and the film *Paris Is Burning*. The metaphorical bodies that appear in Micah are compared with the real bodies that appear in drag in *Paris Is Burning*. I argue that the representation of gender in these works produces what queer theorists have called "genderfuck," but that they do so in a way that resembles Homi Bhabha's conception of hybridity. That is, both film and text reveal the imperfect imitation produced by the colonizing and narcissistic demand for mimicry. This hybridity fucks with hegemonic norms of gender, as well as race (in *Paris Is Burning*) and national identity (in Micah). And yet, if hysteria is read positively, as the bodily expression of resistance to dominating norms, then transgenderists and queers perform hysteria fabulously: with glitz, glamour, and wisdom that give it an enviable flair. As might be expected, this kind of resistance is met with violence in both the film and the text. Yet the violence with which gender transgressions are met destabilizes the structures in film and text by calling into question the ideals upheld as natural, pure, or authentic. Moreover, the hybridity produced in Micah and *Paris Is Burning* is, like hysteria, a liminal state, one that invites alternate identifications. By offering up points of identification characterized by difference, the film and text challenge viewers and readers to interrogate their own responses to dominant textual and social gender norms.

Chapter 5, "Why Girls Cry: Gender Melancholia and Sexual Violence in Ezekiel 16 and *Boys Don't Cry*," looks at the relation between the trauma of losing same-sex loves, the production of gender identity, and violence against women. Ezekiel 16 is a text that describes Yahweh's sanction of horrific violence toward his beloved Jerusalem. *Boys Don't Cry* portrays equally horrific violence toward a female-to-male trangenderist, Brandon Teena, after he has been revealed as biologically female. The sexual violence in both film and text can be read as the acute and traumatic manifestation of what Butler has called the gender melancholia at work in heterosexual identity, that is, a melancholia produced by the ungrieved loss of a same-sex love. Butler's theory of gender melancholia, as well as the Freudian texts on which she draws, show up the traumatic nature of heterosexual identification in film and text, enacted through the matrix of social relations. The gender identifications of Jerusalem and Brandon can be said to be the result of a lost same-sex love. At the same time, the violence against Brandon and Jerusalem might be said to be the repudiation of femininity required for their male aggressors (John and Yahweh, respectively), on their way to establishing heterosexual masculine identifications. Thus, it would seem that the violence in these texts depicts the social enactment of the violent drama of the super-ego, as it appears in melancholia and in post-traumatic stress disorder. This suggests that the loss of same-sex attachments is a constitutive trauma, which haunts the ego through social violence. But remarkably, these interactions also open up various identificatory positions for readers and invite divided gender identifications and sexual preferences. These texts are, therefore, hysterical. They resist the norms of heterosexual gender formation and make available alternative points of identification.

Chapter 6, "Falling Frogs and Family Traumas: Mediating Apocalypse in *Magnolia*," looks at the relation between the apocalyptic revelation of trauma and the hysterical embodiment of that trauma through varying forms of representation. This chapter deals with hysteria on a different register, by reading the film's strangest scene, the biblically inspired falling frogs, as a sort of hysterical symptom that marks the unveiling of the family traumas that cause the dysfunctions in the film's two parallel families. Here trauma is lived out hysterically and cataclysmically with the rain of frogs. But rather than simply occluding the past, the frogs bring with them a recognition of the forgotten past harms of televisual, patriarchal capitalism— a recognition that sets the characters on their various roads to emotional health. Thus, the frogs are revelatory and apocalyptic, and in this fashion they amplify the biblical thematics of the film. Because the frogs' apocalypticism is also intertwined in the film with the trauma caused by television, Benjamin's work dealing with media, memory, and trauma helps to clarify the film's muted discourse on media. The various modes of representation that the film interrogates (television, film, unique art work) are considered in terms of Benjamin's descriptions of modern media, shock, aura, and the interruption of tradition. In this light, it seems that director Paul Thomas Anderson aligns film with the revelatory, apocalyptic, falling frogs, as a medium—unlike television—that has potential to break through oppressive traditions. Nonetheless, the film's apocalyptic imagery is rendered somewhat ineffectual as a liberatory discourse by the history of apocalypse's entanglement with misogyny and colonialism. Thus the political potential that Anderson seems to attribute to the medium of film is also called into question.

How Hysterical ends, then, where it starts, with hysteria's ambiguity. As a strategy of psychic resistance, hysteria seems to be ambiguous in its ability to provoke political resistance. But as a visible marker of trauma, or failed identification, hysteria can offer up alternative points of identification to those that ground the status quo. Thus the arguments in this book move from hysteria's negative capacity to divert attention away from political violence and trauma to its more positive role of creating liminal points of identification that might counteract violent ideologies, before coming to rest on its ambiguity. These kinds of vacillations are perhaps not surprising to find in the material studied, given the range of uses to which both the Bible and popular film are put. The challenge in creating resistance to hegemonic norms of gender, I suppose, rests with the viewer or reader who is able to choose whether to allow hysteria to efface political traumas and violence, or to allow those traumas to touch them through identification with the difference made visible by hysteria.

Chapter 1

Hysterical Phalli: Numbers 16, Gustafsen Lake, *Light it Up*, and Police Brutality

Resistance—that is, resistance to identification with norms of dominant ideology—seems consistently to provoke excessive violence. This is nowhere more obvious than in consideration of police brutality. In the United States, over 200 people are killed by police each year. Some of those shot only inadvertently resist dominant ideology, in particular, the white middle-class norm, by being mentally ill. Many of those killed by police are unaggressive and unarmed people of color, both adults and children, who are resistant simply by the very fact of their skin color.[1] Police and state violence is also carried out on those who have taken more deliberately resistant stances, like the members of black radical organization MOVE, whose residence was bombed by the police in Philadelphia, or members of the Black Panther Party and the American Indian Movement, who were targeted by the FBI's COINTELPRO (see Harry 1987; Abu-Jamal 2001; Churchill and Vander Wall 1988; Shakur 1987). White middle-class activists like myself have only more recently been clued into the reality of police violence in large numbers, having been subjected to increasing police brutality brought on by demonstrations of resistance to current forms of global trade.

However, aggressive response to resistance is not a new concern in Western culture. Indeed, one of its founding texts, the Hebrew Bible, contains prototypes. The squelching of "Korah's rebellion" in Numbers 16 is one such story. In discussion of the relationship between resistance to ideology and excessive violence, Numbers 16 might be fruitfully compared to two contemporary stories of police brutality: the Royal Canadian Mounted Police's brutal siege and attack on aboriginal traditionalists, now known as the Ts'Peten Defenders, in 1995 at Gustafsen Lake (in northwestern Canada); and the too-real filmic representation of violence and intimidation used by the New York City Police Department in response to high school students' protest in the film *Light it Up* (2000), directed by Craig Bolotin. The similarities between these stories come to light when read alongside the discussion of ideological interpellation (a theory of how individuals come to act in accordance with dominant ideology) offered by Marxist philosophers and ideological critics, Louis Althusser and Slavoj Žižek.[2] More specifically, Žižek's psychoanalytic (Lacanian) rereading of Althusser's theory of the subject formed in ideology details the inner workings of ideological interpellation. These details open up the space for thinking a little differently about why the dominant order and the law respond as they do to protesters' refusal to be interpellated.

Both biblical and contemporary narratives in some way or another censor resistance to ideological interpellation. Korah leads a group of supporters who refuse to follow Moses as the chosen leader of the people of Israel. The Ts'Peten Defenders refuse to recognize the provincial government, or in legal terms, "the crown" (Canada technically still being ruled by the Queen of England), and its ownership of land. And the six students (known as the Lincoln Six) who occupy Lincoln High School in *Light it Up* refuse the demands of the school authorities to be quiet about the terrible conditions in which they are forced to learn. In return for these various resistances, all are submitted to drastic punishment and violence. Although the biblical story is not *directly causal* for contemporary responses to resistance to ideology,[3] I would like to point out that, when read alongside Žižek at least, the ideological operation provoking violence is remarkably alike in all of these accounts. The similarities may of course be coincidental, they may be a result of reading with theory, or they may even hint that theoretical writing is not devoid of biblical logic and influence. Nonetheless, a logic very similar to the one inhabiting the violence in Numbers 16 toward "rebellion" on the verge of entry into Canaan operates in these other two more contemporary accounts of resistance to the interpellation. This may indicate a biblical influence operating as a kind of groundspring for increasing intolerance to resistance in the West, which may be important to interrogate.

There are of course qualifications to be made about my treatment of these three accounts of resistance and the move I am making in reading them alongside Žižek. First, they are quite different in many ways, not least in their various statuses as "texts" and the transparency with which they incorporate both official and resistant discourses. Numbers 16 and *Light it Up* are both delimited as discrete texts. The story of Gustafsen Lake, on the other hand, cobbled together from official media reports and from the witnesses of the Ts'Peten Defenders themselves (see ABC 1997; *Above the Law* 1997), is therefore available in more versions than the others; the official and resistant versions of the story are accessible by the general public.[4] In stark contrast, Numbers 16 is much more opaque and does not easily delineate the competing discourses it comprises, though, as I will indicate, it has been pried apart by scholars to posit its official and resistant currents. *Light it Up* lies somewhere between these two poles; it is based in part on actual events and includes representations of official media discourses, but it is shot from the perspective of resistance. By reading these accounts together, thematically and theoretically as I do, I necessarily flatten out some of these distinctions.

Second, Žižek's Lacanian rereading of Althusser is only one out of many theoretical possibilities for consideration of police and state violence; however, his discussion of the realm beyond interpellation (that realm in which excessive violence, call it hysteria, manifests itself) provides a way into thinking through the why and how of the *excess* of violence in a way that takes into account material, ideological, and psychoanalytic structures. My use of Žižek is more than just an exercise in high theory; it is an attempt to think differently about the complex relations and identifications (conscious and unconscious, oppressive and resistant) made between individuals and structures. This sort of theoretical scrutiny of the various processes of ideological identifications may, in some small way, help to open up spaces for new forms of creative identification and resistance. Moreover, Žižek's theorizations enable a critical theoretical account of the real and present problem of police and state brutality in a way that seeks both to emphasize it as a grave reality, and also to show how theoretical privileging of the phallus may be complicit with this violence in more ways than are already obvious.

Althusser and Police Brutality

It may be pertinent to start with the theory on which Žižek builds, that is, Althusser's compelling and well known account of the subject's relationship to ideology. Althusser posits the subject's formation through ideological interpellation (from the French *interpeller*, to question someone, or to demand a response). As he states in his famous essay "Ideology and Ideological State Apparatuses" (1984), "Ideology hails or interpellates concrete individuals as concrete subjects" (1984, 47). In this way, he suggests that individuals respond to the call of the ideological order, and in so doing are transformed into subjects and positioned as compliant. Althusser likens this ideological interpellation to the hailing of a police officer, "Hey, you there," to which the hailed individual turns around as if guilty, and in the act of recognizing the call's address becomes a subject (1984, 48). Thus a person addressed and interpellated by ideology recognizes—or more properly *misrecognizes*—herself in ideology. This process of interpellation might be thought of as an individual (mis)recognizing herself in the image or name given to her through cultural discourses. The individual thus identifies with that image, and conforms to it.

Police brutality is a contemporary problem with which Althusser's metaphor contends. In using the example of a police officer hailing the subject, Althusser of course meant to invoke the law, rather than the individual police officer. What is interesting about his choice of illustration, though, is that it hints at what really might be at stake. His purpose in this passage is not actually to speak about the police and the law, but rather to describe the working of what he calls ideological state apparatuses (religious institutions, political parties, families, schools, newspapers, unions, etc.). The ideological state apparatuses function, without force, to ensure the smooth operation of the state by offering discourses and images with which individuals can identify and understand their positions within the social order and within the relations of production (1984, 18). They hail the individual and urge her to conformity. However, in using the image of the police officer, Althusser seems strangely to mix the work of the ideological state apparatuses with the repressive state apparatus (police, courts, prison, army), those that do use force. Yet, perhaps this overlap between ideological and repressive apparatuses is not so incongruent, since, as he says, the repressive apparatus is necessary for the functioning of the ideological apparatus: "The State apparatus secures by repression . . . the political conditions for the action of the Ideological State Apparatuses" (1984, 24). Police and state repression enable dominant ideology to do its work. Thus, *state violence is a necessary condition for the formation of the subject* through the hailing of the ideological state apparatuses.

The law, for which the police officer stands in, seems, for Althusser, to be another necessary condition for ideological interpellation. In places, Althusser comes close to treating ideology and the law as synonymous, by persistently using the metaphor of law to express the everpresent working and structure of ideology. For instance, he uses examples of religious discourses addressing and interpellating believers to be subject to a preexisting law. Here he gives the example of Moses' obedient response to Yahweh in giving the law to the people (1984, 51–54). Believers become subjects, he argues, in being subjected to the divine law.[5] Likewise, individuals recognize, obey, and are subject to the secular law. In so doing, he argues, they recognize their own position as being in accordance with that law, they recognize (or misrecognize) that "they really do occupy the place it designates for them as theirs in the world" (1984, 52). In other words, ideology, or the law, simultaneously recruits and subjugates subjects, so that individuals believe that theirs is a normal or "natural" subject position. That the individual hailed by the law "turns round, believing/suspecting/knowing that it is for him," says Althusser, shows that the subject is always-already interpellated into ideology (1984, 49).

In describing the always-alreadiness of interpellation, Althusser continues to conflate law and ideology, using an example that reveals the influence of psychoanalysts Jacques Lacan and Sigmund Freud on his conceptualization of the legal metaphor. He borrows Freud's illustration of an infant already called by the "Father's name" before its birth, to describe the pre-given "ideological configuration in which [the subject] is expected" (1984, 50), into which the subject is always-already interpellated. Just as the child is always called by her father's name, the subject does not know a time when she has not been interpellated. Of course, what is important here is that for Freud and Lacan the "name of the Father" is not just a surname, it is also a metaphor for law, though here a more general order of law (e.g., Lacan 1977 [1966], 66–67, 310–11, 321–23). For Lacan in particular, the law is equated with the paternal phallus, which rules against incest (the Father forbids the child's incestuous desire for its mother). The law is, for Lacan, the phallus (1977 [1966], 311). Though Althusser does not draw out the relation between the phallus and ideology implicit in his various metaphors and illustrations, the phallic law is an element, as I will show presently, that gets picked up and built upon in Žižek's rereading of ideological interpellation. That the law is called phallic may be mere semantics, but since, despite protestations to the contrary, it lines up power with the masculine, the metaphor is one that bears some scrutiny.

In sum, there is, in Althusser's work, a relationship between ideology, the phallic law (in ancient, modern, and psychoanalytic terms), which is the condition for interpellation, and the repressive state apparatuses that secure the conditions for interpellation. To be precise, Althusser's account of repressive and ideological state apparatuses indicates that *state violence secures the conditions in which the law, that is the phallic law, can work to ideologically interpellate subjects.* What then, when subjects resist interpellation? It would seem that the repressive state apparatus must go to work to ensure that ideological interpellation will take place; if not, the subject risks elimination.

Ideology Filling in for the Lack in the Symbolic Order

Though state and police violence might be a necessary condition for interpellation, the constant, almost hysterical *excess* of the violence is not accounted for in Althusser's formulation. Here the interrelation that Žižek draws out between phallic law, ideology, desire, fantasy, and social antagonism using Althusser's framework suggests new ways to think about the seemingly irrational excess of violence. Žižek's reformulations show that ideological interpellation takes place through desire for and identification with the phallus/law by means of a fantasy object. As the accounts of excessive violence to be discussed here illustrate, when identification with the phallus/law fails, social antagonism erupts violently.

Žižek renders Althusser's theory of interpellation both more complicated and more phallic by likening it to Lacan's psychoanalytic theory of signification. Žižek's use of Lacan to reformulate Althusser's description of the subject formed in ideology develops the Lacanian underpinnings of Althusser's theory. A number of critics (e.g., Eagleton 1994, 214; Smith 1988, 18–22) have noticed that Althusser draws on Lacan's notion of imaginary identification (very simply, identification with the image): individuals recognize themselves in ideology in a manner similar to the way that the infant, according to Lacan, misrecognizes her reflection in the mirror as a unified whole that she does not necessarily experience in her small toddling body. Thus a person interpellated by ideology recognizes herself in, or identifies with, the image presented to her in ideology and so behaves accordingly. Žižek, in building on Althusser, argues that Althusser does not adequately account for the process by which the external apparatuses of ideology (schools, family, religion) become internalized. Žižek suggests that the Lacanian account of the subject's passage through the symbolic order (Lacan's Other) fills in this gap in Althusser (Žižek 1989, 43–44). For Žižek, the identification that takes place in ideological interpellation is not Lacan's imaginary identification, as Althusser would have it, but Lacan's symbolic identification (identification with language). Lacan theorizes the process of desire and identification that takes place in the subject's entry into the symbolic order. In this process two things happen: meaning comes to be fixed (for linguistic signs), and at the same time subjectivity is formed. Thus for Žižek, ideological interpellation is the moment that Lacan describes as the subject's entry into language, or into what he calls the symbolic order (also called *the Other*).

Žižek uses Lacan's symbolic order (the Other) to describe ideology, though it is not quite as simple as drawing an analogy between them. For Žižek, in entry into the symbolic order, the subject is hailed by, and identifies with, what he terms, following Lacan, the master signifier, or *pinning point* (*point de capiton*, literally, "upholstery button").[6] Instead of identifying with an image, as in the mirror stage, the subject identifies with the symbolic order through the master signifier. The ideological master signifier (for instance, capitalism) fixes the place of the subject within the symbolic order, thus ideologically interpellating and positioning the subject. As Žižek puts it, the subject is "fastened, pinned to a signifier which represents him for the Other, and through this pinning he is loaded with a symbolic mandate, he is given a place in the . . . network of symbolic relations" (Žižek 1989, 113). Put another way, the master signifier, or *ideological pinning point*, makes sense of the subject's place within the symbolic order and organizes the subject's subsequent relations within that order. Here the master signifier functions similarly to Althusser's ideological state apparatuses.

However, the hailing of the master signifier takes effect, not directly through the subject's identification with that master signifier, as one might imagine, following Althusser, but rather more circuitously. In Žižek's terms, interpellation takes place through the subject's identification with the "lack in the symbolic order" that is later filled in, through fantasy and desire, by a fantasy object raised to the status of master signifier, or ideological pinning point. In short, for Žižek, ideological interpellation is the process by which the subject comes to identify with the lack in symbolic order.

What is this "lack in the symbolic order," then, with which the subject identifies? For Žižek the lack is a "strange traumatic element which cannot be symbolized, [or] integrated into the symbolic order" (1989, 133). Elsewhere Žižek calls the lack in the symbolic order "the non-symbolizable traumatic kernel" (1994b, 26). For Žižek this traumatic kernel is social antagonism, a notion—to which I will return—that he derives by modifying Lacanian and psychoanalytic theory. The nonsymbolizable traumatic element is what Lacan calls the Real (to be distinguished from reality). The Real is a concept that Lacan develops from the psychoanalytic tradition on the study of trauma. As a result of trauma, according to psychoanalytic theory starting with Freud, psychic processes are structured around a traumatic event that has been repressed. It is nonsymbolizable, non recognizable, because it has been repressed. This event may be the initial structuring of the drives around an object of sexual desire (e.g., a child's sexual desire for a parent), which is traumatically lost in sublimation, the overcoming of sexual desire through "civilized activity" (Freud 1959 [1908], 185–88; Laplanche and Pontalis 1978 [1967], 432). Or it may also include some other lost, repressed, traumatic event (e.g., Freud's primal scene in which the child sees his parents having intercourse). For Lacan, the Real is that part of the subject that resides in the unconscious, to which the subject no longer has access. The Real is the core of the subject's very being—the structuring of the libidinal drives and needs—which is split off (i.e., repressed) from the subject in its entry into language. Because the subject no longer has direct access to what has been lost, it cannot be symbolized—but it compulsively returns in other ways. It is still always there, at work, reproducing itself in other forms, as symptoms of the loss.

But as Žižek explains it, in Lacan's later writings a traumatic element is understood to structure the entire symbolic order (1989, 133). This non-symbolizable kernel around which everything else turns, then, is the lack in the symbolic order. It "gives rise to ever-new symbolizations [including symptoms and fantasy] by means of which one endeavors to integrate and domesticate it" (1994b, 22; see also 1989, 162–63). In other words, the symbolic order is structured around a lack precisely because that lack is always at work reproducing itself in new symptomatic manifestations (thus constructing the symbolic order). For Žižek, it is with this "lack" that the subject identifies in interpellation. But since the lack is not accessible, as will be explained further on, the subject can only identify with the symptoms that fill in for that lack.

Žižek takes Lacan's later conception of the lack in the symbolic order and moves it specifically onto the level of the social and the political. Influenced by Ernesto Laclau and Chantal Mouffe, Žižek argues that the nonsymbolizable lack in the symbolic order is not so much repressed sexual drives (though this may still be at work) as it is a *fundamental social antagonism*. This, as he puts it, is an antagonism that "is nowhere directly given as a positive entity yet which none the less functions" (like trauma or the primal scene), giving rise to all other kinds of antagonism (1994, 22). It is an antagonism that is too difficult to bear, so it is repressed, but it returns in other ways, as a symptom. Žižek gives the example of class struggle as this kind of nonlocatable antagonism, which both generates other antagonisms and "functions as the point of enabling us to locate every social phenomenon." Žižek's Marxist roots show through when he locates class struggle at the heart of the social order, generating all other social processes and struggles. I will suggest presently that the contests over land or resources found in the accounts I examine here might also be read as a sort of fundamental social antagonism that gives rise to all sorts of other social processes and antagonisms.

However, as noted earlier, the lack in the symbolic order, the fundamental social antagonism, is compensated for, and so hidden, by the ideological master signifier, or pinning point. The ideological pinning point fills in and smoothes over the lack in the symbolic order. Interestingly, in the Lacanian theory on which Žižek draws, the master signifier that comes to fill in the lack is called "the Law," the "name of the Father," and "the phallus" (terms, as I noted earlier, on which Althusser himself draws). Here the patriarchal nature of the Lacanian and Žižekian theory comes to the fore. When Lacan describes identification with the lack in the Other, he speaks in family metaphors of the Other as the mother, and "the lack" as the lack of the father's phallus, which the mother desires. As Žižek explains it, the phallus is that which "gives body to a certain fundamental loss" (Žižek 1989, 154). The phallus is the placemarker of the lack in the symbolic order, it fills in or covers over that lack and holds the place of master signifier. The pinning point/phallus steps in to "unify a given field" (Žižek 1989, 95), filling in the lack in the symbolic order (social antagonism) with itself.

Interestingly, Žižek does not draw out the connection between the phallus and Althusser's police officer and the law. Though he is obviously aware of the relation between phallus and law, he does not choose to make much of it. But because all the components of the Lacanian theory except law figure in his rereading of Althusser, it makes sense to understand the master signifier/phallus as holding the same place as the law in Althusser's formulation. Just as Althusser's subject is actually hailed by some notion of law (the possibility of guilt at breaking the law), so also Žižek's subject is heralded by and identifies with the law. In the readings of police and state violence against protest that follow, I will assume the connection between phallus and law.

But there is another step in all of this: through desire, the subject raises a fantasy object to the level of phallus, and so it actually is the fantasy object that fills in for the lack in the symbolic order. In Lacanian terms, the traumatic element is filled in by a fantasy object because the subject always desires to access that which is lost. This desire is, then, the prototype for all other desires: everything that the subject desires henceforth is merely a substitute for the missing traumatic element. The fantasy object is therefore *a symptom* of what has been lost. Put another way, the only way the subject can know the social antagonism, the unrepresentable lack in the symbolic order, is through something that comes to stand in for that lack. This stand-in acts as the master signifier/phallus/law. But because the master signifier fills in for something absent, it must always be, in some ways, only *a fantasy replacement* for what is absent (*objet a* in Lacan's terminology). The fantasy object stands in as the phallus. Thus it is ultimately with the phallus (or law) by way of a fantasy object (a symptom), that the individual identifies.

This fantasy object, for Žižek, is ideology. Ideology is a fantasy construction that masks this troubling lack in the symbolic order. Yet at the same time, this missing traumatic element, this fundamental social antagonism, can only be accessed through the substitute object of desire, ideology. In a sense, ideology is the only thing to be had. In other words, for Žižek, fantasy/ideology structures social reality around itself (1989, 45–49; 1994, 19–22). Inseparable from ideology, social reality is composed around this fundamental social antagonism. Ideology is the fantasy that both creates social reality and smoothes over antagonism; it is the fantasy object with which the subject identifies, as if it were the master signifier. Ideology, as a fantasy construction, is given the status of phallus. According to this description of ideology, then, social antagonism is regulated by ideology/phallus/law.

Žižek's elaboration of the Lacanian underpinnings of Althusser's account of interpellation enables thinking about how the law is the condition not only for interpellation, but also grounds excessive violence in response to resistance. Žižek's description of the lack in the symbolic order as a volatile, unknowable, yet socially grounded antagonism on which the law rests might give some clue as to the cause for the excess in violence. If social reality, fantasy, ideology, social antagonism, the law, and the phallus are all implicated in each other, it is a rather tight, closed, and totalized system that maintains order. Like a pressure cooker, it seems that the ingredients for explosion are at hand. Resistance lifts the lid, so to speak, on the social antagonism bubbling below the surface of social reality and provokes an eruption. But before looking more closely at Žižek, to see what actually precipitates the violent outburst of the phallus, I turn to three accounts of such violence.

Before going through each of these accounts in detail, let me first cue the ways in which I read these stories with and against Žižek. What I will ultimately be interested in drawing out of these accounts is the relationship between social antagonism (over land and resources), the ideals that motivate the protesters and also the attacks on them (i.e., ideological pinning points), the law, and stand-ins for the law (i.e., fantasy objects raised to the level of law). I argue that in each of these accounts, the having or not having of land, resources, and status generates a social antagonism that is overlooked in the official records by an appeal to some kind of higher order—Yahweh's will, the colonial laws of the land, and the right for law-enforcement agents to enforce order—which might be generally termed "the law." The law is, in turn, represented by Moses, the crown, and school authorities, who, as stand-ins for the law, try to smooth over antagonism by hailing, or, in Althusser's terms, interpellating protesters into maintaining prescribed, obedient roles within the social order. But, in refusing to be interpellated, protesters not only fail to fulfill the symbolic identification required of them, they also recognize Moses, the crown, and school authorities as *symptoms* of the social order, symptoms standing in for the law, which in turn stands in for a central lack or antagonism. This recognition cannot be accomplished apart from another set of master signifiers with which protesters *have been* interpellated and that motivate their protest: holiness, justice, and equality. Yet, in the process of resistance these too are recognized as merely symptoms and are questioned. Finally, this last questioning results in what I will call the explosion of the hysterical phallus, that is, the ugly irruption of that central antagonism in uncontrollable *jouissance*, or, in simple terms, violence. With the latter argument, I take a playful turn—guided by these stories—away from some of the more misogynist notions Žižek builds on (many of them inherited from Lacan): the hysterical woman, the unifying phallus, the vagina as wound, "lack" as the (sublime, feminine) object of desire.

Repression in the Paran Desert

Numbers 16 has come to be a classic tale of dissidence crushed, with Korah figuring as "an archetypal heretic" (Wenham 1981, 134). In this story, Korah the Levite, along with Reubenites Dathan, Abiram, and On, accuse Moses and Aaron of setting themselves up as exclusively holy among the people of Israel. They argue instead that all the people of the assembly should be recognized as holy. Moses tells Korah to appear with his followers before Yahweh the next day. They are to bring their fire censors so that Yahweh might demonstrate to the assembly who is truly holy. He also calls a meeting with Dathan and Abiram, but they refuse to meet with him, saying, "We will not go. Is it too little that you have brought us up from the land of milk and honey to die in the desert, that you must set yourself up over us as a prince?" (Num. 16:13–14). With this response, first Moses becomes furious, asking Yahweh not to pay any attention to their smoke offerings the next day, and then Yahweh becomes furious. Moses again commands Korah to assemble the people the next day with their smoke offerings, Yahweh threatens to destroy the whole assembly, and Moses negotiates the destruction of only the leading rebellious parties. When the contest with divine wrath finally takes place, Korah, Dathan, and Abiram (On is not mentioned after v. 1) are swallowed up by an earthquake, with their whole families and all of their possessions descending to Sheol as a demonstration of Moses' holiness (although the text leaves some question as to whether Korah is swallowed up with the rest of them, since only his tent and his men are mentioned).[7] Their 250 followers offering incense are burned up in a fire coming from Yahweh. The rebels are consumed by an earthquake *and* a fire, when surely one would do. The violence is excessive.

In trying to understand perturbing details like the doubled work of earthquake and fire, and whether Korah died in the earthquake or fire, many scholars have concluded that this story is a composite text (Noth 1968, 121–31; Coats 1968, 174–84; Milgrom 1990, 414–20; Wenham 1981, 141–42; Snaith 1967, 255; Levine 1993, 54–55, 405; Budd 1984, 184) dealing with two issues, land and cultic practice (Levine 1993, 412, 418; Budd 1984, 189–91; Magonet 1982, 6–9). Because the story follows

another rebellion (Numbers 13–14) in which the people do not want to
take possession of the land of Canaan—nearly stoning Caleb and Joshua
for their recommendation to do so—it has been argued that the original
issue in this story was controversy over the conquest of Canaan. Moreover,
it has been suggested (Levine 1993, 424–25; Budd 1984, 191) that for the
Reubenites, Dathan and Abiram, the bone of contention was Moses' insistence that the Reubenites cross the Jordan to fight along with the rest of
the tribes of Israel (Numbers 32), even though their land was allocated
east of the Jordan and so could be possessed without crossing the river
(Josh. 13:14–23).[8] This question of land is thus considered to be an earlier
strand of the tradition, which is later merged into a story about cultic and
Levitical authority, a story that occludes the original settlement issue. As
received, the text tells only of the contest over holiness and leadership
between Moses and Korah. It has been suggested that in this later story the
question of cultic leadership is twofold. First, as noticed by the Rabbis,
Korah was Aaron's first cousin, and may have been slighted when his (hier-
archically) younger cousin Elizaphan (Korah's father's younger brother's son)
was chosen over him to be the prince of his clan (Magonet 1982, 5, 24;
Milgrom 1990, 130). Second, the Korahites, it seems from archeological
and textual evidence,[9] were skilled in cultic arts, making Moses' proclamation of Aaron's unique status all the more insulting (Levine 1993, 430).

While my concern is not to understand the textual, source, or tradition
history of this passage, I would like to frame the issues raised by the
hypothesis of a composite text in slightly different terms. First, the connection through the Reubenites of this story to the issue of land settlement,
along with the story's placement in the book, following the rejected recon-
naissance mission of chapters 13–14, at the very least places the colonial
impulse alongside, if not at the heart of, this kind of divine disciplinary
action for rebellion. Violent punishment of the rebels insures Moses against
further rebellion during the colonization process, or at least it tries. It is
interesting that if conflict over colonization is an issue, even the central
issue, it is nowhere given in this story. If the composite text hypothesis
is accepted, the issue of leadership comes to replace, or stand in for, the
conflict over settlement, and this I will argue fits with Žižek's understanding of the fantasy object—a fantasy that stands in for and smoothes over a
fundamental social antagonism. Lastly, if colonization is an underlying
issue in this story, then the superfluous violence (fire and earthquake) is
doubly excessive because Israel has just previously been violently punished
through defeat in battle, for rebelling and not conforming to Yahweh's plan
of conquest (Num. 14:36–45). What is troubling in the doubled (tripled)
instance of divine wrath (military defeat, earthquake, and fire) is not a
question of textual source, but of overkill, especially because the excess in

violence is specifically related to resistance. However, the issues raised by the suggestion that this story contains a less obvious strand contesting "settlement policy," correspond with the notion of a fundamental antagonism that is smoothed over by ideology.

RCMP Siege at Gustafsen Lake

The excessive violence of Numbers 16 is strangely prescient of a monstrously violent police operation that took place from August 19 to September 17, 1995, in the northern part of the Canadian province of British Columbia at Gustafsen Lake. There the Royal Canadian Mounted Police (RCMP) surrounded eighteen aboriginal traditionalists, who were preparing for their annual sundance. The RCMP moved in 400 police with "dog teams, airplanes, helicopters, Armoured Personnel Carriers, grenades, landmines, M16 and C7 assault rifles, hollow-point bullets— prohibited by the Geneva Convention—and fifty-calibre machine guns" (ABC 1997, 5).

The reason for this excess, this barrage of artillery? The traditionalists, now known as the Ts'peten Defenders, were camping out on their sacred sundance grounds, unceded territory that had been claimed as "crown land" by the government of British Columbia. The crown was putting the land to work by leasing it out to an American rancher (though court testimonies showed that it was not certain whether the land in question was included in the lease). Earlier in the year, some of those among this group had had their lawyer, Bruce Clark, petition the Queen of England (who is still the Queen of Canada) to convene a long-disused "special constitutional court in Britain mandated to hear . . . disputes between indigenous nations and the colonies" (ABC 1997, 6). Those making the petition were confident that this British court would recognize that no treaty had ever been signed for this land, nor indeed for much of the land in British Columbia, and that it was therefore rightfully aboriginal peoples' land. Their appeal to the monarch was based on two legal factors: first, the Queen's administrative obligation under the British law to convene this court; and second, more historically, a 1763 proclamation by King George III recognizing the "right of aboriginal peoples to maintain control of their territories unmolested and undisturbed, within the protection of the British Crown" (Splitting the Sky, in *Above the Law* 1997). The Queen, however, responded to their petition by dismissing her duty on the grounds of "political convention," saying that it was not her practice to meddle in the affairs of the colonies (Dr. Bruce Clark, in *Above the Law* 1997).

It was later that year that the RCMP put into violent action what their own records called "giving the Natives stress out there" (ABC 1997, 7). The "crisis" began when the RCMP escorted a local rancher and a number of ranch hands with rifles to the camp. As they delivered a hand-written eviction notice, one of the ranchers cracked a bullwhip and threatened "to string up some red niggers." About a month later, six men, who were later revealed to be RCMP, dressed in camouflage and carrying assault rifles, were seen creeping up on the camp, so a warning shot was fired from the camp (ABC, 7). The RCMP used this warning shot to justify its siege. During the month that followed, more than 400 RCMP officers were deployed to "secure" the area. The aboriginal defenders refused to leave, arguing that they had a right to the land and to the sundance grounds; they did not, however, aggress the police encircling them. Conversely, they endured continual provocation by the RCMP, including numerous shots into agreed-upon safe zones and accusations of aggression. When the defenders finally agreed to leave the camp, because the danger of police violence was escalating, they were all arrested and charged with attempted murder and mischief endangering lives.

The police offensive, with all its gross injustices, was thoroughly documented by RCMP testimony in the ensuing court case and by the RCMP's own videotapes, in which they are heard admitting to fabrication of stories and media smears, including twenty-four-hour overhead surveillance tapes in which they are seen blowing up moving vehicles (Above the Law 1999). Yet, in spite of all the clear evidence against the RCMP, after a year-long trial (July 1996–July 1997), the court found the defenders guilty. In a shocking display of the racism within the legal system, the judge "prohibited the jury from considering all the major pillars of the defense. . . . He took an unheard of four days to instruct the jury before they retired, telling them which testimony they could consider and insisting repeatedly that they had to accept the law as he explained it to them without question" (ABC 1997, 8).

Interestingly, from the start of the siege until the end of the trial, government and legal officials denied the land issue as a cause for the siege, arguing instead that the issue was one of terrorism and lawlessness. The siege was wholeheartedly supported by the "progressive" New Democratic Party provincial government at the time, with the hopes of winning support for being tough with terrorists. The attorney general, Ujjal Dosanjh, who would later become premier, made the argument at the start of the crisis that "Gustafsen Lake has nothing to do with aboriginal land-claim issues. It's purely to do with the weapons there and the shots that have been fired" (Hume). In the trial, too, the crown lawyer and judge argued that this was not a land-claims issue, in spite of the Ts'Peten Defenders'

statements to the contrary (see Canadian Press). Here the issue of lawfulness comes to stand in for the conflict over land. The media coverage for
the "crisis" corroborated this point of view, portraying the defenders as
fringe, fanatical, and terrorists. As court testimonies revealed, though, this
depiction was engineered in what the RCMP called (as revealed in their
videotapes [*Above the Law* 1999]) a "disinformation and smear campaign,"
including fabricated reports of shootings and aggressions from the camp.
Their campaign was successful, as evidenced by the following national
newspaper report of the trial:

> "[I]t was camp occupants who introduced weapons and violence to the
> standoff at Gustafsen Lake," [Judge Josephson] wrote. "It was that, not an
> act of trespass that required a massive response by police which strained their
> resources to the limit." The sentencing ends a 10-month trial that followed
> the occupation of ranch land in the BC Interior by a small, fringe group of
> natives and their supporters. Claiming the land was sacred and had never
> been ceded to the Crown, members of the group fired at police who tried to
> remove them.
>
> The RCMP spent 5.5-million and brought in more than 400 officers
> to bring the protesters to justice. It was the largest such operation in RCMP
> history (Cernetig).

This report, oblivious, it would seem, to the perverse irony here, indicates
that the chief contention in the eyes of the justice system and the media
was the *aboriginals'* ownership and use of weapons.

NYPD versus the Lincoln Six

The dynamics at work in the unbelievable violence of Numbers 16 and at
Gustafsen Lake can also be seen in the story of police violence in the outer
boroughs of New York City, in the 1999 film *Light it Up*. Focused
on the issue of police brutality, the plot and musical score of *Light it Up*
dramatize the persistent problem of police violence against people of color
in New York City, as well as the increasing criminalization of youth in
schools in poor areas. The action, set in Queens, stages the occupation of
Lincoln High School by six students in defiance of the school's principal,
Mr. Armstrong (Glynn Turman), and his strongman, the school's newest
security cop, Officer Jackson (Forest Whitaker) of the New York Police
Department (NYPD). The opening sequence establishes the school as
a "typical inner-city school": heavily policed, with inadequate funds for
repairs, textbooks, and career development.

The conflict begins after the students' best teacher, Mr. Knowles (Judd Nelson), is given a leave of absence for taking them off campus to try to find a place to hold class, their own classroom being unbearably cold and leaky. Bewildered over the loss of teacher and space to hold class, the students speak out against the principal's decision. Ruffled because of the presence of a visiting superintendent, and conscious that his pension is in the balance, Principal Armstrong tells them to go back to their frozen classroom. They refuse, demanding Knowles' reinstatement. When it is clear that he has lost control, Armstrong calls Officer Jackson to the scene. A struggle ensues between the police officer and two of the students, Lester (Usher Raymond) and Ziggy (Robert Ri'chard). The conflict escalates, in part, because the officer attempts to enforce Armstrong's threats to call the students' parents, thereby unsuspectingly also sentencing Ziggy to extremely violent abuse at the hands of his father. As Lester and Ziggy actively resist this dictate, the police gun goes off in the fray, and Jackson is shot in the leg. Lester decides to take Jackson hostage, and he is joined by Ziggy and four other students. The school is emptied of all but the six who remain. The NYPD rolls up in battalion force to defend the "officer down."

In the course of the standoff between students and police, the plot thickens in several ways. To begin, the students resist the way they are labeled and the underlying assumptions that these labels betray. Their action is portrayed by the media as one of gangsters and criminals. Here again the ideal of lawfulness, i.e., "proper civil behavior," effaces the question of resources. After seeing the extremely negative news report of their action, and having been contacted by a police negotiator, the students formulate demands. They demand that their teacher, Mr. Knowles, be reinstated; that the windows and leaks in the school be repaired; that students have textbooks for every subject; that a career day be established; and that once a month the teachers be tested. In spite of these responsible demands, the police continue to treat the students as less than full citizens. Disdainfully the officer in command responds to the demands: "They got a little power, and now they wanna walk. They got a better chance of getting into Yale." The comment foreshadows the film's ending and draws out the film's critique of the education system, the relation of its quality to class and societal prejudice, and the hierarchies it holds in place.[10]

Second, the story of Lester's own personal trauma is told. He has suffered a grave loss at the hands of the police: his father has been the casualty of police violence. Here the film draws on the well-known incident, reported in the *New York Times*, February 5, 1999, in which four NYPD officers shot Amadou Diallo forty-one times as he reached for his wallet in the vestibule of his home in the Bronx (Cooper 1999; Roane 1999).

In a flashback, Lester watches his father being harassed by the police and being forced to the ground. He sees his father reach for his asthma inhaler. He watches the cops react, shooting and killing his father. In both the film and its prototype, the NYPD is not held accountable, and there is no admission of wrong doing.[11]

Finally, the police violence fatally escalates, as the youths are "brought to justice." At the end of a day-long standoff, the police break off communications with the students and move in, in order to have the problem taken care of before the morning news. In a traumatic climax on the school roof, Lester resists shooting Officer Jackson in his anger. However, the police snipers in the helicopter above, inattentive to the possible negotiations going on below and intent on firing, shoot and kill Ziggy as he runs to Lester's aid. The denouement tells the fates of each of the six. Each of their punishments and subsequent life choices is shown matter-of-factly; but predictably, realistically, the two white students do not face jail time, while the others do.

Light it Up has had some important critiques leveled against it. First, it is undoubtedly somewhat flat in its character development (Monder 1999). Further, the "feel-good" part of Gary Dauphin's assessment of the film as "feel-good agitprop" is somewhat troubling given the seriousness of its subject matter. Even more problematic, as Eric Monder points out, is the endorsement of commercial products, from Coca-Cola to news media logos, which sabotages the film's political message, particularly its message about the inaccuracy of U.S. news media. And finally, "not only does the film pit . . . [a] Caucasian teacher against a horrifically bureaucratic African American principal, but it also establishes this teacher as the students' most noble and intelligent role model" (Monder 1999). In addition, the structure of white privilege is also disavowed in a similar attempt to reverse stereotypes, when the Puerto Rican Stephanie (Rosario Dawson) is portrayed as more inherently privileged, advantaged, and confident than the Anglo American Lynn (Sara Gilbert), who fights for her self-esteem. But while the film can be accused of thus undermining its stance on the issues with which it deals, it is still a rare Hollywood film that focuses specifically on the issue of police brutality toward people of color. The film's treatment of police violence is more accurate than many would like to admit, in its resemblance to real-life accounts collected by the Stolen Lives Project in *Stolen Lives: Killed by Law Enforcement*. My interest in it is as a film is as a fairly realistic depiction of the NYPD in its profiling of people of color, and in its violent response to resistance against systemic racism; as such it is homologous to the other two accounts in its treatment of resistance to interpellation.

Parallels

These contemporary accounts have a number of things immediately in common with Numbers 16. First, in each case, there is a refusal of interpellation and a disidentification with the authority demanding obedience and conformity. Korah leads a group of supporters who no longer identify with Moses and no longer accept the demand that they follow him. Thus when Moses summons Dathan and Abiram, two of Korah's supporters, they refuse to meet with him. Likewise, when the Ts'Peten Defenders are delivered an eviction notice from the rancher leasing the land from the crown, they refuse to recognize the sovereignty of that authority, or their obligation to it. And the Lincoln Six refuse the demands of the school authorities. Stephanie leads the refusals when Armstrong tells the students to go back to class. Lester and Ziggy repeatedly refuse the demands of the police officer, from the beginning of the film until the moment the gun goes off. Lester refuses first to answer to Officer Jackson's appellation "son" ("I'm not your son," he says angrily), then to "assume the position" (that of a criminal under arrest; face toward the wall, hands up, legs spread), and finally to allow Ziggy to be sent home and submitted to abuse.

Second, in each account, the person or body hailing or trying to interpellate the protesters into the dominant order is an agent of the law. As the book of Numbers makes clear, like Exodus and Leviticus before it, Moses is the bearer of Yahweh's law to the Israelites, in both its basic and detailed formulations. For the aboriginal traditionalists, the government of the province of British Columbia both makes and enforces laws, including its own right to certain portions of the land, whether or not granted it in treaty. And in the introductory sequences of *Light it Up*, the audience learns that it is Officer Jackson's first day of work, and that Principal Armstrong has told him that the breaking of rules will not be tolerated. Armstrong makes the rules, and Jackson enforces them.

However, as the public records of these events (in the Bible, news media, and legal proceedings) make clear, these various lawgivers are merely stand-ins for a rather larger idea of law. In all three cases, an appeal is made in the publicized accounts to a notion of law on another register, that order which "good citizens" of course do not contravene; it is the indisputable moral regulator of social behavior and norms. In each case, the specific issue generating the antagonism—i.e., the having or not having of land, space, and resources—is either not made directly present, or is denied, obscured by accusations of lawbreaking. Korah, Dathan, and Abiram are portrayed as wicked rebels, selfishly angry with Moses and Aaron for setting themselves as uniquely holy, but there is no direct mention of land in the story.

The aboriginal peoples are portrayed as renegade and violent terrorists in media reports and by government and legal officials; the land issue is denied. In *Light it Up*, the Lincoln Six are portrayed by the media as criminals and thugs; those commentating upon the occupation refuse to acknowledge the issues of inadequate resources highlighted by the protest, focusing instead on the lawlessness of the students and the plight of the police officer whom they have held hostage. In each case, then, accusations that the grand-scale order of law has been breached obscure the very concrete issues at stake: the having or not having of access to and control over land and resources.

Interestingly, in each case, protesters also represent themselves as questioning the order of law. It is not as if they stand outside of it or believe it to be completely ineffectual—at least at first. Korah, Dathan, and Abiram argue that Yahweh's will is not made known only to Moses and Aaron but that Yahweh is among all the people (Numbers 16:3); the Ts'peten Defenders appeal to the Queen, the ultimate lawgiver; and initially, the Lincoln Six question the right of the police and the principal to make the rules without listening to their concerns; only later do the students develop a list of their own concrete demands. In other words, the protesters reveal the always-alreadiness of their interpellation. Although they are resistant, they do not quite escape their interpellation by the law. Even they initially appeal to legality, rather than make a direct claim to land and resources.

Finally, all three stories demonstrate more violence than possibly necessary to deal with the "threat" to the dominant order. As noted, earthquake *and* fire are Korah's fate for questioning Moses. The RCMP pull a full-scale military operation on eighteen peaceful sundancers—some of whom had merely inquired into legal processes around land treaties—emptying 20,000 rounds of bullets onto the site (clearcutting the trees later, to eliminate the evidence). And lastly, the NYPD are excessively violent to six high-school students who could by no means, on their own, seriously threaten the process of domestic colonization, or even the conditions of their school.

Why in each case the slippage between land and law? Why the excess in violence? Here Žižek's discussion of the relation between ideological signifier, social antagonism, fantasy, and law highlights the ideological operations occurring on a number of levels in these stories. It also enables thinking through the hysterical excess of the violence that the protesters face in each of these accounts. The protesters' refusal to be interpellated into the symbolic order, that is, their refusal of desire for the phallic signifier, makes visible and questions the ideological processes at work, which in turn causes the irruption of the hysterical phallus.

Fantasy Standing in for Social Antagonism

Returning to Žižek's description of ideology as that which stands in for fundamental social antagonism (or lack) in the symbolic order, in the stories I have recounted the antagonism is always bound up with a lack of access to material resources, but the struggle gets played out on the level of law. Thus in the contest over land and leadership between Korah and Moses, the struggle manifests itself over who has Yahweh's will and holiness. In the contest over land between aboriginal traditionalists and the police, the struggle manifests itself over the lawfulness of weapons. In the occupation in *Light it Up*, the struggle manifests itself over who will make and enforce laws, including laws about where and in what material conditions education is conducted. The Real that is operative does not reside within any specific polarity of power, but is rather the fundamental "imbalance in social relations that prevent[s] the community from stabilizing itself into a harmonious whole" (Žižek 1994, 26). This imbalance results from an unequal distribution of land and resources that can be read as that hard traumatic kernel of lack that generates all other struggles.[12] What fills in, and tries to regulate that lack, is the law. And, as already noted, this is not simply specific laws, but rather a more overarching notion of law that is "uncitizenlike" to contravene.

But as noted earlier, the only way that this pinning point, the law, can even be known (since it holds the place of lack) is through fantasy. So a fantasy object steps in to fill the lack of the symbolic order, as if it were the pinning point. In each of the three accounts I explore here, a fantasy object comes to stand in for the law: Moses stands in for Yahweh's law; "the crown" for colonial rule; and the school authorities for New York law. The figure of Moses, as the holy leader, comes as the bearer of Yahweh's law to regulate the difference between those who have power and those who do not in the newly formed social organization of the tribes of Israel. In the antagonism played out at Gustafsen Lake, the fantasy of crown land ("British Columbia"), fills in the disputes over right to property: "the crown" poses as an originary entity, as if it, as a legal body with its own jurisdiction, had always been there as some kind of binding authority. In the conflict at Lincoln High, the authority of a school officer is enacted to smooth over worries of space and resources by demanding that the students comply with school regulations, and that they physically and metaphorically "assume the position."

The fantasy object is necessarily implicated in the social antagonism. As Žižek makes clear, the fantasy object is always a symptom, and like all symptoms it "stands in" for the lack in the symbolic order (that which has been repressed). In other words, the fantasy object is a symptom of the fundamental social antagonism. Elsewhere, Žižek describes the fantasy object as *part of the fundamental social antagonism* that takes on extraordinary fantasy proportions (1997, 26–27). It is a little piece of the social antagonism (the Real) "which persists as a surplus" (1989, 71), and which, through fantasy, is elevated to the position of pure signifier or pinning point.

It might be said that in each of these accounts a little piece of the social antagonism has been elevated to the level of law to unify or smooth out the antagonism. By setting themselves up as the ultimate and indisputable authorities and givers of law, Moses, the crown, and the school authorities are all implicated in generating the antagonism they come to regulate. They are little pieces of the central antagonism of the social order, and as such they act like Žižek's fantasy object raised to the status of phallus. The fantasy object is a symptom that has become an ideological pinning point hiding its role as symptom from those pinned to it in interpellation. The ideological operation par excellence, then, occurs when, through the desire of those interpellated, the fantasy object steps in to smooth over the social antagonism as ideological pinning point/law/ phallus. Moses, the crown, and the school authorities are raised to the level of law, and as such they become ideological pinning points. They (try to) hail the protesters, and elicit their identification with them.

But what of land and resources, the site of all these struggles? I would suggest that it is, in fact, the materiality of land and resources that constitutes the fantasy object, the "real" little piece of the Real that persists as a surplus and that *causes desire*. Žižek describes this fantasy object as an ordinary object that "as soon as it is 'elevated to the status of Thing [ideological pinning point],' starts to function as a kind of screen, an empty space on which the subject projects the fantasies that support [its] desire" (1991, 133). Paradoxically then, fantasy produces the desired object, which at the same time causes the desire that produces it (Žižek 1989, 160). For this reason he calls the fantasy object the *object-cause* of desire (Žižek 1989, 190–97). It seems that land and resources function this way in these stories; they are that bit of material relations around which power plays, and creates antagonism. But in a sense, desire for the land and its resources *produces* Moses (without whom the people would not be moving toward the land), the provincial government, or crown (the result of a long land-acquiring/desiring colonizing mission), and the Lincoln High School authorities (who are installed, it would seem, instead of textbooks and properly equipped classrooms, perhaps to keep the less advantaged away from the prerogatives—such as Yale—of those who own more of New York's resources). In each case, land and resources are elevated to the status of law as the struggle over them is defined in terms of contesting laws (and lawgivers). Land and resources are then that screen[13] on which various ideological fantasies are projected: Yahweh's will and its stand-in, Moses; colonial rule and its stand-in, "the crown"; and New York law and its stand-in, school authorities.

The materiality and substantiality of the land and resources as object-causes of desire is where these accounts of social antagonism and violence differ slightly from Žižek's description of lack, fantasy, and ideology. For Žižek the only thing that has any real substance is fantasy, ideology, the phallus. Even the fantasy object is pure semblance, devoid of any substantial support (1993, 35–36). But, in these stories at least, the land and resources are the material support for other ideological configurations (recalling the theory's Marxist roots). Land and resources, the object-causes of desire,[14] are not lack, but self-sufficient plenitude. Indeed, perhaps plenitude of land and resources is too difficult to bear and this is what provokes antagonism, requiring fantasy to smooth it over. This is certainly the case in Numbers. The spies tell the people, "The land . . . it flows with milk and honey . . . yet . . . it is a land that devours its inhabitants" (Num. 13:27, 32). The land's goodness is jealously guarded; so the people revolt, and the nebulous, nowhere-present of Yahweh's will must be invoked to calm the fear. The fantasy is only needed at the point that the desire for the land produces antagonism.

Ironically, the antagonism for which the fantasy-object-as-phallus stands in can only be seen as "lack" after the very imposition of the fantasy/phallus itself, thus justifying its presence after the fact. This is not to say that the imposition of this fantasy does not have material effects (i.e., I am not returning here to a vulgar Marxism in which ideology is merely false consciousness): it does smooth over the antagonism, and it does affect the land. The phallus is overdetermined by (both determined by, and determining for) the fundamental social antagonism. But, when the fantasy/phallus is pulled back from this scene of "lack"—through the questions posed by those resisting interpellation—the antagonism produced by desire for land and resources can no longer contain itself; it explodes hysterically.

Symptoms Displacing Symptoms

The fantasy comes to be peeled away from the plenitude of the land precisely through protesters' refusal to be interpellated. In each case, protesters refuse to identify with the ideological pinning points that mask the social antagonism. Thus they resist interpellation: they do not desire what is offered to them. Dathan and Abiram refuse to be devoted followers, they decline a meeting with Moses when he calls them. The Ts'Peten Defenders refuse to be law-abiding citizens and respond to the eviction notice in the name of the crown and its tenant. The Lincoln Six also refuse to be "good" citizens by accepting neither the substandard education allotted them, nor the demands of the school authorities to submit themselves to abuse. By resisting interpellation, the resisters recognize these ideological pinning points as symptoms; that is Moses, the crown, and school authorities are recognized as fantasy objects, little pieces of the Real, which as fantasy formations mask or fill out the central lack (1989, 74), the antagonism of the protesters' social orders. Recognized as symptoms, they are no longer desirable.

What is interesting, though, is *how* these fantasy objects—doing the hailing work of the master signifiers, that is, the law—are recognized as mere symptoms of the more deep-seated social antagonism generated by land and resources. It is clear that for the protesters each of these fantasy objects stands in for the law, and that the law is both inadequate to regulate the conflict and a poor substitute for what the protesters themselves invoke as ideal. In other words, the law is deemed inferior to the master signifiers with which they themselves have been interpellated. Korah, Dathan, and the others call for an ideal nonmediated relationship with God in the assembly of Israel (understood as holiness). The Ts'peten Defenders appeal to the Queen's ruling in favor of aboriginal land claims (understood as justice). And the Lincoln Six appeal to an ideal of shared wealth, respect, and dignity for all (understood as equality).

Thus if Moses, the crown, and the school authorities are recognized as symptoms standing in for the (inadequate) law, it is only in relation to these other more desirable master signifiers: Moses in relation to the chosen and holy assembly; the crown in relation to the ability to bring about justice; and the school authorities with respect to the ability to treat economically disadvantaged students as equally deserving of dignity, respect, and protection as those of higher economic standing. Thus the recognition of Moses, the crown, and school authorities as symptoms brings into view the ideals of holiness, justice, or equality with which the protesters have themselves been interpellated. The first set of inadequate master signifiers can only be recognized as such against the second set of ideal master signifiers. At the same time, this recognition reveals the ideological positioning of protesters.

Moreover, the recognition of the symptomatic nature of the ideological pinning points offered to the protesters and rejected by them, which also makes visible the pinning points with which they have been interpellated (holiness, justice, equality), is occasioned by the losses they have sustained. Indeed, in each case, the giver of the law is also the one who takes away those things held most dearly by the protesters. Moses deprives Korah not only of access to Yahweh, but also of his position among the Reubenites. The crown takes away not only the land, but also the aboriginal peoples' constitutional and legal right to it. And not only do the school authorities and law-enforcement agents withhold proper resources and conditions for learning, but the NYPD also claims Lester's father. By withholding the very things that the protesters state they need, these agents of the law *contribute to the social antagonism*, even spur it on, rather than regulate it. It is loss that pushes protesters to understand not only the inadequacy of the law, but its bearers as symptomatic outworkings of a fundamental social antagonism. So protesters are interpellated instead by ideals that they believe might be more effective in adjudicating social antagonisms. Korah, Dathan, and Abiram ask where holiness resides, the Ts'Peten Defenders ask for justice, and the Lincoln Six demand to be treated with the same respect and dignity that would be afforded students in more affluent neighborhoods.

But if Žižek is to be taken seriously, and if Moses, the crown, and school authorities are read as recognizable symptoms that *stand in for the central antagonism*, then it must be understood that the antagonism generated by desire for land and resources is *still at work* within the ideals of holiness, justice, and equality. Once holiness, justice, and equality are *recognized* as ideological pinning points, they too must be understood as symptoms, ideals that smooth over unrecognized problems within the social order, arising from the materiality of land and resources. Thus, refusal to be interpellated by one set of signifiers (Moses, the crown, and school authorities) necessarily also questions the master signifiers by which they are refused in the first place (holiness, justice, and equality). So protesters become doubly aware of the interpellation process.

Beyond Interpellation: Hysteria

But the question still remains: Why the excess in violence? I would suggest that the violence incurred when the law and its stand-ins are not successful in interpellating protesters might be read as a result of a set of complex relations taking place in what Žižek calls the "realm beyond interpellation." This recognition of the symptomatic nature of ideals, I would argue, is precisely the set of interactions that brings on violence in the realm beyond interpellation. And here I would like to play, a little, with Žižek's phallus.

According to Žižek, in the process of the subject's identification with the lack in the symbolic order (the Other), the Other addresses the subject with the question, "What do you want from me?" ("*Che vuoi?*") (Lacan 1977 [1966], 312). The question is asked as if the subject knows why it has the symbolic mandate conferred upon it by the master signifier (Žižek 1989, 113). Since the subject does not know why it has this symbolic mandate, it internalizes and reformulates the question as, "What does the Other want of me?" (Lacan 1977 [1966], 316), thereby also internalizing the desire of the Other, or the symbolic order (Lacan 1977 [1966], 312; 1978 [1973], 214–15). But because the Other desires what it itself lacks, the subject can never really know what the Other desires. Turning to fantasy as recourse, the subject desires and identifies with the fantasy object that stands in, as the phallus, for the Other's lack. "Fantasy appears, then, as an answer to '*Che vuoi?*' to the unbearable enigma of the desire of the Other, of the lack in the Other" (Žižek 1989, 118).

For Žižek, as for Lacan, failure of identification with the desire and lack of the Other (the symbolic order) produces hysteria. Hysteria is the "incapacity of the subject to fulfill the symbolic identification, to assume fully and without restraint" the identification with the lack in the symbolic order, by internalizing the desire of the symbolic order. The hysteric, instead of posing the question, "What does the Other want of me" and then complying, asks, " 'Why am I what you [the Other] are telling me that I am?' " (Žižek 1989, 113). "Why are you calling me with this ideological pinning point?" Because the failure in identification is ultimately a failure to identify with the phallus, it is not surprising that the hysteric is traditionally gendered as female.[15]

So in rejecting the symbolic identification offered to them, in terms of the Žižekian theory at least, it might be said that the protesters in the accounts discussed here are asking, like the hysteric, "Why am I what you are telling me that I am?" In other words, here in the recognition that takes place in resisting interpellation, subjects *do know* why they are taking the position they do within in the symbolic order, and this awareness sends the question in the other direction. Instead of the usual questions, subjects ask of the symbolic order, "What are you really? Why are you *not* what you are telling me that you are? Why are you—holiness, justice, equality—really just a fantasy standing in to hide the central lack that makes up the central antagonism of the social order? Why do you pose as lawgiving and law-supporting, when in fact you have only caused terrible, debilitating loss in the most lawless, unfair, unjust, and unholy fashion?" Or in the more direct words of Stephanie to the police negotiator, "It's all bullshit, isn't it?"

The question it seems, sends the phallus into hysterics. It is the unveiling of the lack supporting the phallus—that central antagonism without which it could not step in with its unifying function, in short, without which it could not come to power—that provokes its frenzy. Although Žižek never speaks of a hysterical phallus per se (for that would surely contravene his Lacanian legacy), he describes it when he expounds upon the phallus "giving body to a certain fundamental loss" (1989, 157). That the phallus is the signifier of castration or loss is evidenced, he argues, when "the demonstration of power starts to function as a confirmation of a fundamental impotence. . . . The more violent its reaction, the more it confirms its fundamental impotence, the more it confirms its fundamental lack" (1989, 157–58). The reverse might also be true: the more the phallus' fundamental lack is confirmed, the more violent its frenzy.

Thus, when protesters refuse interpellation by the master signifiers Moses, the crown, and school authorities, a chain effect begins whereby the master signifiers that represent the symbolic order for protesters are also questioned. Holiness, justice, and equality are caught and questioned in the act of being symptoms, of merely standing in for lack, phantasmically covering it over. In response to this "unmasking," the antagonism that makes up that lack explodes in ugly *jouissance* (another way that Žižek speaks of the Real). Thus Yahweh, the Holy One, causes the earth to swallow up insurgent Israelites and their families; the justice system in British Columbia employs 400 police to try to blow up 18 aboriginal sundancers; and the NYPD's "respect for human life and dignity"[16] sends the police to kill civilians.

Thinking of the violent response to resisted interpellation as the *jouissance* of the hysterical phallus explains, in Žižekian terms, the persistent ugliness of the police (or the equally unpleasant figure of Sheol, which

Figure 1   Hysterical Phalli in *Light it Up*

gapes in the mouth of the earth). For Žižek, the Real is *jouissance*, and *jouissance* is ugly and "always traumatic" (1997, 25). Ugliness is "a *topological category*" designating an object that is "larger than itself." It is something that spills out from the inside. Žižek also uses the unfortunate (but telling) illustration of menstruation as "the exemplary case of such an ugly inside spilling out" (1997, 24; see also 1989, 77; 1994, 182). Here he finds the vagina, as if a wound, to be an appropriate description of that little piece of the Real, the fantasy object. As nonsymbolizable, the Real fits this topological description of ugliness. The Real is ugly because it cannot be symbolized, because its "existence is larger than its representation" (1997, 21).

It seems to me that the phallus, rather than the vagina and its fluid, is the exemplary case of topological discomfort with a tumultuous inside. The hysterical phallus produces *jouissance* par excellence: the lack that is hidden by the phallus explodes in ugly violence. The antagonism in the social order, produced by lack of land and resources, explodes, turning the phallus inside out: the ugliness of military force and police brutality spills out of the dominant order, and Sheol gapes its mouth in the midst of holy colonizing order. The logic is always the same: when dissidents recognize that the guarantors of the social order are not what they seem and through questioning unmask the fundamental antagonism that makes up the social order—it explodes. The legal and democratic orders wield batons or firearms; the Holy One spits out fire.

Chapter 2

Hollywood's Hegel Reads the Bible: *Remember the Titans*, Race Relations, and the Prison Industrial Complex

Remember the Titans (2000), directed by Boaz Yakin, tells the motivational tale of a journey from racial conflict into racial harmony, accomplished through football. This is the Hollywood version of the true story of a high school in Alexandria, Virginia, in 1971, that has been suddenly forced to integrate black and white students, and so also black and white football players. It is the story of the success of Coach Herman Boone (Denzel Washington), who has been sent to T. C. Williams High School to be assistant coach to Bill Yoast (Will Patton). He is soon promoted to the position of head coach as the token black head coach for the region. Boone's promotion infuriates the displaced white coach, Yoast, and his young daughter, for whom this represents both a humiliation and an obstacle to his being honored in the "hall of fame." In the face of the antagonism of Yoast and his supporters, Boone proves himself. He is a tough coach, who requires his team not only to work, work, work, in order to become perfect, but also to integrate and to get along. Through a process of hard work facilitated by Boone's high expectations on and off the field, the youths supersede their inclinations to the contrary: the team perfects its game, and the players overcome the hostilities generated by racism. Even the two coaches overcome their pride and territorializing behaviors and recognize each other's talents.

The overall "message" of the film (and being a Disney production, this message is none too subtle) is that black and white people can get along as equals, that there are a few hurdles to overcome and a few personal issues to work through, but that once these are dealt with, harmonious integration is more or less clear sailing. So the most basic critique of this film is that while it speaks out against personal racism, there is no exploration of what it might take to overcome systemic racism—that is, the way racism permeates and is perpetuated by institutional and economic structures. There is also a more nuanced critique to be made, however, if the subtexts of the film are taken into consideration. One such critique is made by film critic Christopher John Farley (2000), who argues that *Remember the Titans* reinforces two filmic stereotypes: the "Magical African American Friend (MAAF)" (Coach Boone) and the (white) "Bigot with a Heart of Gold" (Coach Yoast). These are caricatures, he suggests, that efface real African American "life histories or love interests" (2000, 14) and "offer the possibility of grace to all bigots in the audience."

The critique that I will offer here takes the position that these two stereotypes are framed by a yet larger, older discourse on relations of domination: the master–slave dialectic proposed by the renowned late-eighteenth-century/early-nineteenth-century German philosopher George Wilhelm Hegel and later revised and elaborated by the twentieth-century French philosopher Alexandre Kojève. Though many—most famously Karl Marx, Kojève, and the African psychiatrist and revolutionary Frantz Fanon—have considered Hegel's master–slave dialectic to offer the possibility of liberation,[1] I argue that as it appears in *Remember the Titans*, the Hegelian discourse works against liberation and encourages viewers' misrecognition of the seriousness of contemporary forms of racism, in particular the new slavery operating through the prison industrial complex.

Moreover, I suggest that the film is thick with biblically enhanced accompanying themes—desire, recognition between masters and slaves, and work-as-perfection—that undermine and even undo the surface celebration of harmonious racial relations. Along these lines, I assess the ideological impact of the Hegelian work to which biblical citation is put in *Remember the Titans*. Beyond a number of vaguely biblical statements made by characters in the film (in references to children of God, sinful pride, the world, etc.), there are explicit references to the biblical texts of Genesis 4 (the Cain and Abel story) and to Isaiah 40:30–31 (the promise that those who hope in Yahweh will run and not grow weary). In laying out the way these citations are used in a Hegelian fashion, I suggest that they are put to the particular ideological work of enabling misrecognition of the current state of race relations in the United States.

The premise for this kind of reading of the film is Louis Althusser's notion of misrecognition in ideological interpellation (for details on interpellation, see chapter 1). For Althusser, when ideologically interpellated subjects recognize themselves in the societal discourses held out to them (that is, they recognize themselves in ideology), it is always a misrecognition, but one that is constitutive nonetheless. He suggests that there is at once a function of recognition and of misrecognition operative in ideology. The recognition function is ideology's ability to produce a response to itself as if it is completely natural or obvious; the misrecognition function is the way that ideology effaces its operation—as well as its intimate connection to materiality—so that subjects think that their responses are spontaneous and free, not ideologically controlled. Or as Althusser puts it, it is "a peculiarity of ideology that it imposes (without appearing to do so because these are obviousnesses) obviousnesses as obviousnesses which we cannot fail to recognize" (1984, 46). In all this obviousness, individuals misrecognize ideology's reproduction of the material relations of production (1984, 57).[2]

Thus it is my contention in this chapter that the citations of the Hebrew Bible in *Remember the Titans* contribute to the way in which the film enables a white viewer (master) to *misrecognize* the increasingly imprisoned (and enslaved) U.S. black (and Latina/o) population's situation. And indeed, given that the film is framed by the voice and narration of Coach Yoast's young daughter, the viewer is initially interpellated as white and innocent, ready to misrecognize.[3] On the surface, the film seems to depict a sort of happy version of Hegel's dialectic of the master and the slave, showing the resolution of difficult race relations through mutual recognition of black and white high-school football players and coaches. But this on-screen recognition constitutes an off-screen *misrecognition* of the actual state of race relations between black and white people in the United States, with the prison industry growing as fast as it is (though clearly there is diversity within the broad categories of "black" and "white"). This misrecognition is enabled through a simulation of *mutual recognition* of the master and the enslaved, when in reality, the system that holds racism in place does not allow for this kind of mutual recognition. The contemporary master–slave relationship exists in a form that is not amenable to the kinds of permutations that the film suggests are possible.

I proceed through the argument in three stages. I first establish how I read this film as Hegelian. Here I draw heavily on Kojève's influential lecture on the dialectic between the master and the slave, which the film's Hegelianism strongly resembles. Because Kojève's lectures on Hegel in France in the 1930s hugely impacted thinkers like Jacques Lacan, Jean-Paul Sartre, and Maurice Merleau-Ponty, it has influenced the way Hegel has been received in culture (as the film seems to attest) and cultural studies.[4] I then move to an exploration of the way in which the biblical citations—taken from the Hebrew Bible and elaborated in later reading traditions—function within that context to produce misrecognition. Finally, I consider how Paul de Man's reading of Hegel's discussion of Hebrew poetry in the *Aesthetics* might affect this analysis.

To be transparent about my own social location, I will say that as a white academic and activist writing about issues that primarily affect people of color and that do not directly affect my communities or family, I am hindered by my own forms of misrecognition. And although I am involved as an ally in antiracist, antiprison organizing in the United States, I cannot avoid also being implicated in the oppressive structures that produce prisons, by virtue of participation in the many privileges that come with structurally reinforced white dominance. This structural culpability will render my analysis incomplete; I offer it nonetheless, in the hopes that it can contribute in some small way to awareness of pervasive white supremacism, as well as the uses to which the Bible is put in culture and race relations.

Hegel, Kojève, and the Titans

Whether conscious or not, the film's narrative remarkably resembles Hegel's dialectic of the master and slave, particularly as explicated by Kojève, though it is by no means a pure rendition of Kojève's reading of that fourth chapter of Hegel's *Phenomenology of Spirit*. Before getting into an analysis of the film, it may be helpful first to summarize the Hegelian themes that it seems to take up. The master–slave dialectic is a philosophical description of the relationship between two conscious beings (humans) in their struggle for autonomy and self-sufficiency. In this relationship, one party gains the status of self-consciousness (Hegel's word for the autonomous *I*, "isolated from everything and opposed to everything that is not I" [Kojève 1969 (1947), 10]). The other party remains dependent and subordinate. As the Hegelian story goes, in an attempt to attain the truth of itself, one self-consciousness must be recognized as an objective reality by another self-consciousness. But that other self-consciousness also requires recognition to achieve true self-consciousness, and so a fight to the death ensues. In the struggle, one of the two realizes that it is better to be alive than dead, so gives up and gives over recognition to the other. The one who gains recognition and so also true independent self-consciousness, Hegel designates the master; the one who gives the recognition, he designates the slave.

As Kojève points out, the fight begins because of a conflict caused by the (philosophical) requirement for self-consciousness to be both objective reality (a thing) and abstract truth (a concept) at the same time (Hegel 1977 [1807], §186–87; Kojève 1969 [1947], 11–12). While recognition as an independent object might give self-consciousness its "truth," it has also to maintain itself as pure, *abstract* self-consciousness. It therefore has to show itself "to be connected to no specific existence" (Hegel 1977 [1807], §187). This detachment from specific existence requires that self-consciousness negate its objective aspect. Thus each self-consciousness tries to kill the other in which its objective aspect resides, and in this attempt also stakes its own life. Only in risking life, says Hegel, can self-consciousness achieve "the truth of recognition as an independent self-consciousness" (1977 [1807], §187), that is, the truth of itself as both abstract and objective reality at the same time. However, if one of the two struggling actually dies, then no recognition takes place, and so self-consciousness does not accomplish its goal. Rather, negation has to take place in a way that both preserves and maintains the objective aspect of self-consciousness—the classic moment of Hegelian dialectic overcoming, or sublation; that movement of negation and preservation at the same time (1977 [1807], §188). Hence the master retains his objective reality in the slave, but at the same time negates that objective reality by making it servile.

Kojève's reading of the master–slave dialectic elaborates a number of salient points that it might be argued are featured in the film (again without making any claims about the intentionality of their appearances there). According to Kojève, before the fight, the two opposing self-consciousnesses are in an animal state, in what Hegel calls natural existence, and the slave remains in the animal state afterward (1969 [1947], 16), in what Hegel calls "thinghood" (Hegel 1977 [1807], §189). The slave works to transform the "thing" that s/he is, which is also the master's self-consciousness as objective reality. The slave's work on the "thing" enables its movement from the natural world to the human world (Kojève 1969 [1947], 17). Thus, paradoxically, the slave eventually becomes master over nature—thus overcoming his animal nature—through his work for the master. As master of nature, therefore, the slave becomes an independent and true self-consciousness, consequently freeing himself. Kojève, whose reading of Hegel makes much of work, suggests that self-consciousness frees itself *through its work*. At the end of the day, because of work, the slave finds himself further ahead than the master. As Kojève puts it, the slave—unlike the master, who is fixed in one position of mastery—is open to "change, transcendence, transformation, 'education'" (1969 [1947], 22). He goes on to expound, "Perfection . . . can be attained only in and by work" (1969 [1947], 23). Only the slave, then, is able to reach perfection, because s/he works.

For Kojève, as for Hegel, work takes the place of repressed desire. The master's desire is to negate the "thing" (self-consciousness as objective reality). Hence, negation is like consumption, or enjoyment, of that "thing" (Hegel 1977 [1807], §190; Kojève 1969 [1947], 24). As pure consuming negation, however, enjoyment can only be temporary, since once the thing is negated, it no longer exists for enjoyment. But in a negation that preserves and maintains (sublation), "work is desire held in check, fleetingness staved off; in other words, work forms and shapes the thing" (1977 [1807], §195). In Kojève's elaboration, the slave "postpones the destruction of the thing by first transforming it through work; he prepares it for consumption—that is to say, he 'forms' it. . . . [H]e forms things and the World by transforming himself, by educating himself" (1969 [1947], 25). For Kojève, then, it is work that differentiates consciousness as human, rather than animal; and it is ultimately only the slave who is able to achieve this, because the work has to be done under particular conditions of repressed desire to be effective. In Kojève's words, it must be "carried out against the worker's instinct or 'immediate interest,' the work must be carried out in the service of another, and must be forced work, stimulated by fear of death. It is this work, and only this work that frees—i.e., humanizes man [sic] (the Slave)" (1969 [1947], 26). Kojève reads this psychoanalytically when he says that the slave's desire is thus sublimated: "the slave can work for the master . . . only by repressing his own desires. Hence, he transcends himself by working— or, perhaps better, he educates himself, he 'cultivates' and 'sublimates' his instincts by repressing them" (1969 [1947], 24).

How does the master–slave dialectic make an appearance in *Remember the Titans*, then? The film seems to depict the relations between black and white coaches and between black and white players as a struggle for recognition. However, the Disney version of the dialectic is somewhat altered; in it, African Americans (historically slaves) and Americans of European descent (historically masters) *recognize each other*. Most of the characters in the film achieve mutual recognition through their hard work together in the training camp and on the field. Mutual recognition is a small modification of the dialectic of the master and the slave in which only the master gains recognition from the slave, and the slave recognizes himself as self-consciousness through the permanence of his own work for the master. In the film, the recognition is mutual.[5] While this difference might suggest that perhaps the master–slave dialectic is *not* present in the film, there are enough other similarities to suggest that the Hegelian narrative is at work (consciously or unconsciously). On the way to the modified end of mutual recognition, several Hegelian themes come to the fore: the struggle for recognition, work as perfection, and work as repressed desire. Yet though the similarities with a Kojèvian Hegel are strong, it is still crucial to interrogate the film's modification of the narrative's standard form. It is precisely this interaction between the Hegelian narrative and its modification that facilitates misrecognition of the grave problems in race relations in the United States. The relations of mastery and subordination that are so apparent in the master–slave dialectic are definitely present in the film, but they are softened by the mutual recognition of the film's ending, so that it seems as if these relations no longer trouble American life in any serious way.

An examination of the ways in which the master–slave dialectic plays itself out in the film begins where one might expect, with the fight for recognition. At the beginning of the film, when the two coaches first meet, a challenge to the fight is issued. Though Coach Boone says that he has come to learn from Coach Yoast, his "make no mistake, I come to win," can also be read as the Hegelian demand for recognition from one conscious being to the other. Just prior to this scene, one of Coach Yoast's star players refers to his new black teammates as "those animals," a slur that, while repeating a common racist image, also brings to mind Kojève's reading of Hegel, in which consciousness inhabits an animal state before the fight. The film also shows the white players to be driven by instincts. They are governed by testosterone, ready to enter into racial violence. Yoast has to "call them off," like guard dogs. Thus the film frames the need for recognition as a need to transcend animalistic stereotypes and instincts. Following this initial encounter, much of the film narrates an ongoing struggle, primarily articulated between the two competing coaches, but played out by the hostile black and white teams that are forced to integrate, as well as by their respective captains, Julius Campbell (Wood Harris) and Gary Bertier (Ryan Hurst). No sooner have they arrived at training camp than the two captains start fighting, and soon the whole team joins in the brawl.

However, Boone does not tolerate this behavior, and he achieves his desired results of teaching the boys to "play like men" and of winning, by demanding work and its correlative repression of desire. The theme of perfection through work is prevalent in the film. As coach Boone says to the team at the start of training camp, "You have come to work, and we will be perfect in every aspect of the game." The pep talk ends with "perfection, let's go to work." In good Hegelian fashion, the work that Boone demands can only be accomplished through the repression of desire. This requirement becomes evident in Boone's initial meeting with the black members of the team, where he calls a joking, singing group to attention (and here, stereotypically, it is the black players that figure desire). In this first encounter with the members of the team, Boone begins by bullying the confident Petey Jones (Donald Faison) into amending his statement, "Football's fun," to its opposite, "Zero fun, sir!" Satisfied, Boone introduces himself, saying, "I'm Coach Boone, and I'm gonna tell you all about how much *fun* you're gonna have this season. We leave for camp . . . 7:29 A.M. If you report at 7:30, you will not be playing football this season, you will be watching."

Throughout the rest of the film, Boone forces his players to sublimate their "instincts." He makes them get up early to run, he denies them a water break during practice ("water is for cowards, water makes you weak"), and he works them late into the night.[6] Among the instincts that Boone dictates against are racist instincts. He forces each player to get to know one member of the opposite faction in depth. One morning, before light breaks, he has the boys run out to the American Civil War battlefield of Gettysburg as a warning: "if we don't come together, right now, on this hallowed ground, we too will be destroyed just like they were." In response to all of Boone's demands, grumbling notwithstanding, the team works hard, both physically on the field to perfect their skills, and emotionally off the field to overcome their prejudice. Their work pays off with perfection: they do not lose a single game all season, and they learn to recognize and appreciate each other.

Work leads to recognition, as is made evident in the scene of the season's final game. At halftime, it looks as if the Titans are going to lose. In the halftime rally, Coach Boone dejectedly tells the team to do its best, "that's all anybody can ask for." Julius respectfully disagrees, "You demanded more of us, you demanded perfection," a reminder that drastically changes the mood in the locker room, as the team commits to work hard to achieve this perfection. Even Coach Yoast is affected and admits he needs Coach Boone's help with the defense strategy for the rest of the game: "I hope you boys have learned as much from me this year as I've learned from you. You've taught this city how to trust the soul of a man, rather than the look of him. And I guess it's about time I joined the club. Herman! I sure could use your help, Ed Henry's kicking my ass out there." When the team walks

Figure 2   Mutual Recognition in *Remember the Titans*

back onto the field for the second half, they are reinspired. To help the team win, Alan Bosley (Ryan Gosling) gives up his spot to Petey Jones, who has been sitting on the bench, because, as Alan explains to Yoast, he recognizes that Petey is the better player. After a series of outstanding plays—in which Coach Boone also takes advice from Coach Yoast—the team wins the game and the championship. The two coaches hold the football in the air together, black hand beside white hand, exchanging words of mutual recognition. Says Yoast, "What you did with those boys . . . you were the right man for the job, Coach," to which Boone replies, "You're hall-of-fame in my book."

If, for Kojève, work transforms the world and perfects historical progress, in the film the football players transform their world through their work, and it is said that this transformation is later extended to the entire community. In fact, according to screenwriter Gregory Allen Howard, one of the real-life inspirations for the film was the unusual success of integration in Alexandria, Virginia, prompted by football: "I started asking around and I kept hearing about this high school football team. . . . I couldn't imagine that a high school team could so affect an entire town. Some say they saved the city" (Anonymous 2000, 63).

Though the film begins with a struggle unto death, the narrative progresses such that both white and black players recognize each other. In this process they are educated, they sublimate their natural inclinations, and they are freed from their racism. I now turn to the ways in which the film's biblical allusions and citations amplify this racially encoded Disney version of the Hegelian/Kojèvian master–slave dialectic.

Genesis 4: Cain and Abel

Significantly, the struggle between the two coaches and their players is framed through reference to the struggle of jealousy and hatred between Cain and Abel (Genesis 4), which of course is a fight unto death. Coach Yoast's little daughter makes the only explicit reference to Genesis 4, saying, "I wanted the hall of fame real bad, just plain old jealousy, as old as Cain and Abel." However, the theme of aggressive, deadly hostility between two brothers repeats in several other places in the film as well. For instance, after they have run to the battlefield of Gettysburg, Boone asks the team to listen to the voices of the dead, which he (mystically, magically) is able to hear and report: "I killed my brother with malice in my heart; hatred destroyed my family." Later, when Gary, the white captain, gives recognition to Julius, the black captain, in a conversation between the two best

players on the team, he says, "I was afraid of you, Julius . . . now I see I was
only hating my brother."

In deploying the metaphor of Cain and Abel, or hostile brothers, the film
inserts a biblical story that has been racialized over the centuries into the
Hegelian framing for race relations. As a number of scholars have pointed
out, Cain has long been read as black—and his blackness as a mark of his
sin—in Jewish apocalyptic writings from the first and second centuries B.C.E.,
writings by the Rabbis, Medieval Christian texts, nineteenth-century U.S.
apologies for slavery, and Mormon texts (Chevillard-Maubuisson and
Marchadour 1993, 275–76; Mellinkoff 1981, 75–80, figs. 16, 20, 22;
Copher 1991, 148–50; Quinones 1991, 48, 52–53, 258 n. 11). So in referring to Cain and Abel, *Remember the Titans* alludes to a text that has a long
history of interpretation as justification for racist practice.[7]

Interestingly, the Hegelian thematics of the film seem to reflect dynamics already present in Genesis 4. The themes of desire and mastery are explicitly present in the text, and the theme of work comes out in the reading
tradition. Both desire and mastery make an appearance in Gen. 4:7, in
which Yahweh responds to Cain's disappointment that his sacrifice is not
favored as Abel's, saying, "If you do good will you not be exalted? And if you
do not do good, sin is one crouching at the door, and its/his *desire* will be
for you, and you will *master* it/him." The ambiguity of masculine singular
pronominal suffixes plays into a Hegelian reading in interesting ways. The
phrases "its/his desire" (תשוקתו) and "you will rule or have dominion over
it/him"(בו תמשל) are ambiguous in that the masculine singular suffix
could, in each case, refer either to the masculine singular participle "one
crouching" (רבץ), or to Abel. To be sure, the closest referent is the participle, rendering "it" (so van Wolde 1991, 30–32; Chevillard-Maubuisson
and Marchadour 1993, 268; Kabasele Mukenge 1999, 424–25). Yet if the
suffixes are read as referring to Abel (so Azevedo 1999, 50–59)— "*his* desire
will be for you, and you will master *him*"—the phrase easily lends itself to
a Hegelian reading, with Abel's slavish desire for Cain, and Cain's mastery
of Abel.[8] Certainly it seems that Cain, perhaps willfully, takes Abel as
the referent, understanding Yahweh to be telling him to master Abel: in the
next verse he masters his brother by killing him in the field (4:8).

However, Cain's mastery is not complete in the Hegelian sense, because,
as Gen. 4:7 indicates, he is ultimately dominated by Yahweh, who confronts
him and tells him what to do. Yahweh dictates that he must "do good"
(hiphil, טוב in order to be exalted, שאת). In other words, like the slave,
he must work. It seems that the reading tradition for this text takes up the
theme of work. As a number of scholars have pointed out, "doing good" in
this passage has been elaborated in the ancient Palestinian Rabbinic teach-
ings in the Targums (Neophyti and Pseudo-Jonathan) into a discussion of

a competitive meritocracy between the brothers.[9] In these Targums, Abel says to Cain, "Because my works were better than yours, my offering was accepted," with which Cain disagrees (Chevillard-Maubuisson and Marchadour 1993, 279–80; Gunn and Fewell 1993, 14–17; Kabasele Mukenge 1999, 430–31; Kugel 1990, 177). But Cain does become a figure of work in both the Jewish and Christian traditions, as the builder of the first city and as the ancestor of those who create culture, art, and technology (McNutt 1999; Paul 1996). As such, he is a figure of sublimation of desire through the "civilizing" work of building society and culture. Further, in more contemporary readings, Cain has also been read as performing work through sacrifice. For instance, Joaquim Azevedo reads the feminine noun חטאת in its sense as "sin-offering," and he reads the masculine participle רבץ ("one crouching at the door") as the male sacrificial animal, following the verb's frequent use to describe animals; in this way he renders the verse's strange mixing of genders coherent (1999, 51–53). Alan Aycock takes this kind of reading in an even more Kojèvian-Hegelian (and psychoanalytic) direction when he suggests—following a structural analysis of brothers or twins as two sides of a single figure—that in sacrificing Abel, Cain sacrifices the animal part of himself (1983, 124).

When read alongside the Hegelian story, then, Cain can be seen as holding together the two positions of mastery (killing Abel) and slavery (working for Yahweh).[10] This dual position resonates with Walter Lowe's suggestion that Cain is the epitome of the divided self, both slave and master, which is, further on in the *Phenomenology*, what Hegel calls the unhappy consciousness (1999, 118; c.f., Quinones 1991, 18–19).[11] Beyond the aspects of Genesis 4 and its reading tradition that amplify the master–slave dialectic in *Remember the Titans*, what is important to notice here is that the film takes up the Hegelian, racially interpreted biblical story in ways that instigate misrecognition. Indeed, the ambiguities of the biblical passage—from Cain's possible misreading of Yahweh's command (mastering Abel, rather than the sin crouching at the door) to his position as both master and slave—prefigure and even structurally support the misrecognition that the film's narrative encourages.

One of the ways the Cain and Abel story supports misrecognition of contemporary race relations is through the film's (Disneyfied) emphasis on brotherhood. The reference to this version of the world's first brothers is also an emphasis on originary unity to which it is possible to return. Such an emphasis on brotherly unity occludes recognition of the fact that African Americans did not originally come to the United States as full members of the family, nor even to be treated as humans. They did not begin as slaves *and* masters. An originary unity in terms of social positionality in the United States cannot actually be established, yet the film suggests, in high liberal

fashion, that this unity, because it grounds humanity, is not only possible
but is in fact actualized in the United States.

In addition, the film turns the tables of historical mastery and slavery by
having the white brothers (Abel) give way to the black brothers (Cain). The
black brothers take on the position of master. For instance, white captain
Gary gives recognition to black captain Julius, acknowledging him as a
brother; Yoast makes the first move in recognizing Boone; Alan gives up his
spot on the field to Petey; and all of the players give Boone recognition by
acceding to his demand for work. In other words, the white men take the
position of slave, giving recognition to the master. This may be a conscious
and conciliatory gesture on the part of the screenwriter Howard, trying to
right the wrongs of the past. Yet it is clearly one of those easy Hollywood
reversals that imply that racial positions are so structurally similar that they
can simply be reversed. This kind of unnuanced and straightforward reversal is a misrecognition of structural inequality between black and white
people in the United States.

On another level, subtle undertones to this reversal emerge when considered against the Hegelian subtext that I have suggested here. In the
words of Fanon, who reads the Hegelian struggle between master and slave
as essential to obtaining freedom, the kind of fraternal recognition represented in *Remember the Titans* is not actually obtained through struggle on
the part of the oppressed. Rather, "the slave . . . has been *allowed* to assume
the position of master" (Fanon 1967 [1952], 219) as the former white master paternalistically tells him, "Brother there is no difference between us"
(Fanon 1967 [1952], 221)—but clearly, historic practices on the part of
white people, such as slavery and colonialism, have ensured differences on
the level of economics and privilege. Further, within the Kojèvian/Hegelian
economy that seems to be at work in the film, this role reversal puts the
white characters in the position of "slaves" who are open to "change, transcendence, transformation, 'education'" (Kojève 1969 [1947], 22), where
the "master," now black, is not. In short, white folk are put in position to
supersede their black counterparts, a move that urges an explicitly racist
misrecognition.

Rising Up on Wings Like Eagles: Isaiah 40

The other biblical citation in the film that I would like to notice,
Isa. 40:30–31, is a bit lengthier, and plays on the dialectic slightly differently. The citation occurs in the midst of a pep rally called by black
members of the team who are concerned about the way the teamwork has

been degenerating since training camp. Big Blue (Earl C. Poitier) starts it off by saying, "Coach Boone brought us this far, y'all. But he ain't gonna be there for us forever, man. So what, we won a few games. Are you all fools to think that's something? That ain't *nothing* y'all. And you know what else, we ain't *nothing* either. Yeah, we came together in camp, cool. But then we're right back here and the world tells us that they don't want us to be together. We fall apart like we ain't a damn bit of *nothing*, man. And you all think we don't want something? Man we ain't want *nothing*, y'all, *nothing*" (emphasis mine). The film's "light-skinned brother," Lewis Lastik (Ethan Suplee), replies rhetorically to this declaration, turning to another teammate, Rev (Craig Kirkwood), "Rev, what's that you're always telling me when I get sick of trying to keep up with my grades and stuff?" Without waiting for an answer, he breaks into song, "Even youths grow tired and weary. Even young men stumble and fall. But those who trust in the Lord will renew their strength." The Rev agrees and sings back, "They will soar on wings like eagles, like eagles, y'all, like eagles, y'all," and Lewis finishes, "They will walk and not grow faint." This exchange encourages the team, and captains Gary and Julius take it up from there, leading the team into a motivational frenzy.

The point here in the film, of course, is that the team pulls *together*, overcomes, and rises up. The scene is highly suggestive of sublation, the movement into the Hegelian higher third term through negation. "Nothing," which is repeated five times, moves into a soaring up on wings like eagles. It speaks of a kind of transcendence that, in this context, resonates with the way that Kojève describes work: the slave transcends himself by working. Here again, the Hebrew text contains elements that might be said to lend themselves to a Hegelian reading in which desire (trusting in the Lord, קוה, "hoping for," "waiting for") is fulfilled in work (running and not growing weary). Though in the biblical text the strengthening of the weak is an end in itself, as proof of Yahweh's attention to the plight of Israel (as opposed to accused inattention [40:27]), in the film, the running, soaring, and not growing weary leads to other victories: the conquest of the team's internal divisions and then, on the football field, the ultimate sublation of being perfect.

Moreover, given the contemporary interpretive context in which this passage is habitually read, it is not too surprising that it gets taken up in the film in terms of negation and exaltation. The film's use of this biblical passage—taken as it is from the introduction to Deutero-Isaiah (Isaiah 40–55)—fits in a certain fashion with the way in which the larger framework of Deutero-Isaiah has been commonly understood by biblical commentators. Many scholars consider Deutero-Isaiah to be both reclaiming Israel's suffering (e.g., the image of the suffering servant) and also universalizing in its attempt to be inclusive of other nations (though this is often considered to be an imperialist sort of inclusion). To take one example of this kind of reading, John Milbank—a theologian responding to a reading of Deutero-Isaiah put forth by biblical critic Norman Gottwald—provides a remarkably Hegelian reading when he writes, "Israel's *nothingness*, her suffering *vanishing*, is rhetorically *converted into elusiveness, her universal mediation*, her elasticity, so that her subjective disappearance is inverted to become a prophecy of *her final imperial rule*" (1992, 64, emphasis mine). In other words, as in the Hegelian master–slave dialectic, here also suffering and negation ultimately gives rise to power. Milbank suggests that the sacrificial quality to Israel's suffering leads to her salvation: "God also accepts, like a sacrificing despot, the excess sufferings of Israel as entitlement to its reconstitution" (1992, 67). Like the slave in the Hegelian story, in this reading, Israel supersedes its negation through the sacrificial work of suffering.[12]

However, the Titans' "nothingness" at the point of the black teammates' biblical intervention has less to do with suffering than with lack of achievement, due to the two sides' unwillingness to recognize and work with each other. But the biblical pep talk works to solve this problem and to bolster the notion that mutual recognition is possible through *working together*. Here again there is a significant discrepancy with the Hegelian story that is important to notice. In the master–slave dialectic, only the slave works. The master simply enjoys and so consumes the products of the slave's labor. In *Remember the Titans*, not only recognition, but also *work* is mutual. This rendition of the Hegelian story, in which everybody works, conflates easily with the capitalist work ethic and the American dream: if everyone works equally hard, everyone can get ahead, or so the dream goes. Analysis of who does the working and who does the consuming is patently lacking in mainstream representations of the possibilities held out by the work ethic. Mutual recognition made possible by mutual work misrecognizes both historical and actual realities of racialized labor relations in the United States.

Further, this familiar citation of Isaiah 40, along with other "inspirational moments" in the film, positions viewers to misrecognize their own place within labor relations. The film aims to evoke a particular feeling in the viewer, a certain kind of longing, call it desire, for this kind of transcendence. But ironically, viewers are not asked to do any work in this film; it's all served straight up for consumption. Viewers are not asked to repress the evoked desire, to extend its fleetingness through work. Rather they consume the football players' work in the film, and the enjoyment thus produced is made clear in the feel-goodness of the film's conclusion. The consumption of the team's hard work interpellates the viewer into the position of the Hegelian master. But this position of mastery is hidden because viewers are meant to identify in some way with one or the other of the characters in the film (all of whom work), thus identifying with those working themselves into transcendence. That is, viewers are identifying as slaves, while structurally occupying the position of master.

Thus, the film's formal placement of the viewer nurtures a misrecognition of race relations in the United States, particularly for those viewers who occupy the structural position of privileged consumers, i.e., white, middle to upper-middle class. Not only does it encourage a misrecognition of the situation at large, then, but also of white, middle-class viewers' positions within the capitalist system that currently, as ever, gives rise to relations of production and consumption in which white Americans are often economically advantaged, as a result of the labor of people of color.

Central among the many contemporary forums for such racialized relations of production and consumption in the United States—including sweatshops, restaurants, and domiciles—is what has been called "The Prison Industrial Complex." A look at work in the context of the prison industry shows an entirely different picture than the one given in *Remember the Titans*, in which work leads to perfected race relations. As prison activists have been saying for a while now, prisons are the new form of slavery in the United States. As such they represent real relations of mastery over labor, relations—in which viewers may be implicated—that the discourse of race and work in *Remember the Titans* patently fails to address.

Given that the film's discourse takes the form of the Hegelian/Kojèvian story, it may be helpful to think through actual relations of mastery, servitude, and race in terms of the Prison Industrial Complex, in order to see more precisely how the neo-Hegelian story contributes to the misrecognition that the film enables. Of course, the argument could be made that Hegel's and subsequently Kojève's concept metaphors cannot be too rigidly mapped onto contemporary relations of domination and race; but I would argue that that is precisely what the film seems to do, and so at least it should be talked about.

Sublation through Work? The Prison Industrial Complex

The prison industry has become one of the fastest-growing industries in the United States, with private prison companies like the Corrections Corporation of America (CCA) netting $25 million in 2001 (Hoover's 2002). With approximately two million people in prison in the United States, the highest rate of incarceration per capita in the world, 70 percent of these people are people of color (A. Davis 1998). African Americans make up 48 percent of incarcerated people, even though they are only 12.7 percent of the population (Prison Activist Resource Center 2002). And though here I am focusing on the incarceration of African Americans, it is crucial to note that the situation is also dire for Latina/os and increasingly so for 150,000 immigrants per year who are detained by the Immigration and Naturalization Service (INS) upon arrival in the United States (and since September 11, 2001, often taken from their homes). Immigrants are detained for up to four years in private prison complexes or in county jails whose beds are contracted out by the INS.[13] In the state of New York alone, nearly 22,000 people, 95 percent of whom are people of color, are incarcerated by the state's Rockefeller Drug Laws (Correctional Association 2001; Schiraldi 2000, 11). The Rockefeller Drug Laws stipulate that first-time drug offenders (which could mean being caught carrying just one ounce, one time, for a friend, perhaps as a way of alleviating poverty) are automatically incarcerated for fifteen years, with no judicial discretion to lower the sentence. In spite of the so-called lack of judicial discretion, 94 percent of the people incarcerated for drug offenses in the State of New York are people of color, while the majority of drug users and traffickers are white (Correctional Association 2001). Similar laws are in effect in other states.

Within this prison industrial complex, prisoners work. While prisoners have often worked in prison, cleaning inside, or working outside on chain gangs or in convict leasing programs (Browne 1996), more recently there has been an upsurge of private corporations contracting out for prison labor (corporations like Compaq, Dell, Microsoft, Motorola, IBM, Victoria's Secret, and Toys 'R' Us, to name just a few) (Prison Activist Resource Center 2002; Parenti 1999, 230–31). Common objects of consumption—for instance computers and computer accessories—are produced by people of color in prison. While wages vary from state to state, the range is very small: some make "minimum wage" (most of which is then taken by the state and given to victims' rights organizations, antidrug campaigns, inmate "trust" funds, etc., leaving perhaps a dollar to the worker), some make under a dollar an hour, and some make nothing at all (Prison Activist Resource Center 2002; Corley 2000).

But as Christian Parenti argues, in spite of the fact that there has been an increase in the political rhetoric of the benefits of prison labor, actual labor for corporations is done by less than 5 percent of those incarcerated. Prison labor is not necessarily economically advantageous for corporations, and it is often subsidized by government. Products made in prison are often not of good quality because of low morale, and production is slow within the bureaucracy of supervision and scrutiny (1999, 231–35). Yet, the praises of prison labor are sung by those invested in the prison industry. This, Parenti suggests, is because "the right wing loves the trope of the toiling convict;

it is the perfect hybrid between moral revenge and economic efficiency" (1999, 237); it provides an image of morally reforming and economically productive punishment. Further, it plays on "the American cult of work as panacea; work as socio-cultural medicine for the slothful classes" (1999, 238).

In this sense, then, it is the *trope* of the laboring prisoner that does the work of legitimizing prisons and the increased subjugation of an impoverished and disenfranchised portion of the population through positing their uplift. But in order to function, this trope requires both real bodies laboring and a large potential workforce, just waiting to be accessed by enterprising corporations. So, it seems that the work done by the imprisoned "slave" (to come back to the Hegelian dialectic) is not always the actual manufacture of objects, but sometimes it is the work of being the physical support for that trope. The "thing" that is worked upon and formed is discourse. Put another way, often the real work that prisoners do, I would suggest, is in the endurance of incarceration. It is prisoners' sheer physical presence within prisons that works upon the trope of reformative labor in prison.

And though the trope of reformative prison labor is increasingly popular, the fact that it constitutes a complete misrecognition of the role that prisons play, and of the particular kind of work that prisoners do, becomes clear when one considers the rapidly increasing construction of supermaximum-security prisons and Special Housing Units (SHUs) (Thompson and Susler 1996). These types of units enforce the sublimation of desires through deprivation of any pleasures. The tiny cells (approximately ten feet by ten feet), in which one or two prisoners are locked down for twenty-three hours every day, are devoid of any natural light. As one prisoner, Florence, puts it, "When the American prison system decided to build these new super maximum security control units, windows in all of the cells were intentionally left out . . . it is a tool used to break the human spirit. . . . It is the cruelest blow" (Kerness 2001, 11). Pastimes, such as television or reading materials, are restricted. In some SHUs, a door in the back of the cell is opened for one hour a day, but prisoners do not go out. In others, prisoners may be let out for thirty minutes to an hour per day (Weinstein 2001). Steve, a prisoner in Tamms Supermax, Illinois, describes his treatment thus:

> Chances are I'll never leave here alive. I'm not gonna try to play it off like I'm an innocent. I'm not. But places like this are inhumane. When they bring you out of your cell, your hands are cuffed behind your back and there is never less than two officers and a lieutenant there. This is only after you are strip-searched, told to open your mouth, stick out your tongue, lift your privates, turn around, lift your left foot, right foot, then bend over and spread your cheeks. This is done every time you are brought out of your cell. . . . I feel love once a month for two hours, while I visit with my mother. Visits are through

glass, and talk is through an intercom. . . . I haven't seen a TV or heard music in three years, since I got here. Until a week ago I hadn't seen an outside building in three years. I was temporarily moved to a wing where I could see a farm a 1/4 mile away and a house trailer a mile away when I looked out the window. That was a luxury (Weinstein 2001, 16).

Those held in SHUs are treated as the most dangerous of the dangerous, although, in practice, this is not whom these facilities house. In reality, SHUs are being increasingly used to punish misconduct in prison (Sanchez 2001, 21), or to punish hitherto unproblematic situations. For instance a new 750-bed gang unit was built in New Jersey, for which people are "round[ed] up . . . to determine gang membership [though] New Jersey has never had a gang problem" (Kerness 2001, 10).

Clearly this kind of incarceration is not designed to reform the prisoner. George Welbourne, warden of Tamms Supermax (described above by Steve) states, "Tamms is not about rehabilitation, it's about punishment . . . some people may never leave" (Weinstein 2001, 16). Rather, as Parenti analyzes it, the role of prisons is a way of managing the contradictions of capitalism: "Capitalism always creates surplus populations, needs surplus populations, yet faces the threat of political, aesthetic and cultural disruption from those populations. Prison and criminal justice are about managing these irreconcilable contradictions" (1999, 238–39). So the "work" done in these prison units can only be that of enslaved bodily support for a system designed to ensure quality of life for another (white middle-class) master population.

However, neither the work of endurance, nor actual labor for corporations, frees the prisoner. Whether done on assembly lines or in SHUs through endurance, work in prison is always forced labor. Indeed, it would seem that current trends in incarceration may reveal serious limitations to Kojève's notion that it must be "forced work, stimulated by fear of death . . . that frees—i.e. humanizes—. . . the Slave" (1969 [1947], 26). What sounds liberatory in the abstract does not bear out on the material level. People in prison are not being freed, physically or mentally, through their various forms of labor. There are worlds transformed, however. There is the world of the inner city, where poverty and unemployment, still rampant, are "officially" diminished because a large proportion of the population (mainly male) no longer resides there. (This of course looks good for those whose governing careers are advanced by lower numbers of poverty and unemployment, but puts all kinds of pressures, financial and emotional, on those left behind.) There is the world of white middle-class Americans who can turn to prisons to feel that they are safe without "dangerous criminals" on the street. There is the rural world of white working-class prison towns, which are glad of some industry. And there is the world of the market, in which corporations managing prisons, or producing things for and in prisons, have become important and favored players. As in the Hegelian story, these worlds are transformed for the benefit of the master; but in contrast to that story, the slave is not freed. Produced within this context, *Remember the Titans* presents a misrecognition on two fronts. First, as elaborated above, the film misrecognizes the viewer's position with respect to this forced labor. By positioning white viewers to identify as workers, working as equal alongside their black counterparts, the film hides white viewers' privileged positioning within structures of production and consumption. It hides the fact that some of the actual manufacture of goods, if done in the United States, is done in prisons by African Americans and Latina/os. Second, with all its glorification of work, the film misrecognizes the role that the trope of work is actually playing in race relations these days in the justification of prison labor and the construction of new, and crueler, prisons. Moreover, it misrecognizes the value of forced labor and makes it seem acceptable. In the film, hard work (at some level forced on the team by Coach Boone) reforms the players and turns them into men. Hard work is what frees the team from their racism, and makes them perfect, able to reach their goals. Moreover, it is what leads them to mutual recognition. Indeed, hard work may be given extra moral weight in its alignment with viewers' desire, roused as it is by inspirational moments like the biblical exhortation to run and not grow weary. Thus the possibilities that the film sees for work, in suggesting that it can free the disempowered and transform the world, are quite different from what is actually accomplished through the trope of work for prisoners of color in the United States today.

To summarize my argument to this point: on the surface, *Remember the Titans* advocates racial harmony and peaceful integration, but, when read alongside Hegel and Kojève, biblically enhanced subtexts emerge that affirm racist structures and encourage viewers' misrecognition of their position within these structures. These subtexts imply that freedom, recognition, and perfection are only possible through forced labor and hard work, yet they misrecognize who it is that actually does forced labor in the United States. Perhaps, then, the film ends up affirming that forced labor, which in reality occurs in places like prisons rather than in football, is the real solution to the ongoing difficulties of racial integration.

Sublime Exclusion

By way of an epilogue, I would reflect upon Paul de Man's suggestion that Hegel's *Aesthetics* may reveal the Achilles' heel of the Hegelian dialectic.

One of the places that this happens, de Man suggests, is in Hegel's discussion of the "Symbolism of the Sublime" in the *Aesthetics* (vol. 1, pt. 2, chap. 2). In a very dense and close reading, de Man deploys Hegel's uses of scripture in "Symbolism of the Sublime" to show how the "all-important distinction [that Hegel makes elsewhere in his work] between the symbolic and the semiotic aspects of language is eroded" (1983, 142). This erosion, he suggests, would necessarily have implications for Hegel's whole system. Without presuming to attempt a critique of Hegel's entire system, I would follow on from de Man's discussion of the sublime, and the attention that he pays to the biblical quotations that Hegel uses in this passage, to consider how it might inform an analysis of the Hegelian dialectic at work in *Remember the Titans*.

As de Man points out, in Hegel's discussion of the sublime in the *Aesthetics*, the Hebraic poetry of the Bible represents the prime example of the sublime art form. For Hegel, content is sovereign over form in sublime art. The sublime work of art expresses only "absolutely clear meaning," that is, "pure Being as the meaning of all things" (Hegel 1975 [1835], 372). Hebrew poetry is sublime, so the argument goes, because in using words (as opposed to images or icons) to describe God, it privileges content and meaning over form. Representations of form or of the natural world in sublime art only serve to exalt the "one substance," that is, the deity. Here Hegel gives the example of Psalm 104, in which "light, heavens, clouds, the wings of the wind [and humans] are . . . nothing in and by themselves but only . . . for the service of God" (1975 [1835], 376). The sublime art form portrays an utterly dependent relation of creation and individuals on God. Again Hegel uses Hebrew scripture (Psalm 90) to make his point about "the nullity of man" before God: " 'Thou carriest men away as with a flood; they are as a sleep, even as grass which in the morning flourisheth and in the evening is cut down and withereth' " (Ps. 90:5–6).[14] What de Man points out is that Hegel's description of the sublime "one substance" in the *Aesthetics* places it outside the dialectic. Where symbolic language represents a dialectic of form and content, the description of the sublime "one substance," de Man suggests, is outside of symbol, outside of representation; it is apostrophe, sign, and trope. For Hegel, the Hebrew language in praise of the Deity is pure meaning, independent of form. As de Man traces Hegel's uses of Hebrew scripture, the sublime emerges as "rooted in the linguistic structure in which the dialectic is itself inscribed" (1983, 149). In other words, the sublime is what grounds the dialectic, while remaining exterior to it[15] (a relation that might be considered similar to Parenti's description of the functions of prisons as exterior to, but grounding for, capitalism).

The choice to use Hebrew scripture, characterized by Hegel as being radically exterior to form, in a Disneyfied Hegelian narrative about racial unity, may reveal the actual radical, racial, social exclusion that is being effaced by *Remember the Titans*. It is interesting to think about the exteriority of the sublime in light of the fact that, as Mark Taylor has pointed out, elsewhere in Hegel's writings (the *Early Theological Writings* and the *Lectures on Philosophy and Religion*), the Hebraic spirit (i.e., Judaism) is the antithesis of Greek beauty. Where the Hellenic ideal was harmony, unification, and identification, the Hebraic (sublime) is "separation and difference" (Taylor 1987, 7). Along these lines, in terms of the film, it may be symptomatic that Hebrew poetry is used (in Hegelian fashion) in a film that seems more Hellenic in its valorization of harmony and unification. If the sublime is thought of as that which makes visible the gap between representation and the unrepresentable (Žižek 1989, 203; Kant 2000 [1790], §§27–28), then perhaps the film's use of sublime Hebrew poetry points to what is unrepresented and unrepresentable for this Hellenic Hollywood production: those African Americans incarcerated, radically excluded, and held outside the social order.[16]

Of course, in the classic Kantian formulation, the sublime gives both pleasure and displeasure: displeasure that representation is inadequate, and pleasure that reason can grasp the incomprehensibility of the unrepresentable and can strive toward understanding it. In other words, the pleasure arises because "the subject's own incapacity reveals the consciousness of an unlimited capacity of the very same subject" (Kant 2000 [1790], §27). This new awareness "elevate[s] the strength of our soul above its usual level, and allow[s] us to discover within ourselves a capacity for resistance of quite another kind, which gives us the courage to measure ourselves against the apparent all-powerfulness of nature" (Kant 2000 [1790], §28).

Transposing this description of the sublime pleasure onto *Remember the Titans*, I might say that the displeasure of the film is that it doesn't seem to adequately represent race relations. But if there is a certain sublimity at work here, then perhaps part of the saccharine, feel-good pleasure of this film is not in what it says or does not say on the surface, but pleasure in the face of the unrepresentable. Perhaps it is this perverse pleasure that the viewer as master experiences, in knowing, maybe even unconsciously, that race relations in the form of the prison industry are indeed too great and too vast to be represented, yet they will still produce much work for consumption. It would seem that in *Remember the Titans*, both Hebrew scripture, and the sublime excluded other of which it is a symptom, give the pleasure of misrecognition.

Chapter 3

Framing the Golden Fetish:
Three Kings and the Biblical Exodus Tradition

Since one way of understanding how things work is to look at examples that do not, in this chapter I look at an unsuccessful attempt to inspire resistance through film. I am interested in why excess (hysterical, supplemental, etc.) *does not* function subversively in *Three Kings*, David O. Russell's 1999 spoof on the United States' 1991 war on Iraq, also known as Operation Desert Storm. It is a film that attempts to be critical of American foreign policy, yet in spite of its strong critique, it fails to generate resistance to U.S. militarism and imperialism. The film parodies the U.S. involvement in Iraq through the adventures of four soldiers, who, on the verge of returning home after the war in the Persian Gulf has been declared a victory, go on an unauthorized mission to steal Kuwaiti gold (stolen once already by Saddam Hussein from Kuwait). After finding the gold and stealing it, they are aided in their flight by Iraqi rebels, whom they then rescue by bequeathing them gold and enabling their escape into Iran.

One might think that parodic as the film is, in repeating the war so as to make some of its failures obvious, it might generate a kind of subversive excess with respect to the United States' war in the Middle East.[1] But the film's possibly subversive moments are recuperated, it seems, into the general ideological work that the film does of supporting U.S. imperialism. As reviewer J. Hoberman puts it, "The movie keeps trying to go conventional, and ultimately it does" (2000, 20). The film ends up glorifying the U.S. military and its self-prescribed role as savior. It presents and honors the ideological signifier of U.S. supremacy. One of the ways that it does this is through both overt and subtle biblical allusions and framing. The film's biblical undercurrents of messianism, exodus, and conquest highlight the way in which imperial or colonial power seems to set itself up as a salvific force that requires an endless exhibitionist staging and restaging of entry into the land. The film mirrors the biblical text's continual reinscription of rescue through exodus and conquest as it repeats, though parodically, the U.S. military's continual need to reenter the land of oil.

I should state here that beyond an examination of how the biblical subtexts play themselves out in *Three Kings*, this chapter is also an interrogation of certain tropes within poststructuralism and their ability to ground a radical politics. One of the most appealing ideas in theorizing resistance is the *subversive excess of signification*—or in other terms, the remainder, the *supplement*—that has become a popular trope in poststructuralist and postcolonial discourse. Excess makes its appearance under scrutiny of the repetitions required to get something started, whether it be a signifier, a concept, an ideology, or a discourse on metaphysics. Repetitions—of a word, an idea, a discourse—congeal into a "unified concept," into "meaning," effacing all discrepancy; yet there are still minute *differences* between the repetitions. Poststructuralists have called these differences—which are required to get discourses and signification underway but are then excluded or effaced— "undecidable," "trace," "supplement," "remainder." These terms have been used by theorists to suggest that the marginal and the excluded can somehow disturb mainstream norms. Poststructural and postcolonial theorists have circulated the compelling notion that the excess produced and excluded in the repetition that structures language is able to be disruptive, to disseminate and mutilate the unity of the signifier, in short, to trouble the waters of hierarchical power relations.

This leftover of signification, it has been argued, perhaps most persuasively by Homi Bhabha, has the potential to disrupt oppressive systems by disrupting stereotypes, providing alternate points of identification, and making sites of power and discrimination visible. Indeed, if the unified signifier is akin to the phallic ideological pinning point, as Jacques Lacan and Slavoj Žižek would have it (see chapter 1), the notion of the subversive, excessive supplement offers up a way to think about how those ideological pinning points can be disturbed. The question is whether the excesses of signification that give mainstream cultural productions such as film their ideological power can also prompt resistance to those ideologies. In other words, does the process of signification in ideologically mainstream cultural products, like Hollywood films, generate a supplement able to disrupt the unity of a phallic ideological signifier?

In the case of *Three Kings*, there are, without doubt, obscene excesses throughout. The preposterous plot is accompanied by myriad other extravagances: chaotic camera movements, an internal view of a gun wound and the bile it produces, a spilled tanker of milk (reminding viewers of the destroyed milk factory in Iraq), and vivid scenes of military stupidity and violence. With these excesses the film tries to be critical, to raise issues that have been left out of public discussion. It dissects the image of the U.S. military as a lean, mean machine and shows it instead to be made up of mainly inefficient and incompetent, if not plain stupid, soldiers. It is also quite direct in its critique of President George H. W. Bush, who called on the Iraqi population to rise up against Saddam and then left them unsupported to die in their attempts. In its repetition of the U.S. war on Iraq, the film opens up the "unified signifier" of the Gulf War by showing what has been excluded. It would seem then that the film produces difference in its repetition of the war, difference that could possibly operate as a subversive supplement. Yet it seems that while this repetition does indeed produce an excess, it is not subversive, it does not have the effect of forcing accountability or redressive action. *Why* then does colonial power's confrontation with its own excessive image not shake it?

By way of an answer, I examine the film's excesses in relation to a number of homologous concepts that have found their way into poststructural discourse: frame, supplement, remainder, excess, hysterical symptom, and fetish. In particular, I look at aspects of the film that operate as framing devices: the biblical citation (repetition) of Matthew 2, which is commonly held to be a repetition of the biblical exodus tradition; the masculine heroic action that circles around the gold; and the women who play supporting roles, framing the men's action and enabling the plot. I argue that in spite of the liminal positioning of the frames in *Three Kings* (and of frames in general), here they do not function subversively; rather, they are mobilized in ways that urge the viewer to forget the violence of the U.S. attacks on Iraq through identification with a messianic position that is bound up in the film with the humanism, colonialism, and commodity fetishism that bolster, rather than resist, American imperialism.

To be clear, I am by no means hostile to poststructural discourse in any of its forms (as, for instance, is Christopher Norris [1992], who appreciates Jacques Derrida, but not Jean Baudrillard, Jean François Lyotard, and Michel Foucault, whom he decries as relativists). I take poststructuralism seriously; but I am curious if, and to what extent, liminal structures (here named as supplement, remainder, or frame) can be de facto subversive and destabilizing, and to what extent, and under what conditions, they are co-opted into working for an oppressive power structure. The answer, I suppose, will have ramifications for considering the question of agency with respect to liminal structures: Will the supplement do its work on its own, or does it need to be activated by some sort of agent? Translating this question into activist terms, can alternative or marginal identities, practices, lifestyles, and structures be subversive on their own? Or do they have to be mobilized through some kind of intentional public voice or oppositional stance to have a resistant impact? Ultimately I suggest the latter, but this is always a negotiation in which political agency is overdetermined by (both determined by and determining for) the supplement.

Framing the Film: The Gulf War as Hysterical Symptom

I begin by situating the film within the discourse of media coverage of the U.S. war against Iraq, using it to introduce the relation between the hysterical symptom and supplement as frame. The notion of excess or supplement is particularly appropriate for a discussion of a film about the war in the Gulf, because the war itself has been thought of as the epitome of excess media spectacle, with its live coverage commented on endlessly by various experts and political analysts. Further, Baudrillard's assessment of the war in the Gulf as *simulacrum par excellence* has introduced discussion of the war into the realm of postmodern and poststructural discourse (and critique of that discourse; see Norris 1992; Cooke 2001, 8–10). Baudrillard's notion of "simulacrum" has become one of the tropes of poststructuralism that have (ironically) achieved quasicanonical status. The significance of Baudrillard's work is that he expands the usual understanding of simulacrum as a material image or representation that does not necessarily possess its proper quality, like an image of a deity that does not contain divine power. Baudrillard takes up the idea of simulacrum to think about the hyperreality of reality, the inability to know or construct reality, except once removed, through its constant simulation. The image not only stands in for the real, it also creates the real. As Baudrillard puts it, a simulacrum is a "generation by models of a real without origin or reality: a hyperreal" (1994, 1).

One of the ways that Baudrillard describes the simulacrum is as a symptom. The symptom, like the simulacrum, is an image of a reality (for instance, an illness or a psychic state) without which that reality cannot be known. There is difficulty in determining whether the symptom is "true" (indicating a real illness) or simply semblance. Indeed, the symptom might even produce reality itself. Quoting the French lexicographer Émile Littré, Baudrillard writes, "simulating is not pretending: 'Whoever fakes an illness can simply stay in bed and make everyone believe he is ill. Whoever simulates an illness produces in himself some of the symptoms'. . . . [S]imulation threatens the difference between the 'true' and the 'false,' the 'real' and the 'imaginary.' Is the simulator sick or not, given that he produces 'true' symptoms?" (1994, 3). The symptom, like the image, forms reality. Baudrillard makes the same point with the psychoanalytic example of the symptom produced by unconscious processes, without which the unconscious cannot be known (1994, 3). In a sense, then, an analyst's interpretation of a symptom determines an analysand's unconscious processes, because they are otherwise inaccessible.

Along similar lines, in essays written before, during, and after the U.S. war against Iraq, now collected in the book *The Gulf War Did Not Take Place*, Baudrillard (in)famously suggested that the war did not take place, it was only a spectacle. The war against Iraq was fought in and through a world of images standing in for reality. In other words, the Gulf War was a simulacrum. Because, Baudrillard argues, the war was won (by the United States) and lost (by Iraq) in advance, all the media hype and spectacle was simply about deterrence and decoy; it was not real war in which real stakes were waged, won, and lost.[2] Baudrillard does not negate the fact that there were many Iraqi casualties in the war, but asserts that they were "the final decoy that Saddam will have sacrificed, the blood money paid in forfeit . . . in order to conserve his power" (1995, 72). In Baudrillard's view, then, the media spectacle that was the Gulf War was one big decoy in a power struggle already concluded; like all simulacra, it was simply supplemental.

Not surprisingly, one of the ways in which Baudrillard describes the hyperreal phenomenon of the Gulf War is as a hysterical symptom, which emphasizes the supplemental nature of that media spectacle. He writes, "Just as the psychical or the screen of the psyche transforms every illness into a symptom . . . so war, when it has been turned into information, ceases to be a realistic war and becomes a virtual war, in some way symptomatic. . . . We must learn to read symptoms as symptoms, and television as the *hysterical symptom of a war* which has nothing to do with its critical mass" (1995, 41, emphasis mine). Though the highly censored media coverage of the war[3] might not have presented "truth" or "reality" as the Iraqi people knew it, at the same time, it created that reality by generating American and international support for the war, and it was in fact the only way that many people had any access to what was happening in the Gulf.

Baudrillard's simulacral hysterical symptom—blurring reality and image, and making visible an absence otherwise unknowable (here, the trauma of the violence of war)—is reminiscent of one of Derrida's most memorable descriptions of the supplement, found in his discussion of the *parergon*, or the frame. In his essay "The Parergon" (1979 [1974]), Derrida contemplates the question of the frame and its relation to a work of art in the course of an argument devoted entirely to the problematic of the frame as it functions in Immanuel Kant's aesthetics. Derrida carefully reads several illustrations in Kant's "Analytic of the Beautiful" of what constitutes the proper object (i.e., the *ergon*, or work) to be considered for aesthetic judgment (1979

[1974], 17). As Derrida notes, in discussing what is intrinsic to the work of art proper, and what is extrinsic, Kant considers only design and composition to constitute the *ergon* (1979 [1974], 18). By way of contrast, ornamentation, color, tone, frames, and the like are not intrinsic to the artwork, they are *parergon* (beside the work). The *parergon* is, as Derrida translates from the Greek, a " 'secondary object,' 'supplement,' 'aside,' 'remainder.' "(Derrida 1979 [1974], 20).[4] A *parergon* is added to an artwork, as Derrida reads Kant, "only because of a lack within the system it augments" (1979 [1974], 22).[5] As the case of columns around a passageway makes clear, the lack that the *parergon* ornaments, or frames, is only made visible by the very presence of the *parergon*. "[The] lack, which cannot be determined, localized, situated, *halted* inside or outside *before the framing* is . . . both *produced by* and *production of* the frame" (1979 [1974], 33). Put another way, the frame produces the very lack that necessitates the frame in the first place.

In response to Kant's understanding of the *parergon*, Derrida asks, in characteristic fashion, how one is really to tell, for instance in the case of drapery on statues, or columns on an edifice, or frames on art (all examples given by Kant), what is external to the object itself, and what is necessary to it. Columns, for instance, cannot be detached from the building (without destroying it), and so cannot be considered strictly external, superfluous. Or taking another example, frames might be quite elaborate, perhaps themselves works of art (for instance, frames that are ornamented by draped figures). To complicate matters, Derrida asks, "And what about a frame which frames a painting representing a building surrounded by columns in the form of draped human figures?" (1979 [1974, 24]). Such an image presents a very thick frame, in which it is impossible actually to delineate the inner and the outer. As he puts it:

> The incomprehensibility of the border, at the border, appears not only at the inner limit, between the frame and the painting, the drapery and the body, the column and the building, but also at its outer limit. *Parerga* have a thickness, a surface which separates them not only, as Kant would have it, from the body of the *ergon* itself, but also from the outside, from the wall on which the painting is hung, the space in which the statue or column stands, as well as from the entire historic, economic, and political field of inscription. . . . The parergonal frame is distinguished from two grounds, but in relation to each of these, it disappears into the other" (1979 [1974], 24).

In other words, while the *parergon* does operate as a sort of delimiting border, it is not precise; it blurs on both inner and outer limits, depending from which perspective it is viewed. The frame is similar to the symptom (hysterical or otherwise), then, in that both occupy the in-between and destabilizing place of supplement. The frame adds to, and makes visible, the lack around which it is constructed; the symptom is that which both substitutes for and adds to the otherwise inaccessible illness or psychic state (in terms of trauma, the symptom is that which is too painful to recall, and is therefore absent). The symptom fills in an absence and adds to it, but is also essential for knowing it, since it is otherwise unrepresentable.

To bring the relation between *parergon* and symptom back to the simulacral media on the war against Iraq, it might be said that the media's endless commentary on the war by military experts and political analysts framed the violence not shown—that is, the lack—that would be unrepresentable and traumatic for television viewers. But without this frame, support for the war could not be generated as effectively. In other words, the media on the war in the Gulf, like and as the hysterical symptom, occupies that privileged place in poststructural discourse, namely, the place of the undecidable, the supplement, the remainder.

But one would be hard pressed, I think, to make an argument for any of the subversive functions of the supplement operating in the media on the war on Iraq. Rather, media coverage of the war in the Gulf seemed only to generate support for the dominant ideology of American imperialism. But perhaps a supplement to the supplement, a film poking fun at media and war such as *Three Kings*, would be more likely to be disruptive. Given the homology I have sketched between supplement, symptom, and frame, one way into a discussion about whether or not supplements in *Three Kings* are subversive is to look at ways in which the film's narrative is framed. I begin with the biblical frame, then move through the framing of the gold by the men's action (in turn framed and enabled by the women in the film), and finally to viewers' positioning within these frames. The film's frames turn out to be the sort of thick, elaborate frames that Derrida describes in "Parergon." The thickness of the frames—that is, the concentric fashion in which each one frames and overdetermines the others, as well as their implication in the historic, economic, and political fields in which they are inscribed—mitigates against the realization of their potential as subversive elements. This failure occurs in large part because viewers occupy particular positions with respect to the political and economic determinants for the war in the Gulf, so that the film's frames operate precisely as symptoms that enable the forgetting of the traumatic violence inherent to those domains.

Three Kings in the Euphrates River Valley: The Biblical Frame

The entry point for a discussion of the biblical frame is obvious. The film's title evokes the biblical story, found in Matthew 2, of the visit of the Magi to the Christ child (modified through time to the visit of the "three kings")[6] and the holy family's escape into Egypt. The gold that the soldiers try to steal also alludes to the gifts of gold, frankincense, and myrrh that the Magi brought to the infant Jesus (Matt. 2:11). The allusion to the biblical narrative comes at the beginning of the film as the four soldiers discuss the action scenario. The thieving party consists of Sergeant Troy Barlow (Mark Wahlberg), under whose command a map indicating the gold's whereabouts is found wedged into the ass of an Iraqi captive; Private Conrad Vig (Spike Jonze), who pulls the map out of the aforementioned ass ("man, I didn't join the Army to pull paper out of people's asses, no sir, not what I signed up for"); Staff Sergeant Chief Elgin (Ice Cube), a member of Barlow's division who has access to translation of the map; and Special Forces Major Archie Gates (George Clooney), who, alerted to the presence of a map by the investigation of reporter Adrianna Cruz (Nora Dunn), crashes the meeting of the other three and takes on the role of commando. As the four discuss the map and the location of the gold, Conrad, in an unusually astute moment, observes that it is "way north of any allied forces," to which Chief Elgin comments, "it'll just be us and the Humvee in the Euphrates River valley." Perhaps encouraged by having contributed positively to the conversation once, Conrad speaks up again, in a more typical fashion (he is unabashedly portrayed as undereducated, moronic white trash; and not surprisingly he is the dispensable member of the party, killed in action): "where they found Moses in the basket!" Exasperated, Elgin corrects him, "that was Egypt," but Conrad, undeterred, begins to hum the carol "We Three Kings of Orient Are," to which he more heartily sets his own lyrics, mixing in a little Janis Joplin, "We three kings be stealing the gold, my friends all drive Porsches, I must make amends." Annoyed by this creative intrusion at such a moment of import and decision, the others quickly shut him up. Though part of the film's parody of Army personnel, Conrad's musical interlude is also crucial for establishing the framework for the plot. Staged as the confusion of a country bumpkin, the film provides a muddled, but surely deliberate, movement from Moses, to Egypt, to the Three Kings, to American capitalist desire.

In setting up the plot this way, the film alludes not only to the biblical story of the Magi, but also to the story of Moses leading the people of Israel in the exodus from Egypt (Exodus 5–15). This is not a surprising intertextual connection, given that the text of Matthew itself interprets the events following the Magi's visits as patterned on the exodus story. As the narrator of Matthew interprets it, the holy family's sojourn in Egypt (occasioned by the Magi's visit to King Herod, whereafter he jealously orders the deaths of all Jewish baby boys in hopes of eliminating the future king of the Jews for whom the Magi search) is analogous to the ancient Israelites' sojourn in Egypt before the exodus (Matt. 2:15). Like the ancient Israelites, the Christ child is eventually called out of Egypt. For this reason commentators have often considered Moses' life—also threatened by a king who tried to kill all Jewish boys—and the exodus story as models for the Matthean story (Allison 1993, 140–63; France 1981, 234; Bourke 1960; Pesch 1994, 167–68; Harrington 1991, 46–49). The film seems to reflect this well-established reading tradition for Matthew 2.[7] On the level of the film's sub-text, this intertextual allusion draws an equivalence between the biblical Egypt and the contemporary Iraq (Pharaoh and Saddam), and between Moses and the filmic kings. Of significance here is the fact that the Magi in the Matthean text are merely supposed to supplement and highlight the kingship of Jesus. Indeed as scholars have pointed out, the first two chapters of Matthew are concerned with establishing the legitimacy of Jesus' messianic, Davidic kingship (Blomberg 1991; France 1981; Pesch 1994; Nolan 1992; c.f. Horsley 1989). But in the film's plot-setting biblical allusion, Jesus more or less falls out of the picture. So there is an absence here, in the parallel between Moses and the soldiers, that the frame establishes: a missing messianic figure. But a hint appears early on that the messianic role will come into play, when Chief Elgin confides to a somewhat surprised Conrad and Troy that he has the "fire-baptized ring of Jesus." (Elgin demonstrates this gift later, by bringing down an Iraqi helicopter with an explosive football—an image that summons up the Hollywood stereotype of the soulful, athletically gifted African American.[8]) At the beginning of the film, then, there is the hint that the men will fill in the messianic gap, because one of them has the firepower of Jesus.[9]

The biblical frame closes up at the end of the film, picking up on the intertextual reference to the biblical exodus tradition with a climatic scene of crisis and release. By this point in the film, the gold has been partially distributed among the fleeing Iraqi rebels, with the rest stashed for the three surviving Americans to come back and reclaim. The party has almost reached the Iran–Iraq border when the U.S. Army, apprised of the AWOL soldiers' whereabouts, intervenes and arrests the renegade men before they can negotiate the passage of the refugees through the border. Barlow, Gates, and Elgin resist arrest in order to continue helping the refugees, despite being severely berated by their superiors (as is Adrianna Cruz, who has been reporting the scene). The Iraqi border patrols arrest the refugees and herd them into a small pen. Amid the chaos, Barlow nearly dies because, hand-cuffed, he cannot reach the valve that releases air from a recently acquired chest wound. He gasps for breath until the soldier guarding him ignores orders and cut his cuffs. In the moment of calm after Troy's near-death experience, the three men decide to sacrifice their gold and to reveal its whereabouts in exchange for the negotiated release of the hostage refugees. On hearing about the gold, Colonel Horn (Mykelti Williamson) decides to

negotiate with the Iraqi border guards to let the captives go into the land
of their potential freedom, Iran. As he walks back, he signals the wrap-up
of the operation (and the film): the helicopter propellers whirl, the music
begins again, and the captives are released into Iran, while the "three kings"
watch on in farewell, eyes brimming.

There is a clear exodus trope at work here. True to the film's opening,
the men are like Moses figures, negotiating the people's crossing out of
enslavement. And true to the biblical text, the men, like Moses, are not able
to cross with the people (Moses having been banned from the promised
land for disobeying Yahweh's commands [Num. 20:1–12; Deut. 3:21–29]).
But the men's "self-sacrifice" in that climactic scene (made somewhat more
serious by the presence of Conrad's shrouded body), also gives them a
Christlike status, filling out the early hint of Jesus' presence with/as them
and making the parallel of Jesus and Moses complete. As savior figures, the
three men step in to fill the lacuna opened up at the beginning of the film
around the figure of Jesus. In this way, the biblical imagery frames the men's
action as both Mosaic and messianic.

However, by making its messiah/Moses figures members of the U.S.
military, *Three Kings* cannot help but highlight what some biblical scholars
have emphasized as the inseparability of the exodus story from the conquest
narratives (see Warrior 1991; Said 1988; Prior 1999; L. Donaldson
1996).[10] With Yahweh's very first promise of deliverance from Egypt, the
Israelites are also told that the exodus will culminate with entry into the
promised land, the land of Canaan. The Israelites are assured that they
will expunge the inhabitants of Canaan (Exod. 3:8, 17; 13:5; 23:23, 28;
33:2; 34:11). Thus the Israelites' exodus is followed by a series of violent
encounters with the peoples residing in Canaan. Time and again the
recently enslaved Israelites destroy cities and peoples, leaving no survivors
(e.g., Num. 21:35; Josh. 8:22, 10:36–42; 11:12–21). Versions of the
exodus and conquest repeat throughout the Hebrew Bible, in its historical
narratives, in its figurative writing, and in its prophetic texts, like a
repetitive hysterical symptom—compulsively repeating some original
trauma. The film builds on this repetition, by repeating/citing Matthew 2,
itself already a repetition of the repeating biblical tradition. Thus the film
merely follows the logic of the exodus-conquest tradition to which it
alludes when it restages yet another entry into new lands. The action begins
after the war has ended—the soldiers should be going home, but instead
they start a new foray into the land of Iraq, only to come again to exodus.
The film even acknowledges that it depicts this kind of colonial restaging
when Colonel Horn says angrily, in response to Gates' dissatisfaction over
the accomplishments of the U.S. military in Iraq, "Your work in Iraq was
over, done . . . whaddaya wanna do, occupy Iraq? Do Vietnam all over?"

Apparently this is precisely what Gates wants and what the film's narrative requires.

Along these same lines, it would seem that on some level *Three Kings* follows an oft-traveled trajectory of intertextual relations between the early Christian text, Matthew 2, and the ancient Hebrew text, Numbers 24. Though there is not any kind of deliberate connection to Numbers 24 in the film, it does have a presence in the reading tradition for Matthew 2 and therefore may lurk somewhere in the wings of the film's narrative, as part of the background to the stories comprising the biblical frame. Indeed, the Magi's guiding star in the east has commonly been read—as far back as the sixteenth-century (Screech 1978, 392, 397)—to connote the victorious star of Jacob over Moab prophesied by the seer Balaam in Numbers 24 (to the great consternation of Balak, the king of Moab, who had commissioned Balaam's prophecy). A number of contemporary scholars have also considered the story of Balaam in Numbers 24—set during the people of Israel's wandering in the wilderness after the exodus—to be background material on which the narrator draws in telling the story of the Magi in Matthew 2 (Albright and Mann 1971, 14; Brown 1977, 193–96; Hagner 1993, 25).[11] Numbers 24 is, to be sure, a text that brings the colonial aspect of the exodus-conquest tradition into focus. Balaam's prophecy in Numbers 24:17 reads, "A star will come from Jacob, and a scepter will rise from Israel. It will crush the foreheads of Moab, the skulls of all the sons of Seth." Thus Balaam's prophecy specifically blesses, and so valorizes, Israel's colonial conquest of Moab.

The implicit connection to a most violent and genocidal text (Numbers 24) suggests that colonial conquest, not rescue, is really what is at stake in the film. Once highlighted, this intertextual connection does make one think twice about the Iraqis who are shot through the head in the course of the action. It also emphasizes the colonial nature of the soldiers' adventure— even if it does end in exodus—designed to steal other people's resources (no matter if they were obtained already once through theft). In short, this intertextual connection brings into view the conquest that the film hides in reversing the order of exodus and conquest. Ending with an exodus obscures the violent conquest that precedes it.

Framing the Gold, Framing the Phallus: The Men's Action

The escapades of the soldiers are so central to the plot of *Three Kings* that they might not necessarily be called a frame, except that they circle around something else: the Kuwaiti gold. The gold is crucial to the story; without it there would be no plot. It motivates the characters by producing desire (e.g., the capitalist desire of Conrad's song, and Gates's appeal to the others to find a way out of their day jobs). It also mediates relations between the Iraqi rebels and the Americans, and between the U.S. military officials and the renegade men. Facilitating human relations and desires as it does, the gold operates (to introduce another related concept) like a fetish, whether that be what Karl Marx (1977 [1867]) famously described as commodity fetish—"a definite social relation between men themselves which assumes here, for them, the fantastic form of a relation between things" (1977 [1867], 165)—or what Sigmund Freud called the substitute for the normal (sexual) object of desire (1953 [1905]b, 20; 1961 [1927]).[12] A fetish is a material object that operates like a symptom or simulacrum; it substitutes for, and also perhaps makes real, something unseen or repressed (Freud's standard explanation of the unseen causing fetish is the castration anxiety caused by seeing the mother's genitals).

As a sexualized object with definite value, the gold can be read as the commodity fetish that arouses the soldiers' desire and compels them to action. In Marx's terms, the gold enables and motivates all the turnings of the plot, all the relations between people, like "an autonomous figure endowed with life of [its] own, which enter[s] into relations . . . with the human race" (1977 [1867], 126). Relations between the various parties in the film are only established through the exchange of this one item. In Freud's terms, the gold is like an object that has been detached from its usual usage, to be elevated or given special sexual status. Certainly the gold is introduced in sexual terms: the idea of the gold is first mentioned in the only sex scene in the film (a banging scenario, between Gates and a reporter); and the map to its whereabouts is found penetrating a man's ass. Moreover, the gold is detached from "normal" social relations of desire and exchange. The gold becomes the sole object of desire, overriding more usual desires: it is detached from the armed forces' (and the soldiers') expressed goal to "liberate," from the soldiers' usual desire to please the hierarchy within the military, and from Barlow's desire to get home to his wife.

Slavoj Žižek's provocative reading of the commodity fetish along Freudian lines (1989, 11–53) raises an interesting question for a reading of gold as commodity fetish in *Three Kings*. Žižek suggests that what is important about the fetish, the symptom, the commodity, is the *actual form* that it takes. More than simply revealing the repressed memory that it represents, the form taken by the symptom or fetish tells of yet *other* unconscious wishes at work. As Žižek puts it, using Freud to liken the commodity fetish to dream-work, it is the dream-work (that is, the particular form of

the dream created by the process of condensation and displacement)—
rather than the manifest dream-content, or the latent dream-thoughts—
that is the key to the unconscious wishes (wish fulfillment) represented
by the dream (Žižek 1989, 14–15; c.f., Freud 1954 [1900], 277–78,
506–8, 644–47). Just as it is crucial for analysts of dreams to pay attention
to the specific forms of the dream-work, Žižek suggests that for analysts of
the commodity fetish, it is the particular form of the commodity that is
important to interrogate (1989, 15). In the spirit of reading the gold in
Three Kings as commodity fetish and symptom, then, it is vital to consider
why commodity fetish takes the particular form of *gold* in the film. Why is
it gold that is so central, rather than, say, the other commodities shown in
the film, stolen from Kuwait and stockpiled by the Iraqi army?

Perhaps Marx's somewhat central description of the function of gold in
Capital has something to say to the question of the specific form of fetish
as gold in the film. For Marx, gold is not actually a regular commodity, but
rather it is that which is exchanged for commodities. It is money. Gold
"thus acts as a universal measure of value" (1977 [1867], 188). Gold, as
money, stands in for the exchange-value of commodities; it "represent[s]
their values as magnitudes of the same denomination." In other words, it is
a standard form used to mark what Marx calls "exchange-value," or in simple terms, price. Exchange-value is determined by labor; it is an element of
labor *abstracted from* a commodity's use-value (usefulness) that gives it a
market value (1977 [1867], 127–31).[13] As a bit of "congealed labour time"
(1977 [1867], 130) abstracted from use-value, exchange-value is, in a sense,
a supplement. Gold makes visible, and at the same time universalizes, this
supplement.

In a highly instructive reading of this universalizing of exchange-value,
Thomas Keenan (1993) shows that Marx connects the production of
exchange-value in capitalism to the development of humanism. Marx
suggests that the universalization of labor through the abstraction process
that produces exchange-value is precisely what gives rise to humanism. It is
only with the idea of equivalence of labor that a notion of human equality
emerges. A human universal, therefore, is "possible only in a society where
the commodity-form is the universal form of the product of labor, hence
the dominant social relation is the relation between men as possessors of
commodities" (Marx 1977 [1967], 152). As Keenan interprets Marx,
"Humanity as such, empty and abstract, alike and equal . . . is indistin-
guishable from the commodity" (1993, 171). This, of course, is only
one of many possible explanations for the rise of humanism. But read in
conjunction with the notion of commodity fetish, as Keenan does, it gives
one answer to the question, "Why the specific form of the gold fetish in the
film?" If gold stands in for exchange-value (abstracted labor time), which

has contributed to a notion of "humanity," then gold can be read as the signifier of humanity, of humanism.[14]

It makes sense, then, that gold, as a signifier of humanism, is central to *Three Kings*. If humanism is understood in its most basic sense as the belief in equality, the human capacity to work together (as equals) for progress, and the ability of the individual to be self-determined and autonomous, it would seem that the film has a profound humanist impulse. The United States is portrayed as a world leader in bringing about progress, in helping others to be autonomous and free. The U.S. military is depicted as the vanguard of progress and rescue, of international solidarity against the inequality of dictatorship. Such a portrayal is not surprising given that the U.S. war with Iraq was waged under the humanist rhetoric of saving the world from Saddam. (However, as made evident by the film's biblical frame—not to mention Bush's "Just War" speech, which borrowed from a centuries-old theological debate to call the attack on Iraq "just"—the United States has never fully managed to leave religion out of its humanist justification for imperialism.)[15]

While critical of some of what happened in the Gulf, the film does not go so far as to leave behind the humanist rhetoric that motivates it. The valorization of liberal humanist values of freedom, democracy, and individualism becomes clear in an over-the-top, tongue-in-cheek, yet telling, scene in which Gates and Elgin try to convince a deserter from the Iraqi army (Fadil Al-Badri) to give them cars (also stolen from Kuwait) for one of their operations. Gates and Elgin begin by assuming, as colonizers are wont to do, that they have a right to share in the resources. When this is greeted by a polite refusal, they assert that they have a right to these resources because they are the American military, there to do the same work as the rebels in "kicking Saddam's ass." The rebel soldier reminds them that they are not, in fact, all equal: "We have no money, to eat, to live. The American army is huge, it has planes and tanks, and we have nothing." To this, the Americans respond, "Look at us, many races, many nations. Many nations, working together. United. George Bush, George Bush wants you, you, to stand up for yourself. Wants all of you to stand up together to fight, to kick Saddam's ass. He wants you to fight for freedom on your own, and then America will follow." In the style of political rally, Gates and Elgin rile everyone up and end with, "God bless America, God bless a free Iraq." Though the scene pokes fun, it also highlights the humanist values motivating the war and still at work throughout the film (as the film's ending makes abundantly clear). It plainly foregrounds the value placed on self-determination and autonomy, as well as the United States' self-understanding as both exemplary and called to lead other nations.

This scene also shows how humanism in the film is implicated in the structure of exchange. Hoberman puts it another way when he says, "*Three*

Kings ultimately becomes its own entertainment allegory—fighting Hollywood style, to occupy the position at which blatant self-interest can turn humanitarian while still remaining profitable" (2000, 20). As the scene makes clear, there cannot be any unity, any rising up together, without exchange, and the gold that makes it possible. When emotions have subsided a little, Gates asks again for the cars: "What do you say, my friend?" Upon receiving the steadfast reply, "Cannot give car," Gates concedes, "Okay, I guess we'll buy 'em." What becomes clear here, as well as at the end of the film when the men offer up the gold in exchange for the refugees' freedom, is that, as Keenan points out, exchange is fundamental to the commodity relationship, and therefore also to humanism (1993, 171–72).

The humanism displayed in this scene also exemplifies what Homi Bhabha calls the colonial demand for mimicry that both disavows and ensures difference (1994, 85–92). Apparently Iraqi autonomy requires Bush's urging and the blessing of the American state. The American soldiers disavow difference, by insisting on the Iraqi rebels' equality and ability to be autonomous, to stand up for themselves. But paradoxically, they also affirm the Iraqis' subordination and difference by emphasizing George Bush's primacy, "George Bush wants you!"

Indeed, the use of gold as fetish, as signifier of humanism, may also indicate the film's embeddedness in a colonial mentality. The gold reminds that the colonial enterprise, like humanism, is founded on exchange, albeit lopsided. As Laura Marks (2000) points out, the notion of fetishism developed as part of the colonial encounter, as part of the exchange between cultures that occurred as colonizers tried to understand indigenous practices of finding power in material objects (2000, 85–96). Moreover, the European middle classes began to forbid fetishes, which made them "available for disgusted/desiring projections" (2000, 87).[16] Along similar lines, the gold in *Three Kings* is only found and used through (forced) cultural exchange. And like the fetish, it is forbidden in large part because of its implication in colonial relations: it has been stolen already once from Kuwait, and it is only made accessible to the soldiers because of the presence of the American military in Iraq (and the forcible extraction of the map from the Iraqi prisoner). The gold is doubly forbidden because the men are acting on their own terms, not at the behest of their superiors— though they take advantage of the space created by the U.S. conquest of Iraq, they are not authorized by the military or political leadership. Moreover, the film's use of the gold as fetish, as something exchanged for the American values of struggle and freedom, acknowledges the dependence of these values on the exchange of the colonial encounter. It marks the war in the Gulf as another such encounter.

Beyond drawing out the connection between the film's humanism and its colonial impulse, I would argue that the specific form of the gold also indicates the megalomaniacal pretensions of the U.S. military. Thinking through the gold leads to a different assessment of the film's wish fulfillment than that given by film critic Stuart Klawans: "this time [as opposed to Vietnam] we don't behave like complete shits" (1999a, 43). Instead, an interrogation of the gold reveals a wish that reads something rather more like, "this time, like other times, rescue through military action validates a feeling of U.S. superiority."

Here a comparison of Marx's discussion of gold with Žižek's discussion of the phallic position of the ideological master signifier is illuminating. Insofar as gold, for Marx, is not itself a commodity per se, but rather that which makes exchange of commodities possible, it is the signifier of pure possibility. As such, it marks a relationship based in fantasy. Marx points out that the relation between gold and the commodity is an imaginary relationship (in the non-Lacanian sense), though it does bear some relation to the actual material substance:

> We may use purely imaginary or ideal gold to perform this operation [of expressing value]. Every owner of commodities knows that he is nowhere near turning them into gold to give their value the form of a price or of imaginary gold. . . . In its function as measure of value, money [gold] therefore serves only in an imaginary or ideal capacity. . . . But although the money that performs the functions of a measure of value is only imaginary, the price depends entirely on the actual substance that is money (1977 [1867], 190).

Gold as an imaginary ideal marks the place of something that is not there, though it must be supported materially on some level.

The analogy is not exact, but the *idea of gold* is something like Žižek's reading of Lacan's notion of the phallic signifier. The phallic signifier, like the idea of gold, marks the possibility of exchange. As Žižek puts it, "as the signifier of pure possibility, the phallus is never fully actualized (i.e., it is the empty signifier which, although devoid of any determinate, positive meaning, stands for the potentiality of any possible future meaning)" (1993, 161). In terms of Žižek's formulation of the ideological operation, fetish is the symptom, or object of desire, raised to the status of the (missing) phallus (see chapter 1 for details). So like Marx's description of gold, in which a material substance is endowed with power through fantasy, a fetishized object is also endowed with power, and raised to the status of phallus through fantasy.[17] In both cases, a symptom, or a supplement, is raised to the status of the phallic ideological pinning point.

It is precisely this phantasmic, fetishistic status of gold, so similar to the ideological phallic signifier, around which all the other relations turn in the film. What is striking is that the idea of gold takes the same place in the film that the United States and its armed forces like to think they take in the world with respect to politics, culture, and quality of life. Just as the gold is the signifier of pure possibility for the men who pursue it (for example, to Barlow it represents the possibility of owning a Lexus convertible in every color), the United States thinks of itself as a nation that signifies pure possibility for its citizens and for the world. It holds the promise of unbounded democracy, cultural production (including film), and high standards of living. Indeed it is the pure possibility called the "American dream" that is invoked by Gates in motivating the others to think beyond their day jobs to the hopes represented in the gold. The American dream becomes the phallic ideological pinning point. But the film also aligns the American dream (represented by the gold) with the chief ambition of the all-powerful American armed forces (obtaining the gold). In so doing, the film shows that American military power is integrally linked to the possibilities afforded by the American dream: the military is the condition of possibility for the signifier of pure possibility. In other words, the film raises the gold to the level of phallus, that is, to the level of pure possibility enforced by the U.S. military. Using psychoanalytic language, it might be said in response to the question, "Why the specific form of the gold?," that the dream-wish behind the work of prioritizing and fetishizing the gold is the wish of the United States and its military to be all-powerful. Not to put too fine a point on it then, in the film the gold might be read as a stand-in for the American phallus.[18] In the words of Žižek, "the phallic signifier [the gold] . . . is a fetish of itself: phallus . . . as it were gives body to its own lack" (1993, 161). It is a narcissistic and self-referential relation. Though the film pokes fun at the phallic pretensions of the military with the abundant phallic imagery in the film's opening shots (the piss pipes, the media microphone, the soldiers spraying water bottles and posing with guns in celebration), it constructs a complex set of frames around the gold and thereby, in essence, ends up glorifying the American phallus. In a sense, the film frames the phallus. Yet, it seems that the (erect) phallus only gains its ideological power to lay down the law, to dominate, through desire for land and resources (i.e., the gold) and the ability to acquire them; it is, therefore, a specifically colonial inflation (see chapter 1).

What I have been tracing here are the sides of the innermost frame for this central item, the phallus. The four sides of this elaborate frame—messianism, humanism, commodity culture, and colonialism—are all implicated in each other. Messianism is secularized in the form of humanist helping, which supports and is supported by commodity culture, which in turn cannot survive without the colonial endeavor to supply raw goods and labor, an endeavor which (to join up the sides of frame) gets coded as messianic helping. This complex set of relations frames, and is made possible by, the empty yet all-powerful position of the gold (as phallus), standing in for the endless

(Western) endeavor to conquer new land and resources.[19] When read this way, messianism, humanism, commodity culture, and colonialism cannot so easily be separated out as mere framing devices; they are implicated in this phallic will to power.

Female Facilitators: The Woman Frame

Though the narcissism of the American military admiring its phallus in the form of gold may be reason enough to understand why this film is not successful in producing resistance, there may be more to it. Here it is necessary to examine another of the film's frames/symptoms, what I will call the woman frame—an outer frame that frames the men's action—which frames the gold—already framed once by the biblical frame. The film demonstrates what media critic Laura Marks says of the media coverage of the U.S. war in Iraq in general: it's one big buddy film (1991, 57), but it still requires support and sustenance provided by women.

From the beginning, the narrative is framed by women in supporting roles. In the opening sequence of the film, reporter Adrianna Cruz sets the scenario with her on-site reporting of the servicemen's celebration of the "liberation" of Kuwait. Still in the opening sequence, the audience becomes privy to a verbal tussle between Adrianna and another female reporter (who is not even important enough to be named in the opening introduction to the characters). The argument arises over the fact that in order to scoop a story, the other woman has seduced Adrianna's escort (who happens to be Gates). In their shrill and hostile exchange—which in a predictable sexist fantasy takes the form of insulting each other about their looks—the media is shown as the somewhat hysterical feminization of the male military machine. Yet, as Colonel Horn recognizes and tells Gates in reprimanding him, the (feminized) media is essential to the war: "This is a media war! A media war! And you better get on board." In contrast to this scene, the film ends with Troy Barlow, his wife, and two babies gathered together in his carpet store. The closing shot is of his wife Debbie (Liz Stauber) gazing at him adoringly. A polarity is thus set up between sexually free and assertive woman and (presumably) sexually monogamous and financially dependent mother. Though the film may be poking fun at both of these positions, it is significant that the sexually free woman drops out of the picture entirely (though she is not actually "autonomous," as she only serves to introduce Gates and the gold) and that the male neocolonial adventure closes with the image of an affirming, supportive woman in a commercial outlet.

In the middle of the film, as a sort of structurally central supporting column, there is the scene of the radically excluded Iraqi woman without whom the heroes cannot and will not act; she is the necessary catalyst for their action. Just as the men have obtained the gold and are about to drive off with it, a situation develops that changes the course of their action. The leader of the rebels, Amir Abdulah (Cliff Curtis), is held captive by Saddam's soldiers, who have just given up the gold and brought their prisoners out into open air. Amir's wife (Marsha Horan) runs to greet and attend to him, whereupon she is taken hold of by one of the guards. As the American soldiers start their truck, she pleads, "Don't go; please, don't go." The Americans look on, disinterested, preparing to leave, until the Iraqi commander gives an order and she is shot in the head. Blood spurts dramatically, excessively, as she falls in slow motion. Gates's head hits the steering wheel in despair, she hits the ground, the tables are turned. The men decide to stay to help. This unnamed Iraqi woman's death prompts them to change from self-interested thieves into selfless heroes.

Thus the woman frame consists of woman as sexual object, woman as hysterical bearer of crucial news, woman (of color) as (expendable) catalyst for heroic action, and woman as faithful, childbearing, support at home. As such, the women in the film are indispensable to the plot and yet not particularly figured in it. They are excluded yet necessary: the classic frame.

Figure 3   Murdered Iraqi Woman in *Three Kings*

The figure of woman, like a colonized land, is central to the production and exchange of the plot, the war, the gold, the commodity.[20]

The woman frame is a very thick frame, inseparable from the sociopolitical context of actual women's role in the U.S. war on Iraq. The women in the film function as Marks, in her analysis of the media on the Gulf War (1991), has suggested that women function in general with respect to contemporary American warfare. As Marks puts it, women are essential to militarism in a behind-the-scenes, effaced, self-sacrificial, and therefore masochistic way. They are background support, "those who work for free on the base, reinforce (male) soldiers' masculinity, train the next militarized generation" (1991, 59). Marks suggests that during the war on Iraq, women's role was symbolized by the ubiquitous yellow ribbons, which, because of their historic links to women's remembrance of lovers at war, "appeal[ed] specifically to women, and specifically to sexually faithful stay-at-homes whose constancy is crucial to the morale of the individual soldiers, and hence of the military as a whole" (1991, 55). Thus even the patriotic symbol of support for the Gulf War was imbued with a traditionally gendered division of labor in which women acted as sacrificial support.

Women play this same self-sacrificial (sexual) role in *Three Kings*. For instance, Barlow's wife is the sexually faithful stay-at-home wife, bearing another generation for the military. She plays a crucial role in moving the plot along when Barlow calls her from a cell phone in captivity. Because she is home and waiting, ready to set things up for his return, she is able to call the U.S. Army, give Barlow's coordinates, and alert someone to his problem and to the whereabouts of the AWOL soldiers. Likewise, the murdered Iraqi woman sacrifices herself by raising her voice to plead for help. Her sacrifice has the added benefit of moving the plot along. Adrianna Cruz also puts herself on the line. She saves the men's careers, ensuring their honorable discharge with her reporting, in spite of being threatened by Colonel Horn (not to mention being held in contempt throughout the film). Even the competing reporter at the beginning of the film—though establishing Gates's masculinity for the viewer and providing him with sexual release before he takes charge of finding the gold—does not seem to get much pleasure from her sexual encounter with Gates; she doesn't even manage to get (any of) her underwear off. It is clearly, from her end, more about information exchange than pleasure, but it seems she gets the short end of the stick. In the film, as in "real life," women frame and self-sacrificially support male military conquest. The lacuna that is left open by this frame is the place for women in key, non-supporting roles.

Hysterical Identifications

So why are these frames, excessive and supplemental and apparently satirical as they are, not subversive? Perhaps the answer is to be found in the contextual thickness of the woman frame. Here Marks's argument that women acted as points of identification for viewers of the media on the war in the Gulf provides a clue. Marks suggests that the media coverage of the U.S. war in Iraq required self-sacrificing women to appear in what she terms "tragic relief breaks" (1991, 60). These features focused on women—for example, the wives of American servicemen—and their emotions, giving the audience points of identification that enabled a tearful, pain-filled pleasure, a masochistic pleasure (1991, 59). Emotional women, as points of identification, Marks argues, filled in for the "lack of carnage and visible destruction" in the media that would have satisfied male spectators; they furnished instead "compensation in an emotional outlet—which was also the locus of female identification" (1991, 58). Marks further suggests that these tragic relief breaks functioned like hysterical symptoms. Hysterics, in Freud's terms, "express in their symptoms not only their own experience but those of a large number of other people; it enables them, as it were to suffer on behalf of a whole crowd of people" (Freud 1953 [1900], 149; cited in Doane 1987, 19; cited in Marks 1991, 59). Likewise, Marks suggests, "the [American] women in pain—and the spectators who identify with them—provide an emotional outlet for the [Gulf War] coverage as a whole. They are an enabling condition of the massive and distanced violence that prevails elsewhere" (1991, 60). In other words, in the media coverage of the war in the Gulf, images of women, like a hysterical symptom, dealt with the affect produced by the violence of the war that had "not been disposed of by abreaction" (Breuer and Freud 1955 [1893–95], 15), that is, had not been discharged in a normal fashion.

It would be convenient for my argument if the women in *Three Kings* played this same role, somehow providing an emotional outlet for viewers such that they would not have to consider the actual imperialist violence that the film tries to critique. But the film does not seem to establish identification with these women. There is no sympathy established with the female reporters, only disdain. There may be more sympathy for the other women, but identification is certainly not encouraged. The Iraqi woman is not even constituted as a character; Barlow's wife is mainly used as a decoy, especially in the scene of Barlow's torture, where his torturer calls to mind the things that Barlow loves—shown in cuts to the Barlows' domestic life—and compares them with his own loss, establishing viewers' empathy with Barlow and perhaps also with his torturer.

The film does, however, pride itself in its ability to arouse affect; this is clear from the caption at the film's opening, informing the viewer that the colors used are intended to enhance the emotional content of the film. What is odd about the film's declaration of enhanced emotion, though, is that in spite of all the excess throughout the film—in color, in music, in violence, in the vacillation between action and calm—the only real affective moment of the film is in the climactic scene in which the refugees are penned up and then released. Even when Conrad dies, there is only tragic calm. But in this penultimate tumultuous and sentimental scene, the viewer is pushed to emotion. Several factors beyond color contribute to the emotional impact of this scene, including music; the subtle uses of slow motion; the focus on the faces, which as Gilles Deleuze suggests are affection-images (1986 [1983], 87–90);[21] and of course the release of the captives. But perhaps even more rousing is the taking of decisive action: Adrianna to cover the story; the soldier to cut Barlow's cuffs; Colonel Horn to negotiate with the border guards; the three men to give up the gold. In each case there is a build-up of tension and chaos followed by release and calm. And in each case there is self-sacrifice, or a risk involved in making the decision. This moment of masochistic helping is captured perfectly in the image of Gates, Elgin, and Barlow holding up cuffed hands in farewell as the refugees cross into Iran. It is most gratifying that the goal of the various sacrifices—rescue—is achieved.

Significantly, this affective scene is part of the biblical frame. The task of dealing with emotion is shifted from the more typical woman frame onto the biblical frame in the film. But, taking a cue from the (thick) woman frame, it may be possible to read the filmic exodus-conquest trope along the lines of the hysterical symptom. The exodus scene, with its emphasis on release of captives, does the work of a hysterical symptom. The audience is able to live emotionally through the familiar cycle of tension and release in the exodus-conquest motif. Like its prototype, the biblical story of exodus-conquest, this scene offers tension and release in the movement from oppression into victory; it occasions a surge of emotions.

As a flashpoint for viewers' emotions, the exodus scene is like a hysterical symptom that facilitates forgetting. The image of the freed Iraqis enables the viewer to forget facts like the frenzied U.S. bombing of many thousands of Iraqi troops in their retreat from Kuwait (Niva 1991, 69–70; Elbaum 1991, 155–56). It effaces the bombing of civilian targets and the utter destruction of water and sewage systems in the country (Harak 1991, 516; Niva 1991, 70). Combined with the film's emphasis on the "liberation of Kuwait" and its digs at the soldiers' dissatisfaction with their fighting time in Iraq, the exodus scenario intimates that it was indeed a clean war, a war that helped people rather than hurt them. (This sentiment is corroborated by the opening shots of the film—following a caption that tells that the war has just *ended*—in which Barlow shoots an Iraqi solider who is signaling surrender, to which Conrad says, "Dag! Didn't think I'd get to see anybody shot in this war." Though it may be argued that this is satirical, the scene still disavows mass slaughter.) While the film does show images of the horrors of war (the internal view of Troy's bullet wound, the birds caught in the oil slick), somehow the force of these images is rendered ineffectual by the film's opening (the liberation of Kuwait) and closing (the liberation of the Iraqi refugees). Closing with an exodus scenario does away with any lasting memory of the violence that attends conquest.

Moreover, it enables the viewer to forget that still, again, in 1999, the time that this film was being produced, the United States under Bill Clinton was bombing Iraq, having started in December 1998.[22] It enables the viewer to forget the disastrous long-term health and environmental effects of depleted uranium used in U.S. ammunition. More recently, when *Three Kings* aired again on NBC in the spring of 2002—at a moment when support for George Bush's military effort against terrorism might have been flagging after the initial fervor—it no doubt facilitated forgetfulness of the violence already inflicted on Afghanistan and planned again for Iraq.

Thus the biblical frame as hysterical symptom is *not* subversive, not only because it valorizes the U.S. military, but also precisely because in the name of a laugh at a *past event*, it stands in for events past and present that are neither able nor allowed to be represented. It blocks knowledge. As hysterical symptom, this framing device deals with the traumatic affect of doing violence so as to make it bearable to a population that may not know, or remember, the violence incurred in its name by political leadership and the military. In short, it may be that the film's production of affect provides an outlet for emotions produced and left unabreacted by the violence of various U.S. neocolonial wars. As noted by commentators (see Tuleja 1994, 29) and by the film itself, Desert Storm helped to expiate the United States in the mind of the public for the atrocities of Vietnam (Adrianna Cruz says to a group of celebrating servicemen, "They say you exorcised the ghost of Vietnam with a clear moral imperative"). In like fashion, *Three Kings* apparently tries to exorcise the ghost of Iraq.

More important, the biblical frame positions viewers to identify with those making the "right decisions" in the exodus scene. Particularly at work is the film's positioning of viewers through the camerawork. Three sequences at the end of the film illustrate well the identifications with the heroes that the film tries to forge for the viewer. In the first sequence, the viewer is urged to identify with the soldier who cuts Troy Barlow's cuffs. Barlow lies gasping on the ground, his hands cuffed behind his back, unable to reach the valve in his chest that can keep him alive. The camera looks up at the soldier guarding Barlow, before it cuts to Gates, who yells, "Cut his cuffs!" The camera moves back to the soldier, who looks increasingly uncomfortable. It quickly refocuses on the chaotic argument between Colonel Horn and Adrianna, before once again moving back to the dying Barlow. By now the viewer knows the urgency of the task at hand. At last, the camera looks up again at the soldier, squirming with discomfort, as he makes the decision to go against his orders. He cuts the cuffs. The decision is marked by a distinctive and satisfying click as he flicks open his pocketknife; it is given weight by the low camera angle, which sets him on a kind of moral high ground. Once the cuffs are cut, the tension subsides again.

The tension mounts again in a second sequence, as viewers are encouraged to identify with the men as they decide to give up the gold. The sequence begins with the camera focused on Gates. A shot then gives his point of view: the refugees being harassed by the border guard. The camera moves to Gates, back to the refugees, then back to Gates. In a series of quick shots, he obtains significant nods from Elgin and Barlow. The camera finally settles on Gates, who says, "We've got the gold!," in order to initiate negotiations for the refugees' passage. This series of shots, beginning as it does with Gates' anguished contemplation of the refugees, highlights the decision that has to be made in the men's silent communication. Once made, the decision gives great relief, as well as a sense that the viewer has been privy to the decision-making process.

In a third sequence, still in the climatic exodus scene, the viewer is positioned to identify with Colonel Horn, the only military official in the field who has the authority to negotiate to set the prisoners free. The sequence is comprised of two (loosely defined) shot/reverse shots. In both pairs, the initial shots are of Gates trying to persuade Colonel Horn, and the reverse shots are of Horn making his decisions. The first reverse shot registers Horn's indecision. Gates pitches it harder the second time: "Return the gold, save some refugees, get that gold star." The second reverse shot registers Horn's decision to do the right thing. With this formal device, the viewer is positioned, with Horn, as the one making the right decision.

Not only are viewers positioned to identify with those making the right decisions, but they are also positioned to identify masochistically, as self-sacrificing heroes, because in each case there is a great personal risk involved in making these decisions (even for Horn, because he cannot be certain that things will end as Gates promises). Along with the three men, the viewer steps in, as a messianic figure, to fill the lacuna opened up by the biblical frame. In a sense, then, the viewer is integrated into the relation of messianism, humanism, colonialism, and commodity culture that frames the gold and the phallus. The viewer becomes part of the *parergon* to the phallus—that which is necessary for it, giving it body. The position of being requisite in the support of the imperialist American phallus would necessarily render null any thought of subversion.

How to Identify with a Disappearing Remainder

There is, however, more to be said, because as a number of feminist film theorists have pointed out, formal urgings of films are not always successful in securing viewers' identifications (see Stacey 1994 [1981], 130–37). Sometimes viewers identify in unexpected ways. I would like to consider what other sites of identification might be available in *Three Kings*, by way of returning to Baudrillard. In an essay entitled, "The Remainder," in *Simulacra and Simulation*, Baudrillard asserts that the remainder is the excluded element through which "reality is founded and gathers strength" (1994 [1981], 143). Because the remainder is excluded, he argues, there is no opposing term by which to judge it; it is itself the division between inside and out. The remainder, or symptom, becomes the norm by which to judge reality (1994 [1981], 145). However, the remainder has expanded, he argues, with the privileging of the excluded element in various liberation movements. The marker of division between the real and the unreal, between the mirror and its image, has grown, so that when "the system has absorbed everything, when one has added everything up, when nothing remains, *the entire sum turns to remainder*" (1994 [1981], 144). As he puts it, "there is no longer even a remainder, due to the fact that the remainder is everywhere, and by playing with the slash [that is, the division between inside and outside] it annuls itself as such" (1994, 146). It is not clear if Baudrillard bemoans or celebrates this expanding remainder; nonetheless, the implication of his essay for resistance is not particularly positive, suggesting as it does that "all the 'liberations' [of the traditionally excluded] that play on the hidden energies on the other side of the slash" (1994 [1981], 146) are merely recuperated into a new form of (simulacral) reality. In this kind of recuperation, the epistemic privilege of those traditionally excluded as other is lost.

It would seem, however, that the way in which I have described the frames in this film—the woman frame, the biblical frame, and the frame of messianism, humanism, commodity fetishism, and colonialism around the gold/phallus—resembles this spreading remainder. The frames that I have discussed have such thick textures that each broaden out into entire fields of intertextual relations, social relations, forms of identification, gender relations, media strategies, and power relations.

But if, even just for the moment, it is considered plausible that the remainder, or the frame, is all-encompassing and structures reality, then thinking subversively is not just a matter of seeing through it to the truth— if the remainder is all there is, then subversion requires reconfiguring it in some way. If, as is increasingly apparent, the public is caught in an ongoing media war—that is, caught within the simulacrum—it would seem crucial to find new ways to confront simulacral reality, to reconfigure it. While this process would need to be more substantively theorized, I might tentatively suggest that such a reconfiguration may be a matter of differently filling in the gaps that the frames construct. For even though frames may open out onto other vistas, they are still occasioned by and establish absence, even if it is then nearly obliterated by the frames' simulacral sprawl. What seems to happen, at least in film, is that the simulacrum broadens out by offering up its own suggestions for filling in the gaps that ground it, and for positioning viewers to fill the gaps in the same ways. But audiences do have a choice about how to fill in the gaps and how to identify, though these choices might be limited in some way by the film's, or simulacrum's, basic structure. What I am suggesting here, though, is that a negotiation with the simulacrum is possible.

So, for instance, to suggest one possibility among others, viewers might choose to fill in the gap left by the biblical frame differently. As I've argued, the biblical frame in *Three Kings* opens up a space around a missing Christ figure. Viewers are invited by the film's formal structure to fill in the gap with themselves, in an identification with the film's messianic heroes. However, a very different configuration might emerge if the viewer filled that space instead with the sacrificially murdered Iraqi woman, perhaps trying to understand what it would mean to identify with her. Such a move would not overturn the structure of the film entirely. To be sure, it would leave messianism and humanism in place, and it would still leave the viewer identifying masochistically. But it would be a different kind of identification. Rather than an identification with a hysterical symptom, produced by traumatic violence elsewhere, it would be, in some sense, an encounter with the trauma itself. In other words, it might force viewers to deal with their own emotions, rather than live through emotions produced elsewhere. This new, liminal identification would not enable the forgetting of the traumatic violence inflicted by a neocolonial war. It would place viewers, American viewers at least, in the position of hysterics themselves, resisting the identification expected of them, yet unable fully to identify with the other position either; that is, unable, as citizens of a colonizing force, to identify fully with a woman whose country had been ravished by colonizers.

Moreover, if viewers were to identify with this figure, she would be endowed with the full range of (the viewers') emotions and possibilities for action (for as long as she remained alive). And though this endowment might only be a narcissistic filling-in of the film's lack of character development, it would still de facto give her—a woman, an Iraqi—the status of a key player; she would become more than just a peripheral, hysterical enabler of militarism. As such, she would fill the gap left open by the woman frame for characters in key, nonsupporting roles. Further, as a central figure, she would not be so dispensable; her death would not be incidental, but rather, upsetting and angering.

Identification outside of the spaces formally opened up for it would necessarily affect the configuration of the film around the viewer, as well as the viewer's response to the film. For instance, in this case, the sense of the distribution of blame for doing wrong and credit for being heroic might change. The American soldiers, rather than the Iraqi soldiers, would be given the responsibility for the death of this central figure. Viewers might therefore respond differently to their action. Moreover, it could be said that it is the Iraqi woman's action that saves the refugees; the men merely serve as vehicles, in spite of their self-serving intents, only set on their course because of her death. It is only a matter of happenstance—thanks to Barlow's stay-at-home support—that the military authorities show up, and so it is really only a matter of chance that the men give up the gold; their hands are forced, as their chances at returning for the gold are dashed. When the American soldiers' heroism is seen in this light, it makes all the more evident the co-dependence of exchange, messianism, and humanism: there would be no humanitarian saving if the (forced) exchange of gold did not take place.

Reading through this kind of identification is not just a matter of wishing the film to be different—though it might be nice if films would do this kind of work[23]—but rather of suggesting that viewers do have options for identification other than the rather narcissistic ones that the film urges. Taking *Three Kings* as an analogy to the larger simulacrum in which we live (what some people might call ideology), it seems that one strategy for making change might be to deliberately look for and choose other sites of identification within the simulacrum. Any attempt to develop a politics that goes beyond the status quo must take seriously the question of the supplement. But the issue is not, then, simply whether the remainder is subversive or not. It is a question of to what purpose those remainders/symptoms/frames are put, and of how to identify with them. Radical politics may require political agency formed in negotiation through liminal identifications with the postmodern, neocolonial, simulacral structure in which the Western world seems sometimes to be caught.

Chapter 4

Zion is Burning: Genderfuck and Hybridity in Micah and *Paris Is Burning*

The Hebrew text of Micah is not generally heralded by transsexuals, transvestites, drag queens, and other gender transgressors as an iconic text. The film *Paris Is Burning*, on the other hand, is. The 1991 documentary of drag balls in Harlem—directed by Jennie Livingston—might then be just the place to start an analysis of the ambiguous and shifting syntactic and metaphoric signs of gender in Micah. To my mind, both text and film exhibit what is technically termed "genderfuck," that is, the mixing of masculine and feminine gender codes in ways that subvert the present bipolar gender system (Bullough and Bullough 1993, 246; Ekins 1997, 41; Whittle 1996). Yet while genderfuck has usually implied some kind of deliberate effort to upset gender, it would be difficult to argue that the genderbending in Micah or *Paris Is Burning* is deliberately designed to undermine gender. However, as I see it, both film and text perform genderfuck, by setting up gender norms that are then repeated in ways that call those norms into question.

It is my contention that the differently iterated signs of gender in both *Paris Is Burning* and Micah produce a kind of genderfuck that resembles what Homi Bhabha has termed *hybridity*, and that the effects of this kind of genderfuck are, as Bhabha suggests, ambivalent: within both Hebrew and filmic texts, exhibitions of genderbending are violently punished, yet these same hybrid presentations of gender also manage to destabilize the reader, highlighting, shaking, and perhaps loosening commitments to oppressive gender codes and the bodily ways in which these codes are manifested. Thus genderfuck emerges on two levels. At the level of text, the differently repeated signs of gender form a hybrid that, though restrained by the text, calls into question the gender ideals upheld as natural, pure, or authentic. On the level of reading, hybridity crosses readers' own entrenchment in gender and fucks with it.

Such an argument picks up on Peggy Phelan's suggestion that the trans-sexualism and transgenderism of *Paris Is Burning* exhibit the kind of post-colonial hybridity Bhabha describes in several of his essays (Phelan 1993, 187–88 n. 3). I do not, however, wish to analyze the lifestyles of transsex-uals in Harlem per se, but rather to look at the hybridity produced by the *filmic depiction* of Harlem drag culture, using this to illuminate the text of Micah. Quite obviously, by using Bhabha's notion of hybridity in the con-text of a discussion of genderfuck, I take it out of its original discourse on postcolonial relations between cultures. However, to do so is in some senses to follow Bhabha's own often catachrestic use of theory, as well as, I think appropriately, to broaden the notion of hybridity to speak of other cultural relations characterized by dominance and discrimination. Bhabha theorizes hybridity as formed through mimicry of a dominant culture. His insights are therefore fitting, given that the film focuses on the imitation of wealthy white culture, and that the Hebrew text too repeats norms that are oppres-sive. To proceed along this trajectory, then, I first give a synopsis of the film and the text, as well as a discussion of Bhabha and hybridity, before finally turning to an analysis of genderfuck in both.

Paris Is Burning

The film uses interviews with a number of well-known drag artists, legendary children and up 'n' coming legendary children, to communicate infor-mation about the ball circuit in Harlem. Through these interviews, the viewer is introduced to the concept of the ball, the competitive drag fash-ion shows around which the interviewees' world is configured. The ball is like our world. The ball is to us as close to reality as we're gonna get to all of that fame and fortune and stardom and spotlight. Following these explanations, scenes from the ball reveal the different categories in which the drag artists com-pete. There are categories for everyone: **Miss Cheesecake**, That means you must not only have a body, but you must be *sexy*; **Butch Queen, Bangee Girl, Bangee Boy,** Lookin' like the boy who prob'ly robbed you a few minutes before you came to Paris's ball; **School Girl, School Boy, O-P-U-L-E-N-C-E,** You own everything, everything is yours. This is White America; **Pretty Girl, Military, Executive,** In a ball room, you can be anything you want. You're not really an executive, but you're looking like an executive, and therefore you're showing the straight world that I can be an executive. If I had the opportunity, I could be one, because I can look like one.

The balls are situated within the social organization of house. Houses replace the families from which young transvestites and transsexuals are expelled. Let's see if we can put it down sharply. They're families, you can say that, they're families.... A house is a gay street gang. A gay house streetfights at a ball. Each house has a mother who reigns. The mother usually becomes the mother because she's the best one out of the group ... to be the mother of the house, you have to have the most power. Take a real family, it's the mother that's the hardest worker, and the mother gets the most respect. Competition between the houses is played out in the balls, they call them competitions, but believe me they're wars, using stylized violence and creative insults, variously called reading, the real art form of insult, shade, I don't tell you you're ugly, but I don't have to tell you because you *know* you're ugly, and voguing, it's like taking two knives and cutting each other up, but through a dance form.

Among those interviewed are: Pepper Lebeija, the legendary mother of the house of Lebeija.... I'm one of the more popular ones, and I've been around for two decades. Reigning, that is; Dorian Carey, when I grew up, you wanted to look like Marlene Dietrich, Betty Grable. Unfortunately, I didn't know that I really wanted to look like Lena Horne. When I grew up of course, you know, black stars were stigmatized; Venus Xtravaganza, I don't feel like there's anything mannish about me, except maybe what I might have between me, down there, and that's my little personal thing; Willi Ninja, they say I'm the best voguer out; and Octavia Saint Laurent, this is not a game for me, or fun, this is something I wanna live. Hopefully, God willing, by 1988 I will fully hope to become a full-pledged woman of the United States.

Each of these personalities expresses dreams for the future. The very femme Octavia Saint Laurent, who has photos of her idol Paulina Ross pinned to her walls, dreams of being a wealthy model. I think if I could just be on TV, or film, or anything, I'd do that with the money. Of course I'd like the money, because I want the luxury that goes with it. But, I want to be wealthy, if not wealthy, content, comfortable, you know. I want to be somebody. I mean, I am somebody. I just want to be a rich somebody. The more male-identified Willi Ninja, who makes a living teaching women how to model, dreams of stardom. [Voguing] is starting to make a name for itself and I wannit to be known worldwide and I wanna be on top of it when it hit. I want to take voguing not to just *Paris Is Burning*, but I want to take it to the real Paris, and make the real Paris burn. And not just there, but to other countries as well ... I would really like to take my whole house and go to Japan ... I wanna be a big star, known generally every corner of the world. Venus Xtravaganza, who because she is pretty and petite successfully hustles as a woman, dreams of being wealthy and white. I would like to be a spoiled, rich, white girl, they get what they want, whenever they want it. They don't have to really struggle with finances. **And Pepper Lebeija, who boasts of popularity, fame, and beauty**—New York city is wrapped up in being Lebeija—**imagines what it would be like to have wealth.** Just imagine if I had the dollars?! That would be too much for the world. If I had the riches and I had the fame, trust me, all of you all in here would be richer boys. Cuz I'm very generous. . . . I'd wanna charter a plane and we'd all fly to Paris.

At the end, the film comes back to visit these dreams with footage from three years later. Willi Ninja has made it big. Now I've got my foot in every little doorstep that you can think of . . . doing a lot of runway work, dancing . . . doing choreography, helping people put their shows together. By way of stark contrast, Venus Xtravaganza is found under a bed after having been missing for four days, strangled, presumably for hustling as a woman and being read as a man. The film ends between these two polarities with Dorian Carey, who comes to terms with the reality of failed dreams. I always had hopes of being a big star, but as you get older you aim a little lower . . . then you feel you left a mark on the world if you just get through it. . . . You don't have to bend the whole world, I think it's better to just enjoy it, pay your dues and enjoy it. If you shoot an arrow and it goes real high, hooray for you.

Micah

Although the text of Micah seems in many ways light-years away from the film, it might be said to contain its own acts in drag (to appear shortly: Samaria and Jerusalem, alias Sam and Jerry; Brazen Zion; and Madame Jacob). Throughout the text, the gender codes of its personified figures—Israel's national identity (Jacob and the Daughter of Zion), cities (Samaria and Jerusalem), and various towns—are constantly mixed and transgressed, on both syntactic and metaphoric levels. For instance, the gender of the "lamenting feminine" towns and cities of Judah (1:10–16) is not always clear, nor is the consistency of their lament. Masculine plural imperatives, "do not tell, do not weep" (אל תגידו, אל תבכו), are followed in the next breath by feminine singular imperatives, "roll in the dust, pass by" (התפלשי, עברי),[1] all of which seem to be addressed in some way to a masculine plural *you* (לכם, מכם) (1:10–11). The addressee also seems to take on active male behaviors, such as harnessing chariots to the steed (רתם המרכבה לרכש), and giving a dowry (תתני שלוחים), possibly to kings (1:13–14). Likewise, an unnamed city to whom a voice calls in 6:9 is initially addressed with masculine forms. It is said that *your* (masculine singular) name will see success (ותושיה יראה שמך). *You* (masculine plural) are called to listen, hailed with the (masculine singular) appellation, "O tribe,"

(מטה) or as some have translated, "O rod"—both of which have masculine connotations (of Israel's organization and governance for the first, and of aggression for the second). Yet at the end of 6:9 and in 6:12, the city also seems to be referred to in the feminine with feminine singular pronominal suffixes. Finally, a similar, though more obscure, ambiguity of a city's gender occurs in 7:11, where a day is proclaimed for building *your* (feminine singular) walls, followed in 7:12 with the nations coming to *you*, suddenly masculine singular, with no indication that the addressee has changed.

This type of shift has kept scholars scrambling to suggest new and improved emendations. Many scholars read these kinds of shifts as corruptions in the text. For instance, in the case of the feminine singular imperative addressed to the masculine plural in the phrase "Pass by, to you" עברי לכם (1:11), scholars emend either the imperative or the prepositional phrase so that gender and number match.[2] I have been more interested, however, in taking the text as it is, and considering the impact of these syntactic shifts on the metaphoric sense of the text; they have been the impetus for thinking about metaphoric gender benders in the book. I call them "acts in drag," but really they're more akin to camp performances than to actual attempts at passing.

Sam and Jerry

The personified city Samaria appears in 1:6–7, vilified, stripped, and made desolate. She'd been behaving in a most assertive and active masculine fashion by collecting the wages of prostitutes. She is not actually accused of prostitution, just of gathering their wages. Interestingly, this is a detail that most often gets emended away to read, "from the wages of prostitutes they [her idols] are gathered." While "pimping" may be a highly anachronistic term, it seems that scholars, even ancient readers of the text (e.g., the versions), cannot fathom the idea that Samaria collects prostitutes' fees.[3] The punishment in Micah for this initiative, this forward economic enterprise, this pimping? Samaria is stripped, as if to ascertain her real "sex," and anything remotely phallic and thrusting, like idols, are cut off. Finally her earnings are burned. Thus she is stripped of any signs of male power, both physically and economically.

The text's punitive response to female economic independence is apparently not effective, because Jerusalem arrives on the scene in 3:10 wearing a similar outfit, in the same category: executive realness. She is running male intellectual trade workers, who sell their political counsel for profit. Her leaders sell their judgment, her priests sell their teaching, and her prophets prophesy for silver. The text marks these intellectual trade workers, with feminine possessive pronouns, as hers. It is she who profits from their activities. But the power granted her in a male role does not last long. The punishment for her assertiveness comes in 3:12, where it is stated that because of these illicit activities, she will be ploughed like a field, figuratively fucked, and turned into a heap of ruins. As with Jerusalem's counterpart, Samaria, the punishment seems designed to assure submissive femininity. Thus Samaria and Jerusalem take their leave, stripped of any male affectation through the text's violent assertion of their femininity. It's not exactly entertainment anymore.

Brazen Zion

You would think that by this point in the text, any would-be gender benders would be too terrorized to venture forth. But no, a very ambiguously gendered character takes the stage in 4:8–14. Brazen Zion is definitely the star of this show. The pleasure of the scene is heightened by the apparent disagreement between the prophet and Yahweh. The prophet wants to see a more feminine Daughter of Zion, while Yahweh seems to encourage a more masculine Zion. The prophet queries—using the only attested feminine form of the verb (רוע)—why do *you* (feminine singular) raise a battle cry (תריעי)? This is hardly ladylike. He suggests instead more feminine behaviors, a birthing and a rescue. But even with these prescriptions, masculine demeanor persists: in 4:10 the woman is described "going out" from the town to give birth, using the verb "to go out" (יצא), which denotes an active comportment reserved in the Hebrew Bible 90 percent of the time for men. Well, 89 percent of the time. In a page of 204 entries in the Hebrew concordance compiled by Even-Shoshan (1997), only twenty-three entries are feminine forms.

In 4:13, Yahweh steps in to encourage this behavior, demanding masculinity, with imperatives like, "arise, tread." The language used here is the language of Kings, of Asa and Josiah crushing Asherah poles (2 Chron. 15:16; 2 Kings 23:6, 15), of the King of Aram treading down the army of Jehoahaz (2 Kings 13:7), of Yahweh treading down the nations (Hab. 3:12).[4] Yet strangely, it is feminine singular imperatives that are used. The demands on Zion remain gender-ambiguous as Yahweh promises to make Zion's body hard. Zion's horn will be iron, a terrorizing phallic symbol if ever there was one, and her hoofs will be copper, to tread down and pulverize (דוש and דקק) many peoples.

Yet in spite of Yahweh's encouragement in the production of Brazen Zion, her gender transgressions are not tolerated. Suddenly, it is predicted in 4:14 that she will cut herself (תתגדדי), which implies an act of mourning or a sign of defeat.[5] The vocative here, "O Daughter of Mourning" (בת גדוד), can also mean "O Daughter of the Troops"—a rather masculine epithet—in a play on the various meanings of the verb גדד ("to cut" or "gather in troops"). Her self-mutilation is followed by a chastisement of her judges, by an unknown masculine plural subject, with a staff.

Madame Jacob

Another trangenderist, Madame Jacob, appears several times throughout Micah. Jacob appears for the first time in 1:5, accused of "transgression"; it is pointed out that Jacob's transgression *is* Samaria (whose fault, as noted earlier, was her penchant for genderbending). It seems that perhaps Jacob shares an inclination to gender transgression with Samaria. When Jacob appears again in 2:12, more hints of genderbending emerge. Here s/he is addressed as the feminine singular *you* (כלך), then, in the parallelism of the next line, s/he is likened to the feminine שארית ישראל, the remnant of Israel (likely those left in the northern kingdom of Israel after Assyria's conquest of Samaria and deportation of its population, see Hillers 1984, 66). A quick survey of the uses of שארית in the Hebrew Bible show that the feminine gender of the noun is matched by a classically female deportment. The remnant in the Hebrew Bible is for the most part passive: either passively preserved, passively led away, or passively destroyed.[6] Swift on the heels of this appellation, it is announced that Yahweh will make Jacob like a flock, also passive, which murmurs, not surprisingly, in the third-person feminine plural.

The next time Madame Jacob makes more than a cameo appearance is in 3:8.[7] Here the prophet announces his potency to chastise Jacob, who has no response to this threat, in keeping with the passive nature of the remnant. Then in 5:6–14, the mixture of gender codes comes to the fore. Jacob appears again as the remnant (שארית יעקב), and here the ambiguity is more thorough. The feminine noun "remnant" (שארית) rather than the masculine "Jacob" (יעקב) should be the dominant grammatical subject, but masculine verb forms are employed. Yet in 5:6, the שארית יעקב displays a feminine demeanor, gentle as night dew from Yahweh, and evasive as rain. But s/he discloses his masculinity in 5:7 when s/he wreaks havoc among the nations like a lion among sheep. This is no passive remnant. The text acknowledges this in 5:8, by slipping into second-person masculine singular forms. *You* (masculine singular) will lift your hand amongst your oppressors, and all your enemies will be cut off. The raised hand (יד) here evokes an image of power perhaps not unlike the iron horn of power sported earlier. (There are instances of ‏ד‎ referring to the phallus, for example Isa. 57:8.)

Once again, the additional privilege accorded through the mixing of genders is not permitted for long before it produces violence. The oracle of Yahweh in 5:9–14 presents a series of violent actions unprecedented in the book. *I* rail against *you* (masculine singular) with promises of destruction. It is almost as if Yahweh is saying: so you wanna be a girl, then be a girl. To be both is too powerful. Therefore I will cut off your ability to thrust (embodied in your horses and chariots) your source of strength (resident in your cities), and anything remotely phallic (like idols or Asherah poles).

Genderfuck, or Just Plain Fucked?

Given the violence that attends the transgression of gender codes in both film (ranging from familial rejection to murder) and text (from rape to castration), can these texts be said to be subversive? Or are hegemonic norms and attendant exclusions simply valorized? With respect to *Paris Is Burning*, some critics would indicate the latter. For instance, in her biting critique of the film, bell hooks suggests that black drag generally denigrates black women (1992, 145–47). Likewise, Judith Butler questions the mimicry of hegemonic norms of gender that are met with "cruel and fatal social constraints," in her reading of the film (1993, 133). Both hooks and Butler make it clear that the question of gender is not separate from the question of race and class in the film. As Butler puts it, gender is merely "the vehicle for the phantasmatic transformation of that nexus of race and class, the site of its articulation" (1993, 130). In other words, the film, and the ball children who are interviewed, worry about issues of race and class, but they do so through the medium of gender. More pointedly, hooks calls the film "a graphic portrait of the way in which colonized black people . . . worship at the throne of whiteness" (1992, 149); she suggests that it does not interrogate whiteness, but rather celebrates it.

Indeed it seems that the film only valorizes wealthy white heterosexual ideals, and sends the drag ball children scurrying off to imitate these ideals. The film makes no apologies for highlighting the mimicry of the dominant culture. Not even five minutes into the film, stills display the white, upper-middle-class heterosexuality that the balls are said to emulate. Time and time again, both the conversation and the camera return to the desire to be a white, wealthy woman, whether it be through shots of white American life, or in the images of white models plastered to Octavia's walls, or simply as a point of reference in conversation. Venus, for example, explains sex trade with reference to the middle-class het relationship: But I feel like, if you're married, a woman, in the suburbs, a regular woman, is married to her husband and she wants him to buy her a washer and dryer set, in order for him to buy them, I'm sure she'd have to go to bed with him anyway to give him what he wants, for her to get what she wants.

This mimicry is most poignantly shown in the dramatization of the category *O-P-U-L-E-N-C-E*, in which a black man with trench coat and captain's hat begins his walk wrapped in an American flag, swinging his arms proudly. The film then cuts to a "real" (white) businessman on the street with a cigar, and to (white) women with expensive jewelry and hairdos. A voice-over says:

> This is White America. . . . Ev'rybody's in their own home. The little kid with the Fisher Price toys, they're not in no concrete playground. . . . This is White America. And when you come to the minority, especially black, we as a people for the past 400 years is the greatest example of behavior modification in the history of civilization. We have had everything taken away from us, and yet we have all learned how to survive. That is why in the ballroom circuit it is so obvious that if you have captured the great white way of living or looking or dressing or speaking, you is a marvel.

In *Paris Is Burning*, whiteness and wealth is associated with America. This is White America. Any other nationality that is not of the white set knows this and

Figure 4   Dorian Carey in *Paris Is Burning*

accepts this till the day they die. And that is ev'rybody's dream and ambition as a minority: to live and look as well as a white person is pictured as being in America. Ideal femininity is also associated with the white American; the most "white"-looking shot of a drag queen is of Dorian Carey with an American flag as a backdrop.

Just as the film repeats hegemonic norms (white, wealthy, femme-female, heterosexual), the text repeats biblical norms (thrusting active male, passive silent female). And just as the norms in the film cannot be separated from race and nation, neither can they in the text. Gender cannot be separated in Micah from the depictions of the nation Israel: her internal hierarchies, her relations with other nations, or her relationship with Yahweh. Like the film, Micah seems to valorize oppressive norms, here for Israel's national identity, articulated through gender. Femininity is almost always associated with Israel and her cities as they are punished (Samaria, Jerusalem, Daughter of Zion, the remnant), while masculinity is reserved for those ruling (Yahweh, leaders, priests, prophets of the house of Jacob). Moreover, these norms have typically been interpreted in terms of Israel's identity as an oppressed people (feminine and punished), rescued and turned into a colonizing nation (by a masculine and invincible leader).[8] As in *Paris Is Burning*, many of the norms in Micah against which the drag acts perform are revealed in visions of hope for a glorious future (2:12–13; 4:1–8; 5:1–8; and 7:8–20). Throughout these visions, the ideal man repeats as a ruler, shepherding. All of these masculine rulers perform aggressive and dominating action-oriented activities, full of "thrusting muscular" energy and phallic imagery (rising up, standing erect, shepherding with a staff). In 2:12–13, Yahweh is the shepherd who gathers his flock (the verbs used are synonyms, meaning "gather" (אָסַף and קָבַץ), and then breaks out of their pen before them. In 4:1–7, it is explicit that the male Yahweh is king, and implied that he is shepherd through the use of the verbs אָסַף and קָבַץ, harking back to 2:12–13. In 5:1–5 the rulers appear to be human substitutes: in 5:3 a ruler from Bethlehem stands and shepherds in the strength of Yahweh; while in 5:4–5 rulers are raised up to lead resistance against Assyria. A particularly violent and perhaps sexual instance of male domination occurs in 5:4–5, where leaders are "raised up" to rule Assyria with the sword and the land of Nimrod in her gates, which plays on the vaginal connotations often associated with the image of gate in the Hebrew Bible (see Magdalene 1995, 333, 346). Finally, in 7:14 there is an appeal to a second-person masculine figure to "shepherd your people, with your staff, the flock of your inheritance."

The corollary to this masculine thrusting is, of course, passive feminine-femininity, which is marked by the image in 2:12–13, 4:6–7, and 7:14 of the people as a flock—amorphous, passive, and dependent, needing to be gathered, rescued, led, and ruled. This helpless grouping is also the remnant. The flock's reward for being properly flocklike is that she is cared for by the shepherd (2:12; 4:7; 7:18). It seems that in these passages of future hope, the ideal relation between Yahweh and Israel is of Yahweh-male-active to Israel-female-passive. The pimping Samaria does not appear at all in these passages. Zion/Jerusalem has much less agency, as she is not an acting or owning subject, but, instead, the place from which Torah and the word of Yahweh go forth (4:2), the mountain (הר ציון) in which Yahweh rules (4:7). The dichotomy between passive and active bears out in the grammar, too, as the feminine verb forms are few and far between. Significantly, within these idyllic passages, feminine forms appear most to address the (feminine) enemy in 7:8–10. She is far too assertive and inquisitive at first ("Where is your God?" she asks), but she is eventually subdued.

As discussed earlier, the punishment for deviance from these norms is severe. Interestingly, the most violent acts of Yahweh's retribution come, not after instances of corruption and oppression, as one might suppose, but after instances of genderbending. For example, the "schemers of evil" who appropriate land and oppress others in 2:1–2 are threatened with some kind of evil that will result in their humiliation (2:3), but the text only describes this humiliation as a kind of taunting (2:4)—a far cry from the stripping of Samaria in 1:7 or the castration of Jacob in 5:9. Likewise, the male rulers of 3:1–2, who are described metaphorically as flesh-eating, are only chided with the warning that Yahweh will not answer them when they call out (3:4). The prophets who lead the people astray in 3:5 are merely threatened with shame and darkness in place of visions (3:6–7). The leaders who deal corruptly in 3:10 are not themselves punished. But the genderbending Jerusalem is violated (3:12).

Colonizing Gaze/Complicit Reading

These texts appear to valorize and enforce oppressive norms, but what is the viewer or interpreter's complicity in this? Do we, as Butler says, "witness and produce the phantasmatic constitution of a subject, a subject who repeats and mimes the legitimating norms by which it itself has been degraded" (1993, 131)? Or are we voyeurs, as Margaret Miles suggests (1996, 171–72)? Are we exploitative? Have the performances of genderbending in film and text become "exotic fetish" (Butler 1993, 137)? Are the camera and I colonizing and fetishizing in our use of other cultures for stimulation and pleasure? Are we complicit in the heinous fact that those interviewed in *Paris Is Burning* all signed releases, so that they were not

entitled to any of the $4 million that the film made (Miles 1996, 175)—
and this after all their longing for fame and wealth as expressed in the film?
Have I produced a reading of Micah that is titillating, yet at the same time
acts as the gender police, scrutinizing the text for transgression and replay-
ing the violence by which the textual characters have been degraded?

If the answers to these questions are in the affirmative, it would seem
that text and film should be rejected. But I fear that a rejection of the film
for the pleasure it evokes through the ball children's imitation of hegemonic
norms might end up blaming those whose agency is shaped, in part, by the
colonizing demand for imitation. Further, it would not allow enjoyment of
the difference and creativity shown on the screen and in the text, nor take
into account the hope that is evident in the dreams for the future, even if
such hope is deemed misplaced. Finally, it would not particularly interrogate viewers' own ideological positioning. Viewers might go away chastised
for their pleasure and for their implication in the colonizing drive, but they
would not be changed. Such a response risks producing apathy: it prompts
the recognition of oppressive tendencies but does not motivate a response
to them.

A-M-B-I-V-A-L-E-N-C-E

But perhaps, as Butler suggests, *Paris Is Burning* (and Micah with it),
"documents neither an efficacious insurrection nor a painful resubordina-
tion, but an unstable coexistence of both" (1993, 137). Perhaps these texts
are profoundly ambivalent in that they both appropriate and subvert hegemonic and oppressive norms of race and gender (1993, 128). The sort
of ambivalence that Butler describes is reminiscent of the ambivalence in
hybridity of which Bhabha has written. Hybridity encompasses a number
of Bhabha's key concepts: ambivalence within the production of discriminatory discourses, revaluation of colonial identities, reversal of domination,
questioning of authority. A closer look at his conception of hybridity and
ambivalence will, I think, be helpful in understanding the ambivalence of
the film and text.

For Bhabha, hybridity is a result of the ambivalence of colonizers' narcissistic demand for mimicry. They should become like us, but not too much like
us. In colonial (and postcolonial) contexts the fear of cultural difference—
between colonizer and colonized—is diminished by colonizers' belief that
their culture is original and authentic, and that other cultures must learn to
emulate this pure and authentic culture. The threat of the real difference
between cultures is therefore contained, *disavowed by*, "the fantasy of origin

and identity," "the myth of origins" that demands mimicry (1994, 67).[9] However, Bhabha argues, in a colonial context the mimicry demanded of colonized peoples by colonizers is never permitted to be perfect; the colonized is never allowed quite to "become one of us." This "desire for a reformed, recognizable Other, as a subject . . . that is almost the same, but not quite" (1994, 86) produces something new, something hybrid. The very demand for imitation that tries to establish one culture as "superior" and "original" also requires that difference (hybridity) be produced. The recognition of difference is crucial for discrimination, but it is always understood in a way that is "entirely knowable and visible" (1994, 71). Colonialist authority . . . requires the production of differentiations, individuations, identity effects through which discriminatory practices can map out subject populations that are tarred with the visible and transparent mark of power (1994, 111).

The resulting categorization of difference is what produces and justifies discrimination (*those people, not from our origin, not like us*). The colonized people must be known and categorized, but not too different. The objective of colonial discourse is to construe the colonized as a population of degenerate types . . . in order to justify conquest and to establish systems of administration and instruction (1994, 70). Thus, the discrimination produced by the strategy of disavowal, the myth of origins, becomes a discrimination between the mother culture and its bastards, the self and its doubles, where the trace of what is disavowed is not repressed but *repeated* as something different—a mutation, a hybrid (1994, 111, emphasis mine). In other words, the feared difference of the colonized people does not disappear with disavowal, but is made visible through the colonized people's (enforced) imperfect imitation of the colonizing culture.

Hybridity, then, is ambivalent in its construction because mimicry is demanded by the colonizing need to disavow difference, but it must also produce difference to be productive within the colonial matrices of power. The discourse of mimicry is constructed around an ambivalence; in order to be effective, mimicry must continually produce its slippage, its excess, its difference (1994, 87). But hybridity is ambivalent in another sense, as well: it puts authority, which depends on the ability to discern difference, into question. In displaying the colonial culture differently, hybridity puts the "myth of origins" into question, and so displaces the dominant culture's own notions about self-identity. The repetition of the "original culture" through mimicry has the subversive effect of unsettling the "mimetic or narcissistic demands of colonial power," by turning the "gaze of the discriminated back upon the eye of power" (1994, 112). Thus, hybridity can be used to reread and reorder dominant discourses, allowing for subaltern voices that have been suppressed in the stifling of difference. Hybridity is the revaluation of the assumption of colonial identity through the repetition of discriminatory identity effects. It displays the necessary deformation and displacement of all sites of discrimination and domination (1994, 112).

Bhabha's discussion of hybridity causes me to consider how *Paris Is Burning* and Micah produce what Bhabha might call hybridity by turning the eye of power back on itself, undermining colonial authority, and, ultimately, fucking with gender. In both film and text, there is a violently enforced demand for conformity or repetition of certain norms. As these norms are iterated differently, hybridity emerges as the excess. The slippage in the repetition brings the constructed nature of the norms into view, thereby questioning their authenticity and veracity and threatening the authority of the demand for conformity. Hybridity brings into view the exclusions and constraints that the construction of ideal norms requires.

Hybridity at Paris' Ball

Paris Is Burning seems to match Bhabha's description of hybridity as produced through disavowal and mimicry. As bell hooks notes, the film depicts a colonizing demand for mimicry. The film seems to disavow difference by focusing on the "realness" of the ball children. Yet, at the same time, the film continually points out that the children are, or have been, anatomically male. It also asserts, as do a number of those interviewed, that the ball scene is part of a gay male (rather than specifically transgender) subculture. The film does not ever allow the drag children to pass as wealthy white women, but points out their difference, tells their "little personal things:" their anatomical operations, I bought her her tits, I paid for them . . . shake those tits Momma; their need to hustle to make money or their need to mop (steal) outfits; their rejection from the normal heterosexual realm, the family. The film ensures that the viewer knows that those who *could pass* as wealthy women, who might not be detected on the street, are doing just that, passing. Often the film shows very real-looking ball walkers, while voice-overs tell the opposite. For example, while footage of the very real performance of the category Bangee Boy rolls, a voice-over tells us that this is only *looking real*:[10] To be able to blend, that's what realness is. When you can pass the untrained eye, or the trained eye, and not give away the fact that you're gay, that's when its real . . . the idea of realness is to look as much as possible like your straight counterpart. Or in the category *O-P-U-L-E-N-C-E*, the voice-over contradicts the eye, saying, "This is White America." The film might as well be saying, "This is *not* White America." These voice-overs point out differences between norms and their repetition. Such revelations of difference produce hybridity. Thus the film produces a recognizable Other.

What might be disavowed in the real-life act of passing is repeated in the film as something different. The trace of what is disavowed is not repressed but repeated as something *different*—a mutation, a hybrid (Bhabha 1994, 111).

The film seems to dwell on the impossibility of the ball children attaining their dreams "legitimately," the impossibility of being white, wealthy, or supermodels, without having to resort to theft and prostitution. The effect is to produce a category of degenerate and deluded Other. Directly following the opulence scene, the camera takes in the dreams of Octavia, followed soon after by an exposé on the nuances of mopping ball attire. Next comes a similar description of the children's need to hustle in order to make money for the balls. The film returns to Octavia's supermodel dreams, before a series of shots builds a frenzy of desire, cutting back and forth between Octavia and Venus, each lying on their beds, dreaming of being wealthy, "normal" women, perhaps married with children. The scene climaxes just prior to the cut to 1989, with Venus determined to realize her dreams. I want this, this is what I want, and I'm going to go for it. Three years later, Willi Ninja is famous, and Venus is dead. As Butler points out, it is no accident that Willi ends up a star, while Venus is murdered (Butler 1993, 130). Willi does not try to pass as a woman, and he is more normatively masculine in his presentation and dance: Ninjas hit hard, they hit fast, an invisible assassin, and that's what we are. We come out to assassinate. Venus, on the other hand, lived and worked as a woman. The message seems to be that any attempt at undetectable mimicry is illegitimate, illegal, even punishable by death. Those presented as successful (Willi Ninja) or content (Dorian Carey, Pepper Lebeija) are hybrid figures: filmed both in drag imitating hegemonic norms, but also in liminal states (out of drag, in the dressing room, etc.). Difference must be made visible.

But on the other hand, because hybridity is the filmic revelation of what might be an otherwise unnoticed repetition of norms, it unsettles the myth of origins, the myth of an authentic and pure white, heterosexual, wealthy femininity, which demands repetition. In scrutinizing transsexual and transvestite mimicry of hegemonic norms of race, class, and gender, new possibilities emerge: it is possible *to look exactly like* the idealized wealthy straight white woman, and be a poor black or Latino gay man or transsexual. It is this very possibility of mimicry that brings into view the constructed (as opposed to natural and authentic) nature of sex and gender. The same thing goes for the privilege attending whiteness. It is not difficult to play a wealthy white woman, with the right clothes and makeup. The main interview with Dorian Carey demonstrates this possibility. Although Dorian appears several times as a woman who could pass as a (white) star in the genre of her idols Marilyn Monroe and Betty Grable, the interview to which the film continually returns is conducted while she applies makeup, and her perpetual powdering acts as a symbol for the constructed nature of gender, race, and class. In the same way, another one of the ball children, Carmen Xtravaganza, shows that with a chin implant, breast implants, and genital changeover, it is possible to be a woman. Yet, her residual man's voice (pointed out by her friend in the film) remains as an excess to expose the constructed nature of her "ideal femininity." This kind of denaturalization in the film asks: If sex, gender, race, and class can so easily be imitated by other "unnatural" means, how authentic and original are they? I might argue that Carmen's voice and Dorian's innumerable makeup kits are what Bhabha calls the "remainder and afterbirth" of the "subject's accession to and erasure in [discourse]." Voice and kit, these are the leftovers of the subjects' erasure in hegemonic discourses on gender. [They] make vocal and visible . . . the struggle involved in the insertion of agency—wound and bow, death and life—into discourse (Bhabha 1994, 184). These are the tell-tale traces left behind that make visible the construction of gender.

Hybridity also puts into question the naturalness of desire—which gives oppressive norms their power—by showing its constructedness. For instance, in one scene, Octavia appears in the most luscious poses for a photo shoot, looking like the perfect object of straight male desire. Looking through the male eye of the photographer and his camera, the viewer might be attracted to her; but the film tells that she is not "really a woman" (though she is infinitely passable). The viewer (interpellated by the camera and her poses as a straight man) might not question Octavia's desire to be a model, nor his own desire for her, except that he *knows* that she is transsexual, and this is unsettling—it turns the male gaze back upon itself. [His] inner dialogue may have gone like this: "I'm really turned on by this woman, and that's how it should be—I'm male and I'm heterosexual." Then . . . that inner voice might protest, "Wait! She's got a penis! She's a man!" And then the real awful truth may reveal itself like this: "Wait, I'm still attracted to this person, this man! But only women and faggots go for men—does this mean I'm a woman? Does it mean I'm a homosexual?" Poor Baby! (Bornstein 1994, 73). Sexual desire, like the structures of sex, gender, race, and class, is dissected by hybridity.

An interview with Pepper Lebeija provides another example of how hybridity at once denaturalizes and puts into question the norms of the heterosexual family and heterosexual desire. Pepper—who identifies as a man who emulates women—tells the story of rejection by his mother. Distressed that her son was wearing women's clothing, and devastated that his breasts were bigger than her own, she burnt up his mink coat and perfume, while he stood by and cried. As Pepper's narrative questions and problematizes the heterosexual ideal of family, and the strictly enforced roles within the family, the camera cuts to the TV, where what appears to be a scene of heterosexual lovemaking flickers. With this move, the camera interrogates the naturalness of heterosexual desire, upon which families are apparently based, by pointing out the mimicry of actors playing in this scene. One might begin to wonder: Are these actors really straight? Is it really a man and a woman rolling about on the TV screen, or could it be two men? The authenticity and veracity of heterosexual lovemaking is put into question, and with it, its "logical and natural conclusion," the heterosexual family.

Not only does the hybridity produced in the film reveal the constructed and interrelated nature of family, gender, desire, and class, but it also reveals the demand to conform to those constructs, as well as the constraints with which hegemonic norms are enforced. The most deeply disturbing of these is the murder of Venus, but constraints also appear on various other emotional and physical levels. The continual threat of violence hangs over the balls. When they're undetectable, when they can walk out of that ballroom, into the sunlight and onto the subway and get home, and still have all their clothes and no blood running off their bodies, those are the femme realness queens. Further, the film tells numerous stories of familial rejection for transsexuals and transvestites. Yet in spite of these constraints, the children still mimic the norms that oppress them. Ironically, though, the steps taken in order to fulfill the ruling class's narcissistic demand for imitation, are those things (theft, prostitution, transgendered mothers) that run exactly counter to the stated values and the proper outward appearances of the ruling-class.

By showing the "transgressions" required for mimicry, the film documents precisely that part of society that has been foreclosed, excluded, abjected (to use Butler's turn of phrase) in the construction of hegemonic norms (i.e., thieves and prostitutes). In revealing the desire that is essential to the maintenance of these norms, the film also reveals what is "not desirable," that which is disavowed most of the time (i.e., poverty and homelessness). What is more, the film heroizes these abjected elements, by showing the creativity, strength, and wisdom with which poor black gay, transsexual, or transgendered people deal with and overcome the odds stacked against them.

In this way, as Butler argues, the film seeks identification of the white, middle-class, heterosexual viewer with excluded elements (1993, 132). By playing on another narcissistic demand—the demand to see oneself as wise, strong, and creative (like the legendary children)—the film builds an identification between the included and the excluded. And though as hooks argues, at one level the film does not interrogate privilege, on another level it does do so by narcissistically inserting privileged viewers into a position of identification with those less privileged. White, middle-class audience members, sitting in the theater in voyeuristic positions of privilege, are asked to identify with those whom they have abjected, those of whom they demand emulation. Now they will want to imitate the children. Yet most audience members would be unable ever to imitate their world, their skills in fashion design, the movement that they have honed, and the type of femininity or masculinity which they imitate. These are, quite literally, *inverted* imitations, ones which invert the order of imitated and imitation, and which, in the process, expose the fundamental dependency of "the origin" on that which it claims to produce as its secondary effect (Butler, 1991, 22). In being asked to identify with something that mimics them, but that they cannot mimic, a gender-normative, white, middle-class sense of self is put into question. The film does more than just fuck with gender, then, it fucks with the average viewer's very sense of self.

Hybridity in the Book

Hybridity in Micah is constructed slightly differently than in the film, in that it is difficult to say that "the acts in drag" are a deliberate effort to mimic a certain set of norms; however, hybridity is still produced as a result of the repetition or re-presentation of signs, it is still punished, and it still puts the authority and authenticity of these norms into question. As noted, the signs that mark hegemonic norms tend to appear in visions of a bright future; I might say, in expressions of desire. These gender norms are then repeated differently, varying each time according to context, to the network of other marks (Derrida 1984, 16). At the same time, the text leaves marks of a struggle to disavow difference, and hybridity is produced as a result of the slippage of this textual disavowal. As in the film, hybridity denaturalizes structures, reveals the constraints that compel homogeneity, and brings the terms of exclusion into view.

The struggle to disavow difference appears in each case, beginning with Samaria in 1:6–7. The first thing that appears in the text is a description of Samaria being stripped and her wages burnt. At first glance, this is typical treatment of a woman in the Hebrew Bible, and should not be unexpected. Rachel Magdalene points out that the stripping of women has been identified by biblical scholars (in particular Hillers) as a Treaty Curse.[11] The stripping of Samaria in Micah disavows the difference of this woman, not only by showing her to be treated in the same manner as many other biblical women, but also by violently divesting her of masculine traits: her phallic idols, her economic independence. It is therefore the violence that brings the hybridity of the passage into view.

A similar thing happens to Jerusalem in 3:9–12, whereby she appears first as typically female. The passage begins with an address to the male leaders, those "building Zion in exchange for blood and Jerusalem in exchange for injustice" (3:10), as if these leaders were in control, as if Jerusalem were just passively constructed, thus displaying the feminine ideal. Yet the text goes on to speak of these leaders as hers; she owns them, she is held responsible for them. As with Samaria, her responsibility for shady transactions is the justification for violence, but it is this very justification, this demonstration of Jerusalem as a degenerate type, that brings difference into view.

The Daughter of Zion's appearance in the text (4:8–14) shows a different kind of struggle to disavow difference. In this case, difference appears at the start of the passage (4:8), where the feminine titles for Zion are paralleled lexically and syntactically with masculine pronouns, thus creating an equivalence in Hebrew poetic terms. The feminine Daughter of Zion (בַּת צִיּוֹן) is lexically parallel to the second-person masculine singular pronoun, *you* (אַתָּה). In 4:8, the title in the prepositional phrase, "to the Daughter of Jerusalem" (לְבַת יְרוּשָׁלַ͏ִם), is syntactically parallel to the second-person masculine singular pronominal suffix in another prepositional phrase, "unto *you*" (עָדֶיךָ). Then in 4:9, as noted previously, her difference is heard in her battle cry, whereupon the prophet tries to prescribe more appropriate feminine (subjugated) roles for her (4:10–11). *Tremble and burst forth, O Daughter of Zion, like one giving birth. For now you will go out from the town, and you will lie in the field. And you will go until Babylon and there you will be redeemed. . . . Now many nations are gathered against you. They are saying, let her be defiled* (תֶּחֱנָף) *let our eyes gaze on Zion.*[12] The figure produced in 4:8 and beyond is recognizably different: *she goes forth* like a man, *she* could be *you* (masculine singular) who is defiled, *her horn* is iron, and *she tramples* nations. The signs of gender here have been repeated, but differently, so that the mix of syntax and symbol produces a hybrid. Yet even this difference is disavowed by the text's depiction of a certain lack of agency, or passivity, on her part. It is the male Yahweh who will arm her with male tools, for male activity. She seems to passively accept.

While the femininity of Brazen Zion is asserted, the feminine behavior of Jacob is disavowed almost completely. Although Jacob is identified with the ideal passive remnant in 2:12, when he appears again—repeats again—as the remnant of Jacob (שְׁאֵרִית יַעֲקֹב) in 5:6–7, it is as a roaring lion, a ruler that raises his "hand" against his enemies. Even the grammatical forms are masculine, and the only sign of the remnant's liking for feminine attire is her gentle appearance as dew from Yahweh; but even here he independently waits for no man (אִישׁ), for no sons of man (בְּנֵי אָדָם). The שְׁאֵרִית יַעֲקֹב in this passage is not the dependent and passive remnant of 2:12, 4:7, and 7:18. In fact, with all the assertiveness and phallic power of the passage, Jacob seems to emulate the book's ideal male ruler more than the passive remnant. All signs of femininity are suppressed. Yet the slippage of this disavowal appears in the excess of the violence: whereas the ideal ruler rules the flock like a shepherd, the שְׁאֵרִית יַעֲקֹב shreds the flock like a lion. Instead of raising his "staff" to rule his people as the ideal ruler does, he raises his "hand"/phallus (יָד) to cut off his oppressor. Jacob doesn't seem to know how to do (or what to do with) the man's-man thing.

Hybridity in Micah, as in *Paris Is Burning*, questions the naturalness and originality of the norms by showing the very *possibility* that things might be otherwise. The possibility that norms might be differently repeated destabilizes the authenticity of the norms themselves. For instance, the text reveals the possibility for feminine figures to take on roles traditionally left to men in the Hebrew Bible (economic independence, ownership, agency and dominance, fighting prowess). In fact, in the case of Brazen Zion, the text indicates that, in spite of the prophet's efforts to the contrary, Yahweh even makes a feminine figure more manly than the ideal man by giving her an iron horn. Yahweh's participation here undercuts any sort of edict, divine or otherwise, for female passivity. Conversely, Madame Jacob reveals the possibility for the traditionally male figure of the leader to be identified with a traditionally passive and divinely protected figure of the nation. Again Yahweh is implicated, since the feminine aspect of the שְׁאֵרִית (the dew) is said to come from Yahweh. In these ways the divine (and therefore natural and authentic) origin of norms established in the text are challenged by the hybrid figures.

Yet the text's violent reactions to hybridity bring into view the constructed nature of norms in a different way. In Micah, the violence seems to be a major clue that something has gone wrong before. In fact, at times, hybridity would perhaps go unnoticed if it were not for the violence that follows it. In this way the very constraints that try to repress difference are what reveal hybridity. For example, Jacob's appearance as a ravaging lion in 5:6–8 seems difficult to understand in any other way than as a future promise of victory (Wolff 1990 [1982], 155; Craigie 1985, 42–43; Allen 1976, 353–54; Hillers 1984, 139; Mays 1976, 121–23). Yet the extreme violence toward Jacob that follows in 5:9–14, seems to indicate otherwise: that Jacob is not victorious, but rather, devastated. The violence begins with the phrase, "there will be in that day" (וְהָיָה בַיּוֹם הַהוּא), a phrase that, as Wolff notes, is a "familiar connecting formula (Hos. 2:18, 20, 23; Amos 8:9; 9:11; Isa. 7:18, 20, 21, 23)" (1990 [1982], 69). This phrase seems to connect the violence of destroying cities and fortresses and horses to what has gone before: Jacob's victorious ravagings. Yet it is difficult to say what precisely the connection is, and this forces a careful examination of the passage. Many commentators solve the problem by disavowing the impact of the connecting formula and the violence, reading it instead as "a kind of salvation saying" (Mays 1976, 125; see also Wolff 1990 [1982], 154; Allen 1976, 356–67). The phrase "in that day" links this with the preceding predictions, and thereby helps determine its meaning. Whereas in itself the oracle is largely negative in tone, the context of the future glorious time makes it appear as the reverse side of the fabric: being deprived of cities, horses, and the rest prepares a time when God will rule unchallenged (Hillers 1984, 72). But it does not make sense that salvation would require such violence here, when elsewhere in Micah (4:1–4) the time of salvation is portrayed as one in which nations and peoples voluntarily lay down their arms. Rather, it seems more likely that the violence here might be a response to what precedes it, and what precedes it is hybridity.[13] Again it is the violence that reveals the hybridity of the passage, and shows the constructed and enforced nature of the norms.

As in *Paris Is Burning*, hybridity in Micah makes visible the elements excluded in the construction of ideals. The violence toward Sam and Jerry reveals the exclusion of women from economic roles in the Hebrew Bible. The disavowal of Madame Jacob's femininity reveals the exclusion of feminine affectivity from the ideal male world. Most notably, Brazen Zion reveals the exclusion of women from the role of empowered warrior. Further, she appears to be the leftover of the exclusion of the warrior goddess from the biblical text. As Tikva Frymer-Kensky observes, "Micah's picture of Zion as active and able to operate outside the city may owe its scope to several Near Eastern images" (1992, 174). For instance, "the Agushaya Hymn . . . describes Ishtar as a fierce goddess who whirls around in her 'manliness,' whose feast is battle, who *goes out* in war" (1992, 67, emphasis mine). These glimpses of excluded elements in the text, both urge consideration of the kinds of violence that might have been in operation to force their exclusion, and, once again, question the "originality" of the "included" norms of the text.

Finally, like the film, the text urges the reader's identification with the hybrid figures at certain points. By addressing the hybrid figures (Brazen Zion and Madame Jacob) as "you," the text interpellates the reader into a destabilized ideology. As the reader responds to each of the text's variously gendered addresses, such as vocatives, imperatives, and other second-person forms, s/he is positioned and repositioned. Each reply to the text's changing "you" requires a slightly different response. The constantly shifting response marks changes in placement within the ideological construct of gender; that is, changes with respect to power and with respect to privilege. As film theorist Annette Kuhn puts it, this "threatens to undercut the subject fixed in ideology . . . [and] highlights the centrality of gender constructs in processes of subjectivity" (Kuhn 1985, 54). The hybridity that fucks with gender might be said, again in the words of Kuhn, to "open up a space of self-referentiality" that not only calls "attention to the artifice of gender identity" but also "effects a 'willful alienation' from the fixity of that identity" (1985, 54).

Dreaming of an End to Gender

Girls are not different from yesterday or the day before. Everybody who is young has a hope and a dream and I don't think it's ever been different in the history of the world (Eileen Ford, Ford Models, in *Paris Is Burning*).

By way of conclusion, I would like to pick up on the hope that is present in Micah and in *Paris Is Burning*. I must admit that my goals (my desires!) for this chapter are political. I hope that it inspires gender-fuck. One might think that all the violence could only frighten readers off from experimenting with gender, but I hope that the encounter with genderfuck might have quite different effects. It certainly had different effects on me. Before I began working on this text, I hadn't ever dreamed I would spend time trying to see if I could perform gender ambiguously: I had rarely evaluated my wardrobe for its gender content; I hadn't ever walked down the street and tried looking at people in the eyes (male cue); I hadn't ever sat on the bus with my legs splayed to see what response I would get as a women in a male position; I hadn't ever shaved my head. I hope that others have the same kinds of liberating experiences after encountering hybridity in cultural and biblical texts.

Further, I hope I have drawn the links clearly between gender oppression and other kinds of oppressions, and I hope that this will give readers reason to interrogate their own commitment to these kinds of oppressions (myself included). More importantly, I hope that the genderfuck produced by the text and film shows the artifice and violence of hegemonic norms and inspires struggle against them.

I want to fuck with gender.
I want to inspire willful alienation from the oppressive ideologies of gender, race, and class.
I want this, this is what I want, and I'm going to go for it.[14]

Chapter 5

Why Girls Cry: Gender Melancholia and Sexual Violence in Ezekiel 16 and *Boys Don't Cry*[1]

Ezekiel 16 and the film *Boys Don't Cry* (1999) are both texts about repeated, excessive, and fatal sexual violence. But beyond that, it might be said that they really have nothing to do with each other. Nonetheless, the relationship between gender and violence in each can illumine what might otherwise go unnoticed in the other. In this chapter, I argue that the sexual violence in both film and text can be read as the acute social outworking of what Judith Butler has called the gender melancholia at the heart of heterosexual identity. When read together, these texts show up the traumatic nature of heterosexual identification, enacted through a matrix of violent social relations.

Boys Don't Cry and Ezekiel 16 are, in fact, remarkably alike in portraying graphic and traumatic sexual violence: stripping, beating, murder. But the significant differences between the two are what urge consideration of gender melancholia in relation to sexual violence and trauma. The film— with its transgendered tragic hero—highlights questions of gender (is this really about violence against a woman?), while the text—with its male competition played out in violence against the female beloved—highlights the question of motivation for sexually violent rage (is this really about Yahweh's love for Jerusalem?). These differences can be put to work, somewhat paradoxically, as a kind of mutual heuristic in an exploration of the formation of heterosexual gender identity and its relationship to violence. Bearing both the similarities and differences in mind, I proceed first by offering a negative assessment of each text (filmic and biblical). I then soften these critiques in a negotiation with each through an exposition of

Judith Butler's conception of gender melancholia, application of it to the texts, and consideration of what these texts might say about gender melancholia and trauma. Here I look at the kinds of gender identifications that seem to be operative for the central characters in the text. I argue that the melancholic (and traumatic) formation of heterosexual gender identity seems to get lived out violently on the level of social interaction, and that this violence is, in part, a repudiation of femininity on the way to establishing masculine identities. Finally, I consider briefly whether reading this way might urge readers to interrogate the kinds of identifications and foreclosures that form their own positions within gender.

Several points of qualification are in order here. First, I am less interested in the actual psychic makeup of the characters that these texts describe, per se, than in what the details of characterization in these two influential texts might reveal about the social construction of gender. In other words, the assertions I make—about Brandon and Jerusalem in particular, but also about John, Tom, and Yahweh—are assertions about what happens in these texts, not about what happens behind them (for instance, the real Brandon, John, or Tom, or an idealized description of the relation between Jerusalem and Yahweh that is not biased by misogyny). Second, the proposition of heterosexual identification as a kind of socially enacted traumatic neurosis— to put it a little too bluntly—is one that can of course only be tentatively sketched out here, and will require more detailed attention at a later date. Moreover, space does not permit me to engage the extensive range of psychoanalytic and critical theory that exists on these questions. Rather, I simply work through a few theoretical links and connections that I have noticed in a limited number of texts, specifically as they relate to the question of gender melancholia and its impact on social relations. Finally, given that Butler predicates heterosexual identification on disavowed homosexual attachment, and that I argue that heterosexuality thus formed gets lived out violently, the argument I am making could run the risk of being read as predicating violence on homoerotic desire. However, I want to be clear that it is not the same-sex attachment that I am accusing here, but rather the prohibition against homosexuality that comes *before* and *causes* the loss of that first same-sex attachment. It is the heterosexual world that must take responsibility for these prohibitions and their results.

Traumatic Texts?

Ezekiel 16 is one of the most disturbing texts of the Hebrew Bible for those concerned about violence against women. Many feminist biblical critics have worked to expose the depths and implications of the misogyny and violence in Ezekiel 16 (Darr 1998; P. Day 2000; L. Day 2000; Dempsey 1998; Exum 1996; Galumbush 1992; Stiebert 2000; Shields 1998; Weems 1995). In brief (because others have done the work of detailed exposition), Yahweh chastises Jerusalem for idolatry, which is repeatedly figured in terms of a woman's sexual appetite for her neighbors, the nations. Jerusalem is accused not only of "whoring" but, *worse*, of giving gifts to her lovers, of pursuing them (Ezek. 16:23–44). She is compared with her mother (an unnamed Hittite) and her erring sisters (Sodom and Samaria), and found to be infinitely more wanton (Ezek. 16:44–52). As if it were not enough that Jerusalem's cultic practices are construed, condemned, and shamed as too-free feminine sexuality, thus criminalizing women's sexuality in the place of idolatry, the text goes on to punish her sexually as well: Yahweh strips her and further incites her lovers and her enemies against her, gathering them to stone her and cut her to bits (Ezek. 16:35–42). Somehow she lives on through all of this and is told repeatedly to bear her shame and never to open her mouth again (Ezek. 16:63).

How then to deal with such violence and misogyny in a purportedly sacred text?[2] Some feminist critics, without trying to redeem the passage, have made a call to read it differently, so as not to justify contemporary violence against women or other groups (Shields 1998, 18) or so as to highlight and work against contemporary problems of conjugal violence (Dempsey 1998, 76 n. 28). This kind of rereading seems the best option for dealing with this text, since it is still firmly fixed within the biblical canon, and since that canon still operates as authoritative in many communities. The challenge is to create a tradition of reading the text differently so that it becomes another kind of cultural influence. What then if this text were to be read, as the film seems to be, as a text with something interesting to say about the construction of gender identity?

There are more similarities between *Boys Don't Cry* and Ezekiel 16 than one might imagine. The film portrays a woman (Teena Brandon) living as a man (Brandon Teena), who pursues lovers throughout small-town Nebraska, giving them gifts and pleasure. Brandon returns to his pleasures time and time again, almost reveling in the variously motivated chases this provokes from angry men. After hooking up with new friends in one of these pursuits, he ends up in Falls City, in love with the local Lana Tisdel and buddies with his killers-to-be, John Lotter and Tom Nissen. As in the biblical text, her/his sexual behavior—which plays out in flirtations of all kinds and then in passionate lovemaking to Lana—is rewarded with excessive sexual violence. After the police identify Brandon as a biological woman, John and Tom strip her, beat her, rape her, and kill her. So, like the biblical text, the film depicts the shaming of a woman, though here a double shame because it exposes a female-to-male transgenderist as a woman, "the pussy" he tries so hard not to be.

Though *Boys Don't Cry* is ostensibly a film about a transgendered man, it hits home as a film of violence against a *woman* who defies heterosexual norms of gender. The film starts out with Brandon as a young man confidently wooing women, but by the end of the film we are in no doubt that Brandon Teena is in fact a woman; the film goes out of its way to show it. In an extended scene, Brandon is stripped, her womanhood revealed in a long zoom-in on her vagina (unusual in film in any case, and unusually long here). In an even more protracted scene, she is beaten and raped twice (by John, followed by Tom), forcing us to witness her penetrability. Following the rape, the film continues to expose her as a woman, revealing her unbound breasts as she speaks to the nurse who examines her and showing her curves in the shower (this latter scene resembles a mainstream, soap-commercial-style pose—shot from behind, off balance, on one leg, with a focus on thighs and hips). Then, before Brandon can possibly have time to recover, Lana is engaging her sexually as a woman. "You're so pretty," Lana initiates, to which Brandon replies in high femme fashion, "You're only saying that 'cause you like me." Not long after this moment of first-time lesbian romance, we see the predictable filmic response to lesbianism: death. Brandon's head is blown off in the film's traumatic climax, as John "takes care of a coupla dykes." Thus the film forces Brandon to admit what he does not believe is true, fulfilling the wish of his frustrated cousin Lonny, who exclaims, "You are not a boy! . . . You are not a boy! . . . Why don't you just admit that you are a dyke?!" Though Brandon replies, "Because I'm not a dyke," the film apparently thinks it knows better.[3]

However similar the violence toward a woman might be in the film and in the biblical text, it has not been subjected to feminist critique in the same way. Whereas feminist biblical critics have argued that enough is enough with Ezekiel 16, that it is profoundly unhelpful as a religious metaphor, let alone as a culturally influential text, the acclaim for the film has been almost entirely positive. The reasons for the film's amnesty from feminist critique, as far as I can see, are threefold. First, the main subject of the film is the tragic end to a transgendered life, which makes it both unusual and iconic for people who are interested in questions of gender identity (see Rosario 2000), thus giving the film a place in the world of alternative film. Second, the film depicts a true story, which makes it seem like an honest specimen of truthtelling, rather than a fictional figment of misogynist imagination (for which Ezekiel 16 as been critiqued). And finally, the film's director, Kimberly Pierce, identifies as queer (2000b, 39), as does its feminist producer, Christine Vachon (Muhammad 2000, 76–77); there may be some tacit feeling on the part of critics that queer feminists could not produce something damaging to women, or that they might stand outside the patriarchal loop.

But "truthtelling" (which somewhat ironically is how the Bible has traditionally been read) and "authorship" ought not to be enough to grant the film absolution from feminist critique: there is no inherent radical political program in watching in detail—as entertainment—the violence that *really happened* to a wo/man. Nor does an author's self-stated identity guarantee an alternative message. Perhaps a more trenchant question to ask of the film, then—as I also ask of the biblical text—is whether or not it has something to say about gender identity and the violence that surrounds gender transgressions. At one level it seems that it does not, because it frames the story in a very traditional way: two boys (John and Brandon) battle it out over a girl (Lana), one boy wins (John), the other boy loses (Brandon) and is punished. Here another very traditional story is also grafted on, with female sexual misdemeanor violently punished.

And yet, there is no doubt that at the same time the film is very moving and has touched many viewers. Moreover, Brandon has been a powerful point of identity for those who struggle with their gender and sex designations (Rosario 2000; Glitz 2000). There are, evidently, more intricate issues at stake than the seemingly stereotypic narratives imply. It is this underlying complexity that I would like to explore, with the help of Butler and Ezekiel 16.

In fact, the plot of the biblical text is slightly more elaborate than that of the film and may provide a way into thinking about the dynamics in the film. In Ezekiel 16, the two male competitors (Yahweh and the nations) attack the object of their desire (Jerusalem), rather than each other (whereas in the film, the contested object of desire, Lana, is one of the few central characters who remain both alive and unincarcerated). Elsewhere, I have argued that the complexity in the biblical text suggests that perhaps Jerusalem is violently barred from her desire for the nations because it mimics, and so competes with, Yahweh's (same-sex) desire for the nations (Runions 2001b). Since the time of writing that essay, I have come to see that one of the problematic implications of that argument is that it could be read as predicating violence against a woman upon homoerotic desire, instead of upon misogyny and heterosexual misconduct. Further, my argument there depended upon the idea that Yahweh's love for Jerusalem is not sexual, but parental (or both). Though I do not think this implausible, it may also be useful to think through the more traditional and predominantly accepted understanding of Yahweh's love for Jerusalem as sexual. However, the basic instinct of my earlier essay—to relate the strange working of the plot to questions of sexual and gender identity—may still be worth following up. I do so here by taking into consideration the unconscious working of heterosexual gender identifications as they relate to violence. It is here that Butler is informative.

Gender Melancholia, Same-Sex Attachments, and Gender Identifications

Butler's writing on gender melancholia—to give a brief and simplified summary here of the basic lines of the theory—is an attempt to engage and move beyond structuralist and psychoanalytic accounts that separate biological sex from gender. In these accounts, patriarchal law is understood to produce gender by imposing itself on essential raw nature, sex. By way of contrast, Butler wants to see sexed bodies and gender as equally discursively constructed. In other words, she sees "sex" constructed in the same operation in which gender and sexual orientation are also constructed. This proposition moves away from the reliance of feminism on essentializing (Western) conceptions of sex and gender, particularly femininity. Patriarchal law is conceived, not as a universal, but rather as a kind of culturally bound set of psychic processes. As such, it establishes culturally specific norms and prohibitions that inaugurate and regulate the means by which people come to identify and live out their gender and sexuality. In interrogating structuralist (Lévi-Straussian) and psychoanalytic (Freudian, Lacanian) notions of the incest taboo as the founding moment for heterosexual assignments of sex and gender, Butler asks whether there might be another taboo operating in the construction of sex and gender, an even more primary taboo, against homosexual attachments. Butler is at pains to point out that homosexual attachment is not something that comes "before" cultural constructions of sex and gender; it is a possibility opened up *within* culture, but on the margins and powerfully foreclosed from dominant culture (see 1990, 77–78).

Working through Freud's influential works, "Mourning and Melancholia" (1957 [1917]) and *The Ego and the Id* (1961 [1923]), Butler aligns the incest taboo with mourning, and the homosexuality taboo with melancholia. For Butler, following Freud, mourning represents a gradual and healthy letting go of a lost love object, a loss that is acknowledged. Melancholia, on the other hand, represents the inhibition of grief, a disavowal of loss, and an internalization of the lost loved object in a way that continues to haunt the bereaved. In other words, in melancholia the lost loved object is "set up inside the ego," or *incorporated* into the ego.[4] Such an internalization, Freud suggests, manifests itself as *an identification with the lost loved object.* Following this trajectory, Butler argues that the heterosexual incest taboo represents forbidden objects of desire that, because they are known, are actually grievable and therefore within the realm of mourning. On the other hand, the strong cultural prohibition on homosexual desire, she suggests, produces melancholia. By creating disavowed same-sex attachments, the prohibition on same-sex love relations creates unknowable, ungrievable, lost loved objects ("I never loved, therefore I never lost") (1997a, 138–40, 147).

Butler underlines the way in which Freud comes to understand melancholia as constitutive for the ego in setting up a primary identification. Because it is foundational for the ego, melancholia, therefore, is *the condition of possibility for mourning.* Thus, for Butler, *gender melancholia can be read as the condition of possibility for heterosexual norms*: the melancholic, disavowed loss created by the taboo on homosexual attachments prepares the way for the incest taboo that governs heterosexual gender. Put another way, in order for the grievable incest taboo (in Freudian terms, the Oedipus Complex) to operate, the child has first to identify with the same-sex parent, so as to compete for the opposite-sex parent. According to the logic of the system, then, this initial identification is accomplished through a loss, that is, the ungrievable loss caused by strong cultural prohibitions against sexual attachments to the same-sex parent (homosexual taboo), which also at the same time *sets up* the prohibition against incest.

Moreover, for Butler this operation not only forms gender identifications, but also constructs *sex* at the same time. The lost object, as it is incorporated into the ego, she suggests—building on Freud's statement that the ego is "first and foremost a bodily ego" (Freud 1961 [1923], 26)—"*literalizes* the loss *on* or *in* the body" *as a sexed body*. The incorporated lost object "appears as the facticity of the body, the means by which the body comes to bear 'sex' as its literal truth" (Butler 1990, 68).[5] In other words, one of the ways in which the loss comes to haunt the bereaved is as "sex." In this way, Butler is able to move away from an understanding of sex as a priori to gender; for her, sex and gender are part of one and the same melancholic operation.

Both *Boys Don't Cry* and Ezekiel 16 might be said to portray the kind of identification with the lost object that is operative in gender melancholia. The gender identifications made in film and text can be read as incorporations of lost loved parental objects. If Brandon is understood as identifying as a heterosexual man, and Jerusalem as a heterosexual woman, then following the theory that I have laid out, it is not surprising to find that their gender identifications and sexed bodies can be correlated to the loss of same-sex attachments. In each case we find parental loss: Jerusalem's mother abandons her in the field, and Brandon's father, it is revealed at the end of the film, is lost to him before he is born. Not only is Jerusalem's mother—the unnamed Hittite—lost, but any remaining attachment to her, or grief over her loss, is foreclosed by the open derision of Hittite identity and the prohibition against Israel mixing with other nations.[6] In this sense, the loss is the double loss of which Butler speaks: a loss that cannot be avowed or grieved. In Brandon's case, though, the death of his father before his birth makes the loss a literal never-never (never loved, never lost), and therefore also ungrievable.

These losses seem to precipitate gendered identification. Certainly the biblical text makes much of Jerusalem's identification with her mother (in spite of not knowing her). As an insult, Jerusalem is told how alike she is to her mother: "all who recite proverbs against you will recite one saying, 'Like a mother her daughter. The daughter of your mother, you are one who loathes her husband and her children'" (Ezek. 16:44–45). Likewise, Brandon might be said to have incorporated the lost father into/as a heterosexual male identity. Indeed he might be seen as an example par excellence of the literalizing effect of the lost same-sex attachment on and in his body, as "sex." Significantly, in the same scene that Brandon admits to Lana that he has never known his father, he tells her that he was born a girl and later took on the identity of a man. The proximity of these two confessions arguably marks Brandon's movement into an identification with this (never known, never loved, never lost) father. That this kind of internalized identification with his lost father might be at work appears in subtle ways: in a quiet moment, without the usual bravado, he offers to sing Lana to sleep with a song that his father had taught him. Further, in two separate scenes Brandon says that he wants to travel to Memphis, and that his father is in Memphis, suggesting a muted wish to be like and with his father. Of interest here is that Brandon, born a biological girl, has later taken on heterosexual male identity, so the primary loss of a "same-sex" attachment (son to father) is in some sense retroactive. This of course bears out the notion that "primary" loss is not so much originary or foundational as negotiated within and through culture.

Gender Melancholia and the Abusive Super-Ego

There is an element of violence in melancholia, normally internalized, but, as I will argue, externalized in the instances of gender melancholia that I am discussing here. Normally, in melancholia, this violence makes itself known in the form of self-reproach; the unavowed loss of the loved object and the subsequent identification with it is made manifest through self-reproach and depression. Self-reproach, which to Freud seems exaggerated and out of proportion in melancholic subjects, is a result of the ambivalence that the patient feels toward the lost loved one (love *and* anger), and represents the rage that should properly be directed toward the lost loved one, but is instead turned inward.

As noted earlier, Freud takes the mechanism of melancholic loss further, to think of the inward-turned loss as actually forming parts of the ego (1961 [1923]). The ambivalence toward the lost object is understood to be configured both as *identification* (ego-ideal) and as *critical agency* (super-ego).[7] As Butler puts it, the ambivalence is "set up as internal parts of the ego, the sadistic part [the super-ego] takes aim at the part that identifies [the ego-ideal], and the psychically violent drama of the super-ego proceeds" (Butler 1997a, 189). The super-ego, or critical agency, acts tyrannically against the object set up inside the ego (Freud 1961 [1923], 51). In fact, as Butler points out—and this will be important to my own argument—in melancholia the super-ego becomes the agent of the death drive, "a kind of gathering-place for the death instincts" (Freud 1961 [1923], 54; cited in Butler 1997a, 188). The super-ego, Freud tells us, also "has the task of repressing the Oedipus Complex" (1961 [1923], 34), that is, of forbidding incest. When applying this to gender identifications then, it might be said that *the violence* operative in the disavowal of the loved same-sex object *is constitutive for heterosexual identifications.*

As I have suggested, both *Boys Don't Cry* and Ezekiel 16 demonstrate the working of gendered and sexed identifications as structured through a disavowed loss. But following from this, it is interesting that neither Brandon nor Jerusalem seem to engage in much self-reproach, signifying anger at the incorporated lost object, as one might expect of melancholic dispositions. Indeed, for the most part, Jerusalem and Brandon appear well nigh "shameless" in their (hetero)sexual pursuits: the biblical text goes on at length about Jerusalem's willingness to make herself available to her lovers (Ezek. 16:23–34), and Brandon seems always to be on the make, unabashedly using the women who fall for him for food, shelter, and money. There are a few brief moments in the film, though, in which Brandon lets slip a little hostile judgment upon the internalized heterosexual male object with self-deprecating comments. During the ritual of dressing—binding his breasts, inserting his penis, slicking his hair—Brandon looks in the mirror and (approvingly) tells himself, "I'm an asshole." And later, when Lana questions him, "What were you like, before all this, were you like me, a girl-girl?," he responds with, "Ya, like a long time ago, and then I guess I was just like a boy-girl, *then I was just a jerk.* . . . Its weird, finally everything felt right."

But, as Freud points out, there is a kind of ambivalence in melancholia, whereby the melancholic subject is both reproach-filled and unabashed about it. In this fashion, Brandon's professions, though reproachful, are accompanied by a distinct lack of regret—and one gets the feeling that Jerusalem would have no regrets, either, if she could speak. But this too fits with Freud's description of the melancholic, who, he says, exhibits a remarkable lack of shame. As he states it, "feelings of shame in front of other people . . . are lacking in the melancholic. . . . One might emphasize the presence in him of an almost opposite trait of insistent communicativeness which finds satisfaction in self-exposure" (1957 [1917], 247). So perhaps this shameless, but at points derogatory, self-display that Brandon and Jerusalem exhibit might be enough to make the case for the operation of gender melancholia in these texts.

But both texts also depict another kind of brutal reproach that culminates in self-abasement. This is a reproach that comes from the outside but finally extorts self-reproach. In the film, John and Tom first shame Brandon by stripping him and exposing his "true sex," then reproach him verbally, "you know you brought this upon yourself,"[8] and finally degrade him further through rape and beating. Their threat to kill him if he reports the rape seems finally to wrest the sarcastic but self-reproachful response from Brandon: "Of course, I mean, this is all my fault, I know." The same pattern of verbal and physical shaming, followed by self-reproach also occurs in the biblical text. Before Yahweh gathers the nations against Jerusalem to strip and batter her, he verbally reproaches her, calling her "whore," "weak of spirit," "adulterous," "worse than other whores" and all other manner of insult.[9] In response to her abuse by Yahweh, via the nations, Jerusalem is said to acknowledge her wrongdoing (self-reproachfully), to accept Yahweh's covenant, and to remain silent (though as Mary Shields points out, we never actually hear her giving voice to her penitence [1998, 7]).

I would suggest that these scenes are in some way reminiscent of the violent drama of the super-ego. Indeed, John, Tom, Yahweh, and the nations might be seen as standing in for the super-ego, performing the function of the tyrannical critical agency through physical shamings and verbal abuses that ultimately lead Brandon and Jerusalem to some form of self-reproach. Not only are their condemnations twofold (physical shaming and verbal reproach), but in both cases death is the final reproach (though somehow Jerusalem lives on after being cut to bits).[10] Thus the tyrannical male figures in these stories can be read as powerful critical agencies that enforce self-reproach on the part of the melancholic figures. And like the super-ego, they also seem to represent a gathering place for the death instincts, driving their reproaches unto death. It appears then that gender melancholia manifests itself in these texts through reproachful super-egos, as expected, but in a slightly altered, externalized form. This externalization of painful processes within the ego, I will argue presently, is similar to what happens in traumatic neurosis.

However, I would like to consider the way in which Brandon and Jerusalem might also represent externalized processes within the melancholic formations of heterosexual identity. To this point, I have tried to show how these texts can be said to depict (heterosexualized) gender identifications under attack by other, external, tyrannical figures. But significantly, these aggressors, also heterosexual, must likewise operate within the matrix of gender melancholia. Their identities, too, would be constructed through loss, identification, and judging critical agency. It might make sense, then, to see how their cruel actions work out their own gender melancholia. I would submit that inasmuch as Yahweh, the nations, John, and Tom can be read as inhabiting the role of super-ego, so also Brandon and Jerusalem can be read as standing in for the lost loved objects of their tormentors (particularly John and Yahweh, on whom the texts focus). In other words, Brandon and Jerusalem might be said to be external incarnations of John's and Yahweh's own disavowed same-sex attachments (John to Tom; Yahweh to the male nations). Certainly some critics have hinted that the relationship between Tom and John betrays some kind of repressed love relationship (Moss and Zeavin 2000, 1228; Dunne 1997); and I have already floated the possibility that Yahweh desires the nations. If these loves are disavowed and so lost, they might also be set up, here externally, as points of identification that can then be both loved and berated. Brandon is the ideal handsome, kind, and daring man, who must also be taunted into self-destructive behaviors, and Jerusalem is the representative of the ideal nation, but one that must also be denigrated. The sticking point here, of course, is that rather than being male points of identification, as one would expect with disavowed same-sex attachments, Brandon and Jerusalem are destroyed as women, the "worst kind" of women at that (dykes and whores).

Repudiating Femininity

But this odd dynamic can perhaps be seen as a moment within the formation of heterosexual male identification that Butler calls the repudiation of femininity. On the way to establishing heterosexual desire through identification with the same-sex lost object, the melancholic heterosexual male must prove that he is not a woman. Butler describes it thus:

> Becoming a "man" within this logic requires repudiating femininity as a precondition for the heterosexualization of sexual desire and its fundamental

ambivalence. . . . Indeed the desire for the feminine is marked by that repudiation: he wants the woman he would never be. *He wouldn't be caught
dead being her*: therefore he wants her. . . . One of the most anxious aims of
his desire will be to elaborate the difference between him and her, and
he will seek to discover and install proof of that difference (1997a, 137,
emphases mine).

Both *Boys Don't Cry* and Ezekiel 16 show male figures performing exactly
this kind of work; in repressing their own same-sex attachments and
establishing identifications with them as masculine ideals, they must first
thoroughly abjure their femininity.

At the very least, reading along these lines makes some sense of several
peculiarities in the biblical text: that is, the strange working of the plot
whereby Jerusalem's competing lovers gang up on her rather than on each
other; the fact that Jerusalem lives on, even after being cut to bits; and
finally an odd spelling that occurs throughout the chapter. As mentioned
earlier, one of the points where film and text do not match up is in the
treatment of "the object of desire." Where in the film, Lana—the contested
object of desire—remains unharmed, in the biblical text, Jerusalem is
destroyed. But if the primary object of desire in the biblical text is actually
not Jerusalem, but the male nations—for instance the sons of Egypt, whose
"largeness of flesh" seems to be of some interest to Yahweh (v. 26)—then
Jerusalem's role can be understood differently. If this same-sex attachment
to the male nations is disavowed, which clearly it is, and so lost, it makes
sense, within the logic of gender melancholia at least, that a stand-in
(Jerusalem) is set up as a point of identification.

Though the figure of a beloved nation (Jerusalem, and also Samaria and
Sodom in vv. 46–52) may be the perfect stand-in object for Yahweh's lost
love, the question remains as to how to make sense of her femininity. That
Yahweh identifies himself with the nation of Israel, and in particular the
city of Jerusalem, is so much received theological wisdom. But as Shields
points out in a discussion of the sister passage to this one, Ezekiel 23,
Yahweh's identity as a powerful deity is *dependent* on Jerusalem as a political entity, he is nothing without her. There is therefore a strange conflation
that occurs between the abuser/abused, subject/object, masculine/feminine
(2001, 151). This is one of the reasons, Shields argues, that Jerusalem lives
on though she has been killed; she is an essential part of Yahweh's identity.
In a sense, he cannot be "caught dead" being her. Yet as Shields notes,
Jerusalem's continued life also poses a continual threat to Yahweh's power.
This threat, I would suggest, resides at least partially in her feminine identification, that thing that Yahweh must repudiate (within himself) in order
to disavow his love for the nations and to complete the accompanying
masculine identification.[11] Freud writes, "The analysis of melancholia now

shows that the ego can kill itself only if, owing to the return of the object-cathexis, it can treat itself as an object" (1957 [1917], 252). Along these lines, the figure of Jerusalem as sexually objectified woman might be seen as enabling Yahweh's male-identified ego to berate itself.[12]

Of particular interest, with respect to the overlap in identity between Yahweh and Israel, is a strange linguistic quirk in the ancient Masoretic Text (circa 1009 C.E., the most ancient complete text of the Hebrew Bible, on which contemporary translations are based). This linguistic phenomenon produces an ambiguity between first-person verb forms (describing Yahweh) and second-person feminine verb forms (describing Jerusalem). Eight times in the chapter, the written consonants spell the first-person singular suffix form (תִי־) (which would predicate "Yahweh"), but are vocalized as second-person feminine forms (תְּ־) (which would predicate "Jerusalem"). They are also corrected (by the Masoretic scribes in the eleventh century C.E.) in the margins to second-person feminine consonantal forms (תְּ־) (vv. 13, 18, 22, 31a, 31b, 43a, 43b, 51). The reverse occurs in v. 59, in Yahweh's speech to Jerusalem, with the feminine consonantal form vocalized as a first-person form (תִּי־). While these orthographical oddities may simply be, as scholars maintain, an archaic second-person form (Zimmerli 1979 [1969], 325 n. 13; Wevers 1969, 122 n. 13; Gesenius and Kautzsch 1910, §44), it is curious that it occurs with a higher frequency in this chapter than in any other chapter of the Masoretic Text. This spelling, which seems to mix second-person feminine and first-person suffix forms, does not occur again in Ezekiel,[13] though it does occur elsewhere in the Masoretic Text, particularly in Jeremiah (e.g., Jer 2:33; 3:4–5; 4:19; 31:21; 46:11). However, the high concentration of this ambiguous form in this particular chapter is at the very least suggestive of an uncertain identification between Yahweh (*I*) and Jerusalem (*you*). In the most notable of its occurrences, an ambiguity appears as to whether *you* (Jerusalem) or *I* (Yahweh) put "my incense" before the images of lovers (v. 18), whether *you* or *I* build your high places (v. 31a), whether *you* or *I* go beyond the call of duty for a regular prostitute (v. 31b), and whether *you* or *I* have a hand in devising your abominations (vv. 43b, 51). With this ambiguity in place, the speech of Yahweh sounds very much like that of the self-deriding melancholic, accusing himself of wrongdoing at the same time as accusing the lost loved object.

The film has (overall) fewer ambiguities of which to make sense. However, one aspect stands out as somewhat difficult to decipher: that is, the relationship between John and Brandon. Clearly Brandon is both in awe of and jealous of John. But John, as opposed to what one might anticipate in response to a newcomer in a small town, is immediately friendly and warm with Brandon (Tom is much more a bully). John fights Brandon's first fight with him; he jokingly shows him how to throw a punch; he tells him of his love for Lana; he sets him up to (dis)prove his manliness in bumper skiing; and he directs him in a car chase, leaning over his shoulder and telling him how and where to drive. Indeed, there are moments, in long, close-up camera shots of John's face, when it seems that John looks at Brandon with genuine love and tenderness. This kind of attitude is not reflected at all in his relationship with Tom, though the film hints that they do have some kind of a special bond ("I'm the only one who can control that fucker," says Tom). But if Brandon, as a point of masculine identification, can be seen as holding the place of John's (incorporated) lost love for Tom (or other men), John's mentorship of Brandon might begin to make some sense.

And though, on the surface, the film mobilizes John's anger at Brandon as jealousy over Lana, perhaps John's tendency to push Brandon into danger is telling both as a kind of identification and as judgment upon that identification. In setting Brandon up to bumper ski, he tells Brandon first that he "can do it . . . don't let 'em scare you," and then (judgingly) that he "can do better than that," not satisfied. Strangely, as he introduces Brandon into the game, he pulls off his own shirt as if he were introducing himself: "this here's a mean prize fighter up from Lincoln . . . very tough" (this comes as a voice-over while John leads Brandon toward the truck; it is not clear who actually says it, or if it is just in John's head). After Brandon's failed attempts to stay upright aboard the hurling truck, John commends him with what could also be read as an ominous, foreshadowing threat, "you're one crazy little fucker, whadd're we gonna do with you?" Later, he urges Brandon on in a reckless car chase, head close, voice low, again somewhat beratingly ("c'mon ya pussy, go faster, y'cocksucker . . . don't stop,

Figure 5   John Identifies with Brandon in *Boys Don't Cry*

don't stop, go faster, go faster"). At one point he mysteriously leans over (in response to Brandon's "I can't see") and looks as if he will fix something (but what?), or perhaps as if to touch Brandon between the legs in a sort of phallic (sexual?) bonding (though the audience can't see that, either), before he leans back in orgasmic bliss. Yet once they have been stopped by the police, John lashes out at Brandon, "don't you never pull that shit again . . . you got me stopped by the fuckin' cops." It is as if Brandon lives out John's fantasies for him, but also takes the heat for them (fantasies that include making love to Lana, though this without John *literally* in the background). Little wonder, then, with this kind of male identification being established, that when John finds out that Brandon is actually a woman, he goes ballistic, frenziedly seeking to establish proof of the difference between himself and Brandon (the "pussy"), with whom he has identified.[14]

The Trauma of Gender Melancholia

These texts might be seen, then, as aptly depicting the workings of gender melancholia. But beyond reading film and text merely as parables of individual psychic processes, I think that it may be possible and even helpful to consider these texts as cultural renditions of the psychic workings of the social order. I would tentatively suggest, therefore, that these texts reveal sexual violence as the *social outworking* of gender melancholia. More specifically, they seem to depict the violent drama of the super-ego, acting as the gathering place for death instincts, externalized and *enacted by others also affected by gender melancholia*. This kind of reading picks up on the notion, advanced by Butler at the end of *The Psychic Life of Power* (1997a, 178–98), that the social metaphors in Freud's writing make way for a consideration of the relation of the psychic to the social (Butler notes that Freud uses language of institution and polity to describe the psyche [1997a, 178]). Butler seems to see this relation along the lines of ideological interpellation, that is, the means by which an ideological social prohibition, like the prohibition on homosexuality, comes to be imprinted on the individual psyche (1997a, 190–98). But another possible way to look at it might be to consider how these kinds of interior psychic relations come to be externalized and lived out on the level of the social.[15]

To this end, I find it productive to think about the film and the biblical text alongside the muted connection that appears between melancholia and traumautic neurosis when *Beyond the Pleasure Principle* and *The Ego and the Id* are read together. I have already outlined the connection, drawn out by Butler, that Freud makes in *The Ego and the Id* between melancholia and the death drive, whereby for the melancholic the super-ego acts as a gathering place for the death instincts. Given then that Freud suggests that the death drive is operative in melancholia, and given that he develops the idea of death drive out of his consideration of trauma and loss in *Beyond the Pleasure Principle*, it seems pertinent to consider the nature of the relationship between trauma and melancholia, then specifically between trauma and gender melancholia.

In trying to understand why the ego will withstand unpleasure in spite of the pleasure principle (by which instincts continuously seek satisfaction), Freud begins *Beyond the Pleasure Principle* with a discussion of the compulsion to repeat. He notices—in the famous example of his grandson's game of *fort-da* (1955 [1920], 14–17)—that children, in their play, will repeat unpleasurable experiences as a way of renouncing instinctual satisfaction, but also as a way of mastering certain unpleasant experiences. What I would like to notice here is that the unpleasant experience of reality that the child deals with in this game—reality that gets in the way of instinctual satisfaction—is *the unpleasant experience of loss*, both of the child's mother (leaving the room) and of the child's father (away at war).

This discussion of unpleasant but productive repetition then leads Freud into a discussion of trauma and traumatic repetition compulsion, whereby the person who has been traumatized engages in a similar process of uncannily repeating the traumatic experience in order to master it. Freud speaks of trauma particularly in terms of fright, as a forceful stimulus for which the external protective system of the ego is unprepared. The ego then works to shore up the breach in the ego's protective shield, through repeating the unpleasurable experience so as to master it (1955 [1920], 26–33). The actual experience of trauma is so sudden and so violent that it is repressed, and so therefore returns in alternate forms (dreams, etc.). As Cathy Caruth puts it, since trauma cannot be known, traumatic repetition is always the attempt to reclaim a "missed experience" (1996, 60–63). In some ways, this mirrors the structure of melancholia, which is the psychic working-out of a loss for which an individual is unprepared, and in which the loss is unknown or repressed (twice-lost) (Freud 1957 [1917], 245).

Moving on from the discussion of trauma in *Beyond the Pleasure Principle*, reflecting more generally on why it is that individuals are driven to repetition, particularly of past unpleasurable experiences, Freud concludes that human organisms are essentially conservative, seeking a return to the past, to the time before life, which is ultimately death. Thus Freud rounds out his discussion of unpleasurable repetition by proposing the notion of death drive, that urge in the ego to return to "an earlier state of things" (1955 [1920], 38). In a sense, then, in the death drive, the ego works to restore what has been *lost to it* in the passing of time. Three years later, in *The Ego and the Id*, he relates the death drive to melancholia and the functioning of the super-ego. The super-ego, as the gathering place for the death instincts, is the internalized mechanism that enforces renunciation of instincts, which enforces mastery of the instincts through repetition.

It seems—and perhaps this is an obvious point, but I think it still bears mention—that Freud's discussions of trauma and the repetition of unpleasurable experience (culminating in the development of the notion of death drive) are based in some sense on the idea of *mastering an incommensurable loss*.[16] Freud's appellation of the super-ego as a gathering place for the death drive goes beyond just describing its destructive impulse: it is a repetitive mastery of loss. In the unpleasurable experience of the super-ego's judgment upon the lost object, the ego puts itself in the position wherein it has, once again, but in a different form, to try to master the unpleasurable experience of loss. This is the same kind of loss (unprepared for, then repressed) that provokes melancholia. Thus, the loss that causes melancholia can perhaps be said to be in some way traumatic. The melancholic's tendency to repeatedly berate herself is one means of trying to master this loss, just as the traumatized individual constantly tries to master the "lost" encounter by means of reencountering the trauma.[17]

A similar link can be made between trauma and the loss of same-sex attachments that give rise to gender melancholia. That is, part of the reason that the loss of the same-sex love is disavowed—as with a loss that brings on melancholia rather than mourning—is the ego's unpreparedness for this loss, and its unwillingness to accept it. Further, if, as Butler argues, this loss is constitutive for heterosexual identification, then perhaps *the loss of same-sex attachments is a constitutive trauma*, which the ego, via the super-ego, seeks to master.

This way of thinking about the connection between gender melancholia and trauma prepares the ground for thinking about how gender melancholia might operate on a social level. What is interesting in Freud's discussion of trauma, and what—as I think these texts show—is applicable to gender melancholia, is his argument that while at times the ego relives the trauma actively, through dreams, at other times these repetitions occur as if by chance, as if by some external daemonic force that causes the ego to constantly confront the same traumatic experience (1955 [1920], 21–23, 36). He hints, though does not develop as fully as one might like, that this seemingly external manifestation is actually generated internally. When internal unpleasures become too great, says Freud, "there is a tendency to treat them as though they were acting, not from the inside, but from the outside, so that it may be possible to bring the shield against stimuli into operation as a means of defence against them" (1955 [1920], 29). Given my discussion of the film and text, I would suggest that when the super-ego's threats become too great in the trauma of gender melancholia, then perhaps they are externalized and acted out on the level of the social. Indeed, as Freud writes in *Inhibitions, Symptoms, and Anxiety*, the "loss of an object . . . and the threat of castration are just as much dangers coming from outside as, let us say, a ferocious animal would be" (1959 [1926], 145).

This kind of social working-out of psychic processes may be possible because of the liminality of the ego. As others have pointed out for other purposes (e.g., Prosser 1998, 40–41; Butler 1993, 58–59), in *The Ego and the Id*, Freud also describes the ego, particularly the system of perception-consciousness within the ego, as a (bodily) surface that forms *a borderline between internal and external* perceptions and processes (1961 [1923], 24–27). He writes, "A person's own body and above all its surface, is a place from which both external and internal perceptions may spring" (1961 [1923], 25). Moreover, the ego mediates between internal and external "excitations" and processes. It would seem that at points, external excitations are rolled into the ego's work, and perhaps stand in for unpleasurable internal excitations. Because the super-ego is part of the ego (the borderline between the external and internal worlds), its judgment may come, at times, from the outside.

The way that gender melancholia seems to be worked out on the level of the social in these two texts suggests that the primary loss of same-sex attachments operates in the same way as traumatic events, as described by Freud. In other words, like trauma, the loss of same-sex attachments gives rise to uncanny, repetitive, seemingly "daemonic" encounters with destructive forces. The loss of a same-sex love is traumatic. Thus it would not be surprising to find that the self-reproaches to which the gender melancholic is inclined seem to come from without, as life-destroying dangers. These externalized melancholic self-reproaches might be thought of as repetitive encounters with the externalized super-ego, also called the death drive, as a result of the traumatic event of the loss of the loved object. Perhaps this makes sense of why, in the film, Brandon repeatedly seeks out and revels in unpleasurable chase scenarios,[18] and why in Ezekiel 16, Jerusalem is said to repeatedly take pleasure in the very thing that angers Yahweh most. This reading points to the conclusion that if gender melancholia produces the norm (heterosexuality), as Butler suggests it does, then the norm inherently lends itself to violence—and to traumatic violence at that.

Readerly Identifications

In sum, I have tried to show that both Ezekiel 16 and *Boys Don't Cry* do indeed have something interesting to say about the construction of gender.

I have tried to indicate how both texts demonstrate Butler's conception of gender melancholia lived out on the level of the social, as the traumatic reenactment of the primary loss of same-sex attachments. More specifically, I have tried to show that these texts lay out the ways in which the construction of heterosexual identifications and identities, predicated as they are on traumatic loss, lend themselves to violent externalizations of melancholia.

There is, however, an added layer of complexity in all of this, when readerly identification is taken into account. Identifying as a woman, I initially experienced *Boys Don't Cry* as a text of terror, as traumatic, and to this I would most certainly add Ezekiel 16. But as commentary shows, other readers have engaged with these texts differently, more positively. A number of feminist biblical critics have shown how male scholars writing about Ezekiel 16 identify with Yahweh, and see Ezekiel 16 as fundamentally about Yahweh's goodness (L. Day 2000, 224–27; P. Day 2000; Runions 2001b). Likewise, those writing about the film have shown how many viewers, both straight and transgendered (Rosario 2000, 31; Giltz 2000; Pierce 2000a), have identified with Brandon as a male hero, charmer, and, especially, as daring self-inventor (Anderson 2000, 54; Moss and Zeavin 2000, 1227; Pierce 2000a; Brooks 2000, 44).

Yet it is interesting to note that both texts are structured in such a way as to invite divided identifications. As Shields points out, readers, as addressees of the biblical text, are invited to identify with whores, but (especially if readers are male), there is "pressure . . . to identify with YHWH" and therefore to identify as both women (whores) and men (Yahweh) (2001, 150). Along similar lines, Linda Day suggests that perhaps in refusing to acknowledge Yahweh's behavior as problematic, commentators, though taking the part of Yahweh, are in a sense also identifying with abused *women* before they decide to leave their partners (2000, 227). I would also add that with the reversibility of the pronouns *you* and *I* in general, the reader is invited to respond as *I* to the text's *you* and as *you* to the text's *I*, which places the reader alternately in the position of Yahweh and of Jerusalem. Further, the ambiguity between the first- and second-person feminine forms in Ezekiel 16, discussed above, also lends itself to a kind of transgendered cross-identification.[19]

Boys Don't Cry may provoke a similar kind of divided identification. In an interview, film director Pierce states that she deliberately tried not to demonize Tom and John, but to characterize them so that the audience could identify with them as well as with Brandon (2000b, 40). Certainly John is a likable and warm character in his unabusive moments. And in the portrayal of Brandon's gender ambiguity, the viewer is also invited to identify both as male and female. In this way, viewers are given a wide range of identifications: cruel straight men, ideal straight men, and abused women (or, in psychoanalytic terms, critical agency, ideal identification, and repudiated femininity). Readers are also invited to consider, and perhaps to identify with, a wide range of sexual preferences: as men liking women, as women liking women, as men liking men.

Moreover, if these texts can be said to mirror each other in some way— and I hope I have shown that they do—then, read together, they might provide an eye-opening reflection of readers' favored points of identification. For instance, if those readers who identify in some way with Yahweh can see that Yahweh is much like John and Tom (all of whom may be much like readers' own super-egos), then perhaps they might find this reflection disconcerting enough to consider loosening their identification with Yahweh. Likewise, those (especially straight) film viewers who identify with Brandon (as a straight man) might see that he is not that different from Jerusalem, and that both are figures of repudiated femininity and disavowed loved objects. Perhaps this might further interrogate opinions about the revered American ideal of self-invented heroes, and shed light on the violence and exclusions that support the "extolled virtue . . . [of] the 'self-made man,'" which apparently drew viewers to Brandon (Anderson 2000, 54).

Indeed, Brandon repeats the figure of the "self-made man" in a way that shows up the contradictions, the conflicts, and the subtle differences that get rolled over by such a stereotyping designation. In repeating such an icon of "freedom" so differently, Brandon is in a sense a hybrid figure (see chapter 4). Hybridity opens up a point of identification for viewers that does not fill quite the same ideological role, nor incite quite the same kind of longing, as does the notion of "self-made man." In other words, Brandon allows viewers to identify differently, to identify with difference. Similarly, the reader of Ezekiel is pulled into identification with Jerusalem, on top of a more habitual identification with Yahweh against Jerusalem. Elsewhere I have described these kinds of identifications as "liminal identifications," after Homi Bhabha (Runions 2001c). Such identifications necessarily challenge readers' and viewers' habitual identifications, precisely because they offer other images in which readers and viewers can recognize themselves.

By way of parting reflection, I might say that if readers and viewers identify, perhaps differently, with those having same-sex attachments or non-gender-normative identities, they might also begin to unearth and confront the disavowed primary attachments that underlie their own gender identifications. In other words, these texts might prompt readers to think of their own never loved and never lost same-sex attachments. Thus, these texts provide a way of "tracing the ways in which identification is implicated in what it excludes" (Butler 1993, 119). If so, it would seem that, read together, Ezekiel 16 and *Boys Don't Cry* remind readers that every heterosexual identification— in the words of Brandon Teena[20]—is a gender identity crisis.

Chapter 6

Falling Frogs and Family Traumas: Mediating Apocalypse in *Magnolia*
with Adrienne Gibb[1]

Released on the eve of the millennium, in December 1999, the film *Magnolia* has been called apocalyptic, a label it earns in part because of its use of cataclysmic biblical imagery (e.g., falling frogs, flooding rains). But going beyond the biblical imagery, the apocalyptic—and so also biblical—nature of the film lies, in part, in its *unveiling* activity; in this case, the unveiling of traumatic patriarchal structures and incidents that fuel the hysteria, rage, woe, and fear in the characters that make up the film's two dysfunctional families. But the apocalyptic nature of the film might also be read along the lines of Walter Benjamin's postbiblical apocalypse: the interruptive messianic "time of now," a notion—when illuminated by his views on media, and in particular, film—that is especially fruitful for the argument here.

Benjamin's reflections on media, memory, and trauma assist in reading *Magnolia*, as it seems self-consciously to use various forms of media to set the stage for this kind of apocalyptic unveiling and interruption of the effects of patriarchal family trauma. The film disturbs patriarchy—aligned in this film with television (the two fathers of the two parallel families have both made their careers in television). It does so by recollecting particular histories and by introducing other forms of media, such as individual art-works and historic film footage. Against the televisual medium, *Magnolia* lays out contrasting registers of temporality and representation, from the early filmic register of newsreels in the precredit sequence, through the tele-visual register that dominates the whole film, to, finally, a brief but crucial glimpse of a handmade image: a painting bearing the caption, "But it did happen." In thus deploying contrasting forms of media, the film inserts the past where in the televisual world it has been disavowed; it envisions the end of time as the end of a present that is totalizing, amnesiac, patriarchal, and televisual.

But this critique of patriarchy may find its limit in the film's demand for a return to salvation, originary truths, and evolutionary time. The film's call for chronology and teleology through traditional apocalypse may undermine the potentially liberating movement of the film by insisting on a kind of time and imagination that has been critiqued as particularly Western and patriarchal (see Bhabha 1994; Keller 1996; Quinby 1994). Here Benjamin's "time of now" is helpful in thinking about how *Magnolia* might present a different kind of apocalypse, one that encourages viewers to grasp hold of their own experience in order to resist traumatic abuse. Nevertheless, the use of apocalyptic themes and images in the film remains ambiguous with respect to critique of patriarchy and may serve only to highlight the problems with apocalypse itself.

Patriarchy through Television

Magnolia plays quite deliberately with feminist critiques of television as an enabler of patriarchy and traditional family roles (see Brundson 1997; Spigel 1997). As film critic Diane Sippi puts it, "*Magnolia* links the cultivation of misogyny to commercial television and its role in the home" (2001, 9). The drama of the film pans through scenes of abusive fathers and their children, particularly those of two parallel families, connected through television. The film is intense in its portrayal of the everyday disasters within these two white, upper-middle-class families. Both fathers are major figures in the television industry. One, Earl Partridge (Jason Robards), lies dying of cancer, cared for by homecare nurse Phil Parma (Phillip Seymour Hoffman). Partridge is the owner of the television station in which much of the story line unfolds. He is also the father of Frank T. J. Mackey (Tom Cruise), star of the "self-help" seminar for men, *Seduce and Destroy*. As disclosed during the course of the film, Frank does not speak with his father because Partridge abandoned his first wife Lily (Frank's mother) during her fatal bout with cancer, leaving his son at age fourteen to care for her. Partridge's young, beautiful, and slightly hysterical second wife, Linda (Julianne Moore), aggravates the estrangement between father and son by her hostility toward Frank and her jealousy of any attention he might receive from his dying father.

In the parallel family, Jimmy Gator (Philip Baker Hall), who has also been diagnosed with cancer, is the renowned host of a game show, *What Do*

Kids Know?, that airs as part of Earl Partridge's network. Jimmy Gator is the father of Claudia Wilson Gator (Melora Walters), a hard-core coke addict who refuses to speak to him because, as becomes clear, he has sexually abused her. Claudia becomes romantically involved with do-gooder police officer Jim Kurring (John C. Reilly) in a meeting provoked by her neighbor's complaint of noise (caused by Claudia's fight with her father when he comes to tell her he is dying, as well as the loud music she subsequently plays). Kurring is himself a caricature of TV serial cops, out to help people, to "make a save, correct a wrong, or right a situation." It is in Kurring's world that the margin to the film's white middle-class universe—that is, what lies beyond the televisual frame—appears. During the course of his duties, Kurring investigates a murder in what appears to be a low-income neighborhood, in the home of the black woman Marcie (Cleo King), who is somehow related to the preteen, prophetic rapper (Emmanuel L. Johnson) who offers to help Kurring solve the mystery. This story line is ultimately erased; it fizzles out by the end of the film, serving only as a prop for the narrative, thus marking its status as marginal.

Sandwiched between these two families and their frames are two more generations of TV offspring: former quiz kid Donnie Smith (William H. Macy), a forty-something, lovesick kleptomaniac, still bitter at his parents for making him perform on *What Do Kids Know?* and stealing his prize money; and contemporary quiz kid Stanley (Jeremy Blackman), whose aired-live child's nightmare of peeing his pants causes him to revolt against the game he is playing and ultimately to stand up to his father's driving abuse.

Television dominates the filmic universe of *Magnolia* visually as well as narratively. The establishing shots that serve to introduce the characters make this abundantly clear, beginning with a television frame that fills the screen with an advertisement for Frank T. J. Mackey's instructional video series. The camera then moves to Claudia, the parallel TV offspring to Frank, in a scene in which she makes an exchange of sex for cocaine, during which a television in the background plays a brief retrospective of her father's thirty-year career as host of *What Do Kids Know?*. Moving in through the televisual frame to Gator's life and career, we find within it another TV screen, displaying genius kid, Stanley, on Gator's show. Once again the camera moves in through the televisual frame to view Stanley's world. His father rushes him out the door to school with his bags and bags of books, berating him all the while (to the sounds of Frank Mackey announcing *Seduce and Destroy* on a television in their home). Parallel quiz kid Donnie Smith is also introduced through a television screen showing a rerun of *What Do Kids Know?*, before the camera moves in to show the neurotic adult Donnie having his perfectly straight teeth fitted for braces. Finally, the camera moves—sans TV screen—to Earl Partridge, the progenitor of this close-knit TV world, with his wife Linda, and his nurse Phil. These introductions are all bound together by the voice of Aimee Mann singing, "One is the loneliest number that you'll ever do." The televisual frame continues to confront the filmic frame throughout *Magnolia*. This intrusion of the televisual frame does more than highlight the film's critique of television. It also spells out television's relation to capitalism (infomercials and stores filled with TVs) and to sexist and androcentric interests (porn flicks and monster-truck racing).

Sexism and paternalism run rampant throughout the various vignettes in the way women are spoken of and to (particularly evident in the depiction of Linda), but those responsible for sexism are not portrayed altogether without irony. For instance, Frank T. J. Mackey's appallingly misogynist seminars are introduced to the viewer with a shot of Mackey, backlit in a most phallic way, accompanied by the dramatic music of *2001: A Space Odyssey* (an allusion that recalls that film's obsession with the phallic column). Mackey's choreography moves his body through representations of phallus, Christ figure, and action hero. Later, the film pokes fun at Mackey's narcissism as he gives an interview for national television. Mackey, pumped up, panting, and posing in his underwear, is obviously disappointed when the interviewer finally tells the camera to roll after he has dressed. ("What? I thought we were rolling.") With a similar kind of irony, Officer Kurring, who works both arrogantly and comically in his investigations, patronizing those he interrogates, continually loses his phallus. He drops his billy club upon first meeting Claudia; later he loses his gun, praying frantically to God to help him find it. A more serious, yet still tongue-in-cheek display of the backfiring of phallic will occurs at the end of the film, after Jimmy Gator has been confronted with his abuse of Claudia. Gator tries to shoot himself in the head, but to no avail. A falling frog hits the gun he is firing, causing it to misfire to shatter a TV (announcing a steal at $39.00) instead.

Falling Frogs

To be sure, the falling frogs, which come at the end of a torrential rain, are the film's oddest feature, and as such bear some attention. Certainly the significance of the frogs has troubled critics. Kent Jones complains in *Film Comment* that the frogs are not tied into the rest of the movie, that they offer "no moral, psychological, [or] thematic resonance" (2000, 38). But as Mim Udovitch points out in her interview of director P. T. Anderson, the frogs may be a reference to "the work of Charles Fort, the early-twentieth-century scientific skeptic and compiler of paranormal phenomena, who said that a society's existence could be judged by the health of its frogs" (2000, 49). The frogs in *Magnolia* are both paranormal and unhealthy as they fall from the sky to splatter and smear across every surface. As an indicator of societal health, the falling frogs answer the questions asked at the film's opening regarding odd occurrences, chance, and destiny, by placing strange happenings within the realm of unhealthy social relationships.

But the film also makes it clear that the frogs are in some way biblical. The clue to this is a sign held up briefly by a TV studio audience member reading "Exodus 8:2,"[2] indicating a verse that tells of Moses' threat to Pharaoh of the plague of frogs, in advocacy of the people of Israel's exodus from Egypt. This narrative and symbolic turn has led liberation theologian Mario DeGiglio-Bellemare to give the frogs in *Magnolia* moral significance in the light of that theological tradition's valorization of the exodus story as a metaphor for exodus from oppression. DeGiglio-Bellemare reads the frogs in the film as the precursor to "an exodus from structures of sin that enslave and destroy lives" (2000, 11). It may be that in spite of their seemingly random appearance, the frogs are thematically and psychologically integral to the film in a way that resonates with DeGiglio-Bellemare's reading. Namely, the frogs mark the moments for each of the characters in which the logical results of the patriarchal TV legacy are challenged. As the frogs fall, almost all of the central characters undergo some kind of personal transformation as they become able to understand their personal histories differently. The frogs do seem to mark an overturning of structures in a way that could be read as liberatory. But this overturning of structures might also reflect another kind of biblical influence—especially given critics' assessment of the film as millennial—that is, apocalypse. In fact, some biblical scholars have interpreted ancient Near Eastern apocalypse, and in particular the biblical Revelation of John of Patmos,[3] as a resistant, liberatory discourse, motivating its audience to political resistance to the Roman Empire (see Fiorenza 1985, 181–203; A. Y. Collins 1984, 77–94). Thus, it seems as if the film is using the exodus imagery apocalyptically (perhaps taking its cue from the book of Revelation),[4] building on the liberatory and resistant premise of the exodus to suggest the same for its own apocalyptic themes.

Apocalypse Now

Apocalypse is a word and a genre that has far outgrown its biblical, or more properly, ancient Near Eastern, roots.[5] As the recent turn of the millennium approached, a number of literary, biblical, and cultural critics turned their attention to things apocalyptic. As Jacques Derrida—who has been hailed, perhaps overhastily given the extensive scholarship on the subject, as "the foremost theorist of apocalypse in the late-twentieth-century" (Dellamora 1994, 7)—points out, the biblical sense of the Greek word *apokalupto*, is *to reveal* or *to disclose* (Derrida 1984 [1981], 4). And indeed, as John J. Collins shows in his delineation of the genre of ancient Near Eastern apocalypse, revelation of eschatological truths—that is, truths usually imparted by otherworldly figures (mostly saints or patriarchs, not frogs) about the end of the current order and the beginning of a new order—is a central component of biblical and other ancient Near Eastern apocalypses (J. J. Collins 1979, 6–8).

At the same time, Derrida pushes his definition of apocalypse to include notions of unveiling, overturning, catastrophe, and the sublime. Other cultural and literary critics have likewise looked at biblical and postbiblical apocalyptic narratives in similar terms. What qualifies as apocalyptic for these critics is broadly focused as visions of the end of time, from narratives of doom and catastrophic destruction, to utopic new worlds. Though the content of these narratives is quite diverse, ranging from Augustine's *City of God* to Hal Lindsey's *The Late Great Planet Earth*, their structure is similar, often using fantastic images with cosmic import to move from disaster to hope for a new world, in ways that strongly resemble biblical and ancient Near Eastern apocalypses.

Within the movement from doom to utopia, twentieth-century scholars of apocalypse have identified a number of rhetorical and political functions for apocalyptic texts. Of these, several aspects are important to highlight as pertinent for a reading of *Magnolia*. First, apocalypse deals with a sense of imminent crisis (O'Leary 1994, 16; Kermode 1967, 28); it gives voice to the worry of an impending disaster in cosmic language that helps to makes sense of that crisis. As scholars have pointed out, the understanding of what causes crises is usually bound up with some notion of evil or societal ill (O'Leary 1994; Keller 1996; 1997). Second, apocalypse insists on a particularly linear way of understanding history: it envisions the future as the cosmically appropriate or deserved outcome of history and its bearing upon the present. As Frank Kermode puts it, people "in the middest make considerable imaginative investments in coherent patterns, which, by the provision of an end make possible a satisfying consonance with the origins and with the middle" (1967, 17). In other words, imagined endings enable the present and the past to cohere. It would seem that the imagination of a catastrophic crisis followed by a radically antithetical utopia is a way of dealing with an actual crisis in a way that matches up with presuppositions about origins. Apocalypse supplies cosmic reasons and outcomes for contemporary crises and their solutions. Variously proposed utopias are seen as a kind of salvation from the crises and catastrophe, often to be achieved by a saving agent (often divine, individual, and male, as the biblical Revelation attests). Apocalyptic narratives of history and its "end" can therefore ground a range of political positions and actions.[6] Lastly, in spite of the apocalyptic strategy of posing a definitive end to time as the definitive result of history, that end is always deferred because the end never arrives, its posited arrival is always pushed back (Derrida 1984 [1981], 23–27).[7] As Kermode observes, this deferral of the end renders apocalypse a discourse that enables transition and smoothes out crises of transition (like those required by technological change); the end becomes "immanent rather than imminent" (1967, 101), and the past is brought together with the future (1967, 100).

Magnolia and Apocalypse

The falling frogs in *Magnolia* are certainly fantastic and catastrophic in their plague-like import.[8] They are not, however, the only apocalyptic element in *Magnolia*. Other portentous images include the torrential, threatening rain; the cryptic reference to the Worm and the Flood in the testimony of the child "prophet" to Kurring in his murder case; the likening of children to angels; and the references to (phallic) figures aiming at salvation and control of destiny. Salvation figures are both exemplified and at the same time mocked in the characters of Officer Kurring, who lives for "the save," and Frank Mackey, whose self-help is all about controlling destiny. ("Because in the end of the day, *Seduce* may not be just about picking up chicks, sticking your cock in; it's about finding out what you can be in this world, defining it, controlling it, and in saying, I will take what is mine. And whatever, if you just happen to get a little blow job out of it, hey, what the fuck, why not?") But beyond quipping at themes of doom and salvation, the film might be said to ask cosmic questions. The opening narration tells of seemingly random, arbitrary events and catastrophe, hinting that they are not mere coincidences. It thus posits questions of relationships: What connects things in the universe? Are these relations arbitrary, random coincidences? Or do they have significance? Are they connected below the surface? The allusions to sacred (biblical) texts suggest that there is a significance; but while grounded in ancient Near Eastern notions of apocalypse, the larger thematics of the film—like so many other uses of apocalyptic images in art and media—move beyond these particular sources.

Indeed, the overall structure of the film, moving as it does from personal crises and impending catastrophe to personal triumphs and reconciliations, is apocalyptic. When in the January 2001 issue of *CineAction* Diana Sippi lists *Magnolia* as one of several apocalyptic films that appeared at the end of the millennium, she defines apocalypse in a more or less conventional way as "the end of the world as we know it: a representation of irretrievable, possibly cataclysmic loss" (2001, 5). But though she wishes to leave the definition of apocalypse at that, her essay turns around the hope for film also to represent that place, left by the loss, wherein a new world can arise: "a new vision—a world both artist and spectator create—[that] can teach us to approach any place, on or off the screen, with cautious veneration, owing to its potential ambiance, its dynamic life, or its latent spirit" (2001, 5). In this way she seems implicitly also to include in her definition the usual utopic counterpart to the cataclysmic destruction of apocalypse: the opening out onto something new. And this hope for something new is the potential she sees in *Magnolia* in all its "simultaneous crises and nerve-shattering crescendos and plunging meltdowns" (2001, 7). She writes of the film:

> Placing apocalypse in *Magnolia* is not about tracing the trajectory of frogs. It is about playing a role as a visitor on that street and then as a resident on our own. It is a matter of noting the nexus of person and parent, family and work . . . faux euphoria and buried fear in every household because they really happen. Pegging the time and place, venting rage and woe where they belong, putting sadness and dismay into their proper quadrants, is the only hope for setting things right (2001, 9).

Here Sippi suggests that the film urges the viewer to aid in the transformation of social life through proper placement of rage, woe, and fear. She seems to understand apocalypse not only as the end of time, but also as a kind of transformational political discourse.

Before returning to this question of the film's apocalyptic rhetorical efficacy as a transformational discourse, it may be helpful first to explore in a little more depth the apocalyptic nature of the film. The frogs are perhaps more important than Sippi suggests, in that they bring the biblical roots of apocalypse together with this particular cultural manifestation of it. Not only do they allude to biblical plagues and new beginnings, but they also mark an unveiling and an overturning of unhealthy and traumatic social relations within the patriarchal world of television. And yet, as will be discussed further on, apocalypse in *Magnolia* is highly ambiguous with respect to the actual kind of social transformation it urges.

Walter Benjamin: Apocalypse, Media, Memory, and Trauma

The apocalyptic working of the film can be understood in a more nuanced way when considered alongside the film's juxtaposition of different kinds of media in its critique of television. The film's depictions of TV, painting, and film are linked in the interconnected story lines to the characters' varying abilities to remember and mediate their own traumatic pasts. Interestingly, the frogs mark the moments in which these media and their distinctive temporalities confront one another, and in which the characters recognize and move beyond those aspects of their past that are traumatic and have blocked change. This interrelation of media, memory, and trauma within the film is brought into focus by the early-twentieth-century writings on modernity and media by the German Marxist philosopher and essayist Walter Benjamin. Particularly helpful are Benjamin's notions of aura and shock as they relate to his thinking on history, memory, and the potential for revolutionary politics. Because a number of Benjamin's essays contain both psychoanalytic and apocalyptic elements, they are apt for thinking through the relation of media, trauma, and apocalypse in *Magnolia*. This is not to say that the film is deliberately Benjaminian, but rather that considering it alongside several of Benjamin's essays offers a way of reading its apocalyptic elements together with its treatment of various forms of media.

To summarize the argument that will follow, one of Benjamin's last essays, "Theses on the Philosophy of History," presents an apocalyptic theorization of history, which provides an interesting frame for his notions of aura and shock. "Theses" has implications for thinking about aura and shock as they appear in two other of his essays also collected in *Illuminations*, namely, "On Some Motifs in Baudelaire" and "The Work of Art in the Age of Mechanical Reproduction." The Baudelaire essay contains some of Benjamin's thoughts on art, memory, and collective experience, while the artwork essay considers the relationships between art, media, and politics. In these two latter essays, Benjamin aligns aura with unconscious memory, experience, and premodern media such as painting, whereas he aligns shock with stimulus overload, conscious memory, and modern media such as photography and film (and also Charles Baudelaire's mid-nineteenth-century lyric poetry). However, as Miriam Hansen (1987; 1999) indicates, Benjamin's discussion of film can be read as blurring the lines between aura and shock,[9] between conscious and unconscious memory, between stimulus overload and experience in a way that envisions the rupture of the inevitable progress of technology and history.[10] Thus when considered alongside "Theses," this blurring of aura and shock can be interpreted as constituting something of an apocalyptic moment. Further, *Magnolia* can be read as illustrating this kind of apocalyptic overturning of technology and its logical conclusions; the film achieves this reversal by aligning the medium of film with the medium of painting, over and against the medium of television.

In "Theses on the Philosophy of History," Benjamin's various and cryptic reflections on history circle negatively around the possibility of political change, or revolution, through "progress." In criticizing a notion of progress, aligned in social democracy and fascism with technological advances, he pits "homogeneous, empty time" that cumulates in historicism's images of the past and of progress against a messianic time that is a rupture, an arrest of time's progression and history's progress (1969 [1940], 262). This rupture, Benjamin suggests, operates like a shock (1969 [1940], 262) in a confrontation with the kind of tradition that grounds a future of progress; it is "an image of the past" that constitutes a "moment of danger" that challenges tradition (1969 [1940], 255). He goes on to say, "in every era the attempt must be made anew to wrest tradition away from a conformism that is about to overpower it. The Messiah comes not only as the redeemer, he comes as the subduer of Antichrist" (1969 [1940], 255). Here the Antichrist seems to be conformist historical tradition grounding "progressive" outcomes (later he gives the example of the understanding of the *tradition* of Protestant work grounding a notion of "improved conditions" for society, while actually exploiting nature and the laborer [1969 [1940], 258–59]). Over and against an understanding of history as tradition, Benjamin suggests that the messianic caesura comes through an understanding of history and its relation to the present, "the time of now" (1969 [1940], 263), "the notion of a present which is not a transition, but in which time stands still and has come to a stop" (1969 [1940], 262). This moment "blast[s] open the continuum of history" (1969 [1940], 262).

In short, history is not worth telling, for Benjamin, if it does not relate to the concerns of the present in a way that does not blindly follow the tradition of the past. In this respect, Benjamin's view of history is quite different than that of traditional apocalyptic thought, in which the past, present, and future are seen as logically and consequentially continuous, and in which the present is merely a transition into a preordained future (i.e., a kind of history grounded in tradition). Rather he envisions a moment of radical break in the inevitable flow of history that takes into account the concerns of the present.

The notion of shock evident in "Theses on the Philosophy of History" is more substantially outlined in other of Benjamin's essays (1969 [1936]; 1969 [1939]), where it is also contrasted to experience. For Benjamin, experience is tied up with memory and tradition; experience requires a connection with history through memory—specifically, unconscious memories (or memory traces), what he calls *memoire involuntaire* (1969 [1939], 158–61).[11] As he puts it, borrowing from Henri Bergson, experience is "a matter of tradition . . . the convergence in memory of accumulated and frequently unconscious data" (1969 [1939], 157). (Though he critiques Bergson's romanticism, he preserves this notion of unconscious data, and elaborates upon it by way of Marcel Proust and Sigmund Freud.) Experience, for Benjamin, is also a matter of community or the collective. He argues, "where there is experience in the strict sense of the word, certain contents of the individual past combine with material of the collective past" (1969 [1939], 159). The loss of experience is a loss of connection to memory, to tradition, and to the collective.

The assault on experience comes through repeated shocks. In "On Some Motifs in Baudelaire," Benjamin explores the way in which Baudelaire's poetry deals with what Benjamin calls "the increasing atrophy of experience" in modern life, through its shocks (1969 [1939], 159). For Benjamin the effects of modernity—in forms such as urban industrialization, crowds, Taylorized production, and industrial warfare—impact humans as shock. In part, shock replaces experience with an excess of information (for instance, he gives the example of storytelling—which relays experience—being replaced by information [1969 (1939), 159]). The excess of stimuli and data also increases the need for voluntary memory that serves to store information while reducing involuntary memory (unconscious memory) and thus also "the scope for the play of imagination" (1969 [1939], 186).

The modern life, however, is characterized by more than just jarring information overload; rather, it is a series of repeated shocks. Benjamin suggests, quoting Freud, that shock, like a traumatic event, threatens to "break through the [psyche's] protective shield against stimuli" (1969 [1939], 161). To recall briefly, in Freudian psychoanalytic theory, the structure of trauma is such that original traumas are repressed and only known in their accidental yet compulsive repetition. Freud describes trauma, in *Beyond the Pleasure Principle*, as occurring when some unexpected shock or upset breaks through the external protective shield of the perception consciousness system. Psychic energy then works to shore up the breach and remaster intruding stimuli, but the trauma itself cannot be known. Memory traces are laid down, but they cannot be accessed voluntarily. The trauma becomes, as Jacques Lacan puts it, an "encounter forever missed" that sustains fantasy (1978 [1973], 60; see also chapter 5).

As Benjamin reads Freud, if the protective shield does not function well, then the traumatic moment becomes an unconscious memory trace, accessible only through some other distorted afterimage, like dreams or random objects that one encounters. However, if the protective shield does function well, it parries the shock, and those moments remain in consciousness and

are not laid down as memory traces. The protective shield does not, therefore, allow those moments to enter into the realm of experience; rather
those moments "remain in the sphere of a certain hour of one's life" (1969
[1939], 163). In other words, they remain on the level of information,
or of a series of lived moments, and do not seep down to congeal on the
level of tradition or history. What happens in modernity with its over-
abundance of shocks, Benjamin goes on to suggest, is that the protective
shield becomes trained to parry shocks more effectively, so that fewer and
fewer unconscious memory traces are laid down (1969 [1939], 161–62),
hence the atrophy of experience.

The bombardment of shock in modernity is quite a shift from premodern times, when experience was transmitted through the unique artwork.
Benjamin terms the ability of an art piece to pass on experience, or to
encode *memoire involuntaire*, "aura." His formulation of the notion of
aura occurs as a questioning of the impact of technology on "art in its traditional form" (1969 [1936], 220). Aura refers to the "ritual function"
(1969 [1936], 224) of works of art in the premodern period, through
which they were able to legitimate and lend authority to traditional social
structures and values. For Benjamin, aura is the authority and uniqueness
attributed to a work of art based on its singularity, "its presence in time and
space, its unique existence at the place where it happens to be" (1969
[1936], 220). This singularity of the artwork means that it gains authority
through its relation to tradition and history (1969 [1936], 220–21), starting with its use "in the service of a ritual—first the magical, then the
religious kind . . . even in the most profane forms of the cult of beauty"
(1969 [1936], 223–24). The notion of distance or unapproachability,
arising from its "cult value," is fundamental to the concept of aura (1969
[1936], 222–23).

The aura of an artwork resides for Benjamin not only in its uniqueness,
its relation to tradition and to cult, and the distance it maintains from its
viewer, but also in its ability to call up these *memoires involuntaires* (1969
[1939], 188). Benjamin speaks of the auratic artwork being able to "look
back" (1969 [1939], 188–89). He writes, "to perceive the aura of an object
we look at means to invest it with the ability to look at us in return" (1969
[1939], 188). This might be thought of as an ability of the artwork to
rouse the memories of the viewer, enabling him to "take hold of his experience" (1969 [1939], 158). In other words, the auratic artwork prompts
the viewer to remember and to access her experience. Baudelaire's poetry
attests to the disintegration of the aura (1969 [1939], 194), in part because
the figures he describes do not return the gaze, immersed as they are in the
consciousness—heightened by shock—required by the city and the crowd
(1969 [1939], 189–91).

Over and against the auratic artwork, Benjamin positions cinema, the epitome of modern shock. He writes in the Baudelaire essay that, "in a film, perception in the form of shocks was established as a formal principle" (1969 [1939], 175; see also 1969 [1936], 238). Reflecting upon the difference between film and the auratic artwork in "The Work of Art in the Age of Mechanical Reproduction," Benjamin suggests that the reproducibility of films and photographs renders them transitory and detached from tradition (1969 [1936], 221). Based on the principle of shock as it is, it would seem then that there is no hope for film as art, or as anything of much value. By contributing to atrophy of access to unconscious memory and of experience, film seems only to contribute to forgetfulness and to the impoverishment of society in general.

But where in the Baudelaire essay Benjamin seems vaguely nostalgic about the loss of aura and the connection of art to tradition, in the artwork essay he seems to celebrate the "emancipat[ion of] the work of art from its parasitical dependence on ritual" (1969 [1936], 224).[12] In the age of mechanical reproduction, art is no longer embedded in ritual and tradition, but is instead, like film and photographs, designed to be reproduced for exhibition to the masses (1969 [1936], 224–25, 234). With reproduction, authenticity and the attendant notion of "pure art" become irrelevant, giving way to the possibility for art's social and revolutionary functioning (1969 [1936], 224).

Along these lines, it would seem that Benjamin sees a positive role for film in its concomitant ability to break with tradition, and also, surprisingly, to access the unconscious. No longer does art keep the auratic "phenomenon of a distance," but, with the technology available to film, the camera is able, like a surgeon, to dissect reality (1969 [1936], 233–34) and to analyze human behavior much more precisely (1969 [1936], 235–36). Filmic techniques such as slow motion reveal hidden aspects of movement and behavior, including those habits that would normally remain opaque to consciousness. As Benjamin puts it, "the camera introduces us to unconscious optics as does psychoanalysis to unconscious impulses" (1969 [1936], 237). So where in the Baudelaire essay the disintegration of the aura and of experience is occasioned by shock, it seems that, in the artwork essay, by imputing to cinema the ability to probe the unconscious, Benjamin is suggesting that perhaps film enables an encounter with experience and *memoire involuntaire*; but film does this in a way that is not allied with cult, authority, and tradition, but rather with the concerns of the present.

Indeed, it is the combination of the break with tradition, the ability to represent reality more intimately, and the proximity of its represented subject matter to the viewer (versus the auratic artwork's distance), that gives cinema its political and apocalyptic potential. As Benjamin puts it, "the technique of reproduction *detaches the reproduced object from the domain of tradition* . . . and in permitting the reproduction to meet the beholder or listener in his own particular situation, it reactivates the object reproduced" (1969 [1936], 221, emphasis mine). In other words, film takes the object it represents out of the realm of tradition and brings it together with the viewer's present, the "time of now." Benjamin goes on to suggest that "these two processes lead to a tremendous shattering of tradition which is the obverse of the contemporary crisis and renewal of mankind [sic]" (1969 [1936], 221). This assessment of the *potential* of film in "The Work of Art in the Age of Mechanical Reproduction" resonates with the notion of messianic time in "Theses on the Philosophy of History." When these two essays are read side by side, there is a hint that perhaps Benjamin thinks of film as having the capacity to perform a sort of messianic function, by inserting the "time of now" into the perception of the reality represented by film, blasting understanding of that reality out of its traditional framework.

Put another way, the radicality of Benjamin's take on the potential of cinema might be the suggestion that through "unconscious optics," film brings to consciousness the realm of the unconscious and involuntary memory. In so doing, film brings the "time of now" (consciousness) to meet the time of *memoire involuntaire*, tradition, and experience. As Benjaminian scholar Miriam Hansen puts it:

> Benjamin readmits dimensions of temporality and historicity into his vision of the cinema, against his own endorsement of it as the medium of presence and tracelessness. The material fissure between a consciously and an "unconsciously permeated space" opens up a temporal gap for the viewer, a disjunction that may trigger recollection, and with it promises of reciprocity and intersubjectivity (1987, 217).

Thus film, while heightening consciousness through shock, perhaps at the same time enables consciousness to comprehend the unconscious optic, or in other terms, to experience the auratic. And it does so in a way that is not bound up with unchanging tradition, but rather with transformation in the present. Following this line of argument, it would seem that cinema may be able to blur the lines between shock and aura by making the link between consciousness and experience rather than increasing alienation from experience through shock; but it is able to do this in a way that avoids the pitfall of allowing art and experience to be governed by unswerving adherence to tradition and cult.[13]

When Hansen's reading is grafted onto Benjamin's apocalyptic language, film seems to take on a messianic role. The clash in the medium of film— between the conscious realm of information and disjointed lived moments, and the unconscious realm of history and experience—takes on the redemptive function of enabling recollection and mutuality. In some ways, film's unconscious optic might constitute the "moment of danger" or "image of the past" that Benjamin envisions operating as an apocalyptic shock or messianic rupture that disrupts tradition. Indeed, *Magnolia* seems to function in this way in its attempt to work through the trauma produced in (and productive of) the amnesiac tradition of television, by activating memory and experience through certain apocalyptic shocks.

Televisual Atrophy of Experience

Magnolia presents a critique of television that can be read in the Benjaminian sense of a critique of the atrophy of experience in the age of mechanical reproduction. Though Benjamin was writing before television became a dominant cultural influence, TV might be seen as the ultimate medium of shock, not only because of the speed and ubiquity of images that the medium allows, but also because of the type of "information" with which it bombards the viewer. Moreover, where the careful camera techniques of film can trigger involuntary memory and thereby access experience, live-time TV is without such benefits. The way television is represented in *Magnolia* epitomizes the lack of experience, memory, and genuine collectivity that Benjamin suggests characterizes modernity. In *Magnolia* the televisual—for which memory is nothing more than the reified data or collection of factoid information exemplified in the quiz show—relates to Benjamin's notion of consciousness, which forecloses on experience by barring memory. Television seems to represent a forgetting of history by way of an eternal, patriarchal present. The temporality of television as part of the thematics of the film is bound up with the very technology and history of the medium, its technical "liveness," and its relation to the collective, in a way that highlights the capitalistic and patriarchal factors in television's contribution to the atrophy of experience. The film indicates that all these aspects of television produce trauma that prohibits the characters' ability to reach down to the level of experience.

One of the ways that *Magnolia* makes this critique of TV is in presenting the world of television as a dysfunctional collectivity, seemingly playing with early (1940s, 1950s) discourse on television. As television critic Lynn Spigel notes, television from its very beginnings was a technology and medium invested with the potential to bind together disparate elements—in the varying forms of ideas, people, families, communities, nations—into a unified, homogeneous whole. Spigel quotes the president of NBC,

Sylvester Weaver, as stating that "television would make the 'entire world into a small town, instantly available, with the leading actors on the world stage known on sight or by voice to all within it'" (1997, 216). Along these same utopic lines, as television theorist Richard Dienst points out, popular discourse in the early days of television even vested it with the ability to create a kind of world peace, a kind of harmony in homogeneity (1994, 4–6). From its early history as media, the televisual with its new capacity to offer total and "instantaneous visibility" was "imagined as an all-encompassing, putting-into-view of the world" (1994, 4). In this way television was envisioned as a new kind of collectivity, a kind of global "abstract totality" (1994, 6).

Yet while the television industry purported to present the televisual as a totality, *Magnolia* reveals that the televisual logic is not only incomplete but also distorted. The film presents television as forming a totalizing, tight-knit social system, creating strong links and correspondences between people. Yet although television in the film seems to fulfill its promise of generating and linking collectivities, it only does so in their dystopic, almost grotesque aspect. In the filmic universe of *Magnolia*, the televisual is allowed to appear as a totalizing force; everything in the film is interconnected through it and gains its significance from it. As 1940s popular discourse promised of the newest household appliance (see Spigel 1997),[14] and as contemporary sitcoms attempt to depict (see Probyn 1997), television in *Magnolia* unifies the collectivity; it brings the family together. However, in *Magnolia*, the televisual is the gloomy counterpart to the illusions of the collectivity offered by television, with its pretensions—indicated by its happy TV-family of sitcoms and commercials—as the unifying force in the family. The televisual in the film unifies the collectivities as dysfunctional families, or rather, it shows them to be distinctly lacking in community, producing alienated individuals. Moreover, the film reveals television's "global, abstract totality" to be one that is markedly white—controlled and dominated by white patriarchs—deliberately excluding narratives that don't fit, as shown both by Kurring's dismissal of the young black prophet's story, and the film's truncation of Marcie's story.

Magnolia sets up television and the collectivity it creates as one answer to the question it poses at the outset: "Is there something that binds together all the strange happenings in the world?" By way of an answer, the film offers the negative image of the dystopic family and its intersection with the technology of television and its production. The producers of televisual images are also responsible for "producing" traumatized children: Claudia, Frank Mackey, little quiz kid Stanley, and adult quiz kid Donnie Smith. All these TV offspring are alienated in some way from their peers, from intimate relationships and from healthy community; they exemplify the atrophy of experience through a medium that typifies shock effects.

The traumas that this film highlights are produced not only by the television industry and its shocks, but also by fathers and by capitalism. The doubling of the characters and their link through the fathers in the television industry bears out the idea that the traumas here are the traumas produced through patriarchy in an ultracapitalist form, television. There are links between patriarchy, television, and the economics of the industry throughout the film, from the specter of the dying Earl Patridge's TV fortune, to Stanley's controlling father telling other parents of quiz-kids, "Let's make some fucking money here people." In this way, the film indicates that the technology of late patriarchal capitalism produces trauma.[15]

As one might expect in a discourse on trauma and technology, *Magnolia* plays with the idea of memory. The film indicates that television production is a decidedly amnesiac process, one based on omission or forgetfulness. Technically speaking, as Dienst explains, the composition of the TV image on the level of electrons is simultaneous to its reception—there is no need to store the image as in film. The composition of the televisual image is produced as an electronic signal and "cannot deliver an image all at once" (Dienst 1994, 20). Instead, its composition is always in progress: "A televisual image has to be established and sustained on screen moment by moment. With transmission, images and sets of images pass the time and fill out the current: in this sense television is always 'live'" (Dienst 1994, 20). This simultaneity or "liveness" of television differentiates it from the filmic image, whose "here and now" of presentation is divided from its "then and there of production" (Dienst 1994, 20).

Magnolia follows this logic in which television is an eternal present, a space of no past, memory, or history. This temporality is exemplified in the game show *What Do Kids Know?*, a live broadcast. What history this TV show does have, as offered in the brief retrospective about host Jimmy Gator's career, is based on an illusory world that TV projects; for instance, Jimmy is portrayed in the retrospective as a family man, but the film tells of his frequent "real-life" extramarital liasons. Further, the illusion of the show is punctured as its production process unravels in Jimmy's collapse and Stanley's revolt. The show's image of "liveness" is shown up as no more than a staged and scripted performance.

The characters in *Magnolia* are all caught within the "liveness" or present of television time. They are unable to remember, mediate, or work through their respective pasts. Such a forgetfulness is, of course, part of the structure of trauma or shock. Trauma creates an "impossible" history, one that is so unthinkable it cannot be experienced fully at the moment of its occurrence; rather, it is repressed. In a sense, the traumatized individual is caught within an eternal present, unable to look back and so unable to move forward. Frank Mackey typifies this kind of effacement of the past, refusing to acknowledge the trauma of being abandoned by his father at the time of his mother's illness and death. Mackey tells his interviewer that, "facing the past is an important way of not making progress. . . . The most useless thing in the world is that which is behind me." So on one hand, television seems to be completely detached from tradition and experience in *Magnolia*, and on the other hand, it is fully implicated in the oppressive tradition of patriarchy and capitalism.

Static Image as Unconscious Optic

Against television, the film seems to privilege and promote itself as a medium, but it does this in part by way of another medium, ostensibly the most static medium presented in the film, that of a painted image. This image appears to us in a brief, oblique flash, following a climactic revelation in which Claudia's mother realizes the guilt implied by Jimmy Gator's forgetfulness ("I don't know what I've done") in the face of her accusation that he molested their daughter. As she arrives at Claudia's door, in the cathartic moment of her reconciliation with her daughter—made more intense by the fright caused by the concurrent rain of frogs—a side pan only partially reveals the image: it shows a woman seated, looking reflective, with a small caption underneath, "But it did happen."

The moment and the image of the painting generates a crucial affective moment of the film, occurring at the climax of the falling frogs; through its appearance we can unfold the inner workings of *Magnolia*'s preoccupations. By providing a glimpse into the past of one of the characters, the image organizes into significance the earlier behavior of various characters, a significance effaced within the televisual logic. It offers a way to understand the breakdown that occurs in each of the narratives before the apocalyptic rain of frogs: Linda's hysterical suicide attempt, Claudia's flight from Jim, Frank's judgmental silence during his interview, Stanley's refusal to continue playing on the game show, Donnie's drunken remorse over the toilet bowl. It affirms that in each case something "did happen" to cause the characters to be the way they are. The moment is classically apocalyptic in the sense that it reveals or unveils truth.

However, the image might also be read as a kind of "unconscious optic," and as such it might participate in a more Benjaminian kind of apocalyptic moment. As an immobile media, it is a moment that might otherwise pass by unnoticed, were it not frozen and zoomed-in on; thus distilled, it allows the viewer a glimpse into Claudia's unconscious memory. As such it carries with it elements of aura and of shock, both of which enable it to participate in a "countermediation" that serves to interrupt the dominant temporality of television. The televisual structure of disavowal and forgetfulness is pierced by the sudden, if brief, appearance of the reminder, "But it did happen." That reminder comes as an "image of the past" that flashes up, in Benjamin's memorable phrase, as "a moment of danger." In this sense it is a shock that stops the televisual tradition's inevitable progress. It forces the present and the past to meet.

But the radically different temporality with which the image intervenes into televisual time can also be said to be auratic in some way, linked as it is to unconscious remembrance. If Benjamin's aura is the experience of investing an object with the ability to "look back," or the experience of a kind of reciprocity with the past, the looking back in this case reveals a concealed history of child abuse that flashes out in scandalous significance. Moreover, like the auratic artwork, the image is unique in time and space. And because the camera makes the image only partially visible to the viewer, all efforts fail to bring the image closer, to get a better look; the image retains a certain kind of auratic distance from the viewer. It is only in its arrested and distant state, like a partial still life of the unconscious, that it can provide a true image of memory, one that resists the live-time of television, that interrupts and provides a persistent and contrary truth to the bland, oblivious flow of televisual time and narrative. Time stands still in a way that blasts open the televisual continuum.

Film as Access to the Past and Experience

The shock of the painting is accompanied by another shock, the rain of frogs, which highlights the moment's significance and aligns the medium of film with that of the unique artwork. By affiliating the filmic frogs with the static image, the film builds an alliance with the painting as an alternative form of media, thus privileging itself as medium. Certainly, as a medium that is technically comprised of repeated images, film is more aligned with the static image than with the ongoing, everpresent signal of television. This affinity between the unique artwork and film is built over and against television (as attested by the frog-induced shattering of the TV screen).[16] In building this alliance with the static artwork, the film seems to indicate that it sees itself as in some way auratic. If the frozen image is a static shock that brings into view the forgetfulness of trauma and asserts the past, then the frogs are shocking in the same way. They, too, like the shocking, yet still auratic, artwork, push the characters to access the past and experience. Thus the film takes on a Benjaminian apocalyptic status, as a medium able to blur the lines between shock and aura in a way that interrupts the oppressive tradition of television and its dysfunctions.

However, reading through a Benjaminian lens, there are a number of factors that obstruct the film's easy alignment with aura. Where the painting is able to bring together artistic elements of aura and of shock, it is more difficult to see how the film could claim auratic status. The repeatability of image in cinema (as opposed to the uniqueness of an auratic artwork), as well as the reproducibility of the film as a whole and its formal use of "shock effects" are all attributes of cinema that militate against the film easily taking on this kind of auratic status. Yet *Magnolia* manages to perform an apocalyptic overturning of these categories, by insisting on linking present behaviors to the past and in proposing a different kind of collectivity. In so doing, it does seem to blur the lines between aura and shock in the Benjaminian transformative and redemptive manner of apocalypse (though for the moment I will hold open the question of just how transformative the apocalyptic impulse of this film really is).

Nonetheless, this redemptive recuperation of alienating shock effects is not immediately evident. To begin with, the technical structure of film resembles the structure of trauma (rather than apocalyptic transformation). Like cinema, traumatic neurosis is always replayed. To recall, if trauma is caused by a breach in the psyche's protective mechanisms, it is by repetition of the trauma in forms unrecognizable to the traumatized individual that she psychically tries to regain mastery of that breach. These repetitions often appear to be accidental or random. (The famous example of this in Freud is the woman who continually marries husbands who die [1955 (1920), 22].) Thus as Derrida points out regarding Freud's notion of the unconscious and memory in general,[17] trauma in the Freudian sense entails a specific temporality of deferral: the traumatic event is never actually encountered, it is always deferred, encountered through later repetitions of it. The same thing might be said of film with respect to the moment it captures. That moment is never played live (as in television), but is always deferred, played later, in a series of repeated, minutely changing images. Neither film nor trauma offer ready access to experience.

The first half of *Magnolia* emphasizes the repetition (and reproducibility) characteristic of cinema, subtly linking it to the repetition produced by trauma. Not only does the actual medium of film seem to mirror the structure of trauma, the narrative of this particular film seems quite consciously to depict various kinds of repetition compulsions. *Magnolia* plays with the idea of repetition in the doubling of the families, in the characters' constant repetition of their own phrases, and in the relentless rain and ominous music that run throughout. Notably, addicted repetitions are part of the film's portrayal of traumatized TV collectivity, particularly in the compulsive behaviors of the characters—sex (Frank), drug use (Claudia, Linda, Earl), theft (Donnie, "the prophet"), infidelity and abuse (Earl, Jimmy), even knowledge (Stanley). The Aimee Mann song to which the entire cast sings along, as the rain pours, explicitly outlines the repetition compulsion (and also its link to the impossibility of desire [see Lacan 1978 (1973), 53–64]): one after the other, the cast sings, "once you thought, when you first began that you got what you want; but its not going to stop, its not going to stop, until you wise up." Thus the behavioral repetition in the film highlights the connection between the repeatability of the medium of film and the repetition compulsion that follows trauma.

But in *Magnolia*, the frog fall is the cataclysmic and shocking—though seemingly random and disconnected—apocalyptic repetition of the pervasive rain. The frogs do not bring the doom that the rain threatens, but rather they mark the "wising up" to repetition and to trauma. After the frogs fall, each of the characters is able to "make good," as it were, and to break out of their doomed cycles through reconciliation and recovery. The deferral is not eternal, the apocalypse does arrive. This working through of trauma comes, as the static image of the painting suggests is necessary, through the revelation and recollection of specific histories. With its repeated phrase, "the book says, we may be through with the past, but the past ain't through with us," the film insists on the resurfacing of unconscious memories and the remembering of the past. Where the painting can only hint that the past must be remembered, the film can actually reveal the missing historical pieces. The film unveils traumatic incidents through the unraveling of the various family narratives: Donnie Smith's parents' extortion of his prize money; Frank's abandonment by his father; Jimmy's sexual abuse of Claudia.

The frogs shock and recall the past in a different way than the scandal of the static image: they are shocking as live but wounded flesh, falling, smashing, quivering, and bleeding. They are like uncanny *bodily* symptoms of something else that might be at work. In this sense, they might be seen as the hysterical symptom of the trauma of the televisual world. Reading the frogs as hysterical symptom fits well with Benjamin's thinking on the potential benefits of filmic shock. As Hansen points out, Benjamin proposes—in an aspect of his work that is easily missed by readers of the English translations—that the shock of film might be helpful in working through trauma. Hansen notes that in all but the last version of Benjamin's artwork essay (which is the version found in *Illuminations*), he includes the Freudian idea of innervation (1999, 313–14), or "conversion" of the unrepresentable traumatic experience into a bodily symptom in the hysteric (1999, 316; Breuer and Freud 1955 [1895], 285). Hansen argues that "Benjamin, unlike Freud, understood innervation as a two-way process, that is not only a conversion of mental, affective energy into somatic, motoric form, but also the possibility of reconverting, and recovering, split-off psychic energy through motoric stimulation" (1999, 317). In other words, shock or sensory stimulation (as occurs through film) might have a positive effect on the psyche, enabling it to work through trauma by "producing emotion in the beholder through bodily movement" (1999, 317) or through "sensory-aesthetic effects" (1999, 335). Hansen goes on to suggest that "the concept of innervation intersects with the notion of an optical unconscious" (1999, 337), as one way of producing "a bodily collective innervation [in the sense of reclaiming psychic energy, or experience] as the condition of an alternative interaction with technology and the commodity world" (1999, 340).

In *Magnolia*, the frogs unquestionably have a sensory effect. When they first slap into Jim Kurring's windshield and ooze their way down it, the viewer is physically startled, just as Kurring is. So while the falling frogs might be said to represent a Freudian conversion into a bodily symptom for the film's characters, jolting them into memory and recognition, they might also provoke for the viewer the kind of innervation of which Benjamin speaks. To be sure, for the characters in the film, the frogs constitute the kind of shock that can recover their experience, lost in the amnesiac tradition of the capitalist, patriarchal, televisual world. Indeed, read as symptom, the frogs can, like an "unconscious optic," be seen as auratic, as a small window onto the characters' past and onto experience.

Thus the falling frogs mark a Benjaminian apocalyptic disturbance of the totalizing and closed, serial, televisual logic represented by the film, perhaps even an exodus from it into a remembering of the past and a more hopeful future. The film depicts the end of time as the characters know it, the end of time as the end of the eternal, patriarchal, televisual present.

Figure 6   Fallen Frog in *Magnolia*

Moreover, it does this through the unveiling of the past, the revelation of those defining traumatic moments. The past makes sense of the crises that the individual characters live in the quotidian, in a way that points toward a more hopeful future. Thus the film presents a strong critique of capitalist patriarchy and the traumas this system creates.

The falling of frogs is also apocalyptic in that it reveals the interconnectedness of the film's discourses on media, cosmic order, trauma, and memory. The film intimates, by aligning the frogs with the static image and its caption, that perhaps there is something more at work in the universe than mere chance: a connectedness to the past. The painting's caption, "But it did happen," echoes Stanley's amazed wonder at the frogs, "this is something that happens!" Both allude to the initial narrator's precredit pronunciation, "These strange things happen all the time."[18] The film hints that coincidence is continuous with the past, but that catastrophic coincidences might be replaced with serendipity if memory were wakened. These hints crystallize into assertions when, after the tumult of the falling frogs has jarred Earl from his morphine-induced stupor briefly to meet Frank's eyes before he dies, the film cuts back to the opening sequence and its discussion of random events. After this unlikely reconciliation, the narrator concludes (again) that "Strange things happen all the time. And so it goes, and so it goes. And the book says we may be through with the past, but the past ain't through with us."

Thus the film insists on the past in a way that does not anchor it in tradition. The film inserts the time of now into the telling of the past. As implied by the caption, "So Now Then"—which signifies both past and present, and which appears just before the recapitulation of the precredit sequence following Earl's death—the film is only interested in the past, in experience, as it pertains to the solving of present dysfunctions. Moreover, the shocks in the film disrupt tradition in such a way that the future does not simply represent the logical conclusion of the past. The past is pulled away from blindly following the televisual tradition of capitalistic patriarchy. The continuum of history is broken open as the past is startlingly brought together with the time of now, the moment when each of the characters recognizes the past and is reconciled with it. In this way, the film seems to suggest a kind of apocalyptism that is more Benjaminian than strictly biblical, one that is not interested in future punishment and the transition to eventual utopia, but in which the time of now disrupts tradition. Put in other terms, by privileging a unique and cataclysmic moment (and the falling of frogs is most definitely a unique moment in cinema), yet by insisting on *memoire involuntaire*, *Magnolia* both epitomizes shock and contravenes the very aspects of film that contribute to the atrophy of experience, allying itself instead with the auratic artwork.

What is notable, though, about the way in which the characters break out of their patterns is that they do it not only by remembering the past but also through the help of others, that is, through collectivity. Jim Kurring, would-be savior, helps Claudia through withdrawal by believing in her and affirming her as "a good and beautiful person." He also helps Donnie, playing beneficent judge by "forgiving" him and allowing him to put back the money he has stolen from his boss's safe. The young "prophet" helps Linda when he finds her overdosed in her car and calls 911. Frank—who both confronts his past and visits Linda in the hospital, signaling possible reconciliation—is helped both by the TV interviewer who pushes him to remember his "actual family history" and by his father's nurse, Phil, who tracks him down and calls him to Earl's deathbed. Thus the film imagines a different kind of collectivity, one built on mutual aid rather than abuse and alienation. The collectivity that the film envisions is one built on experience. That is, the collective in *Magnolia* derives from the wisdom garnered by the memory traces of the traumatic. Here again the film pits its own medium and narrative against the dysfunctional isolation caused by the world of television.

So Now Then . . .

Yet it should be noted that even the desire for genuine collectivity finds its limits in a medium, perhaps conditioned by the film's production in Hollywood, that reinscribes traditional roles of men saving women, African Americans enabling Anglo Americans, police officers playing the role of judge. Indeed these traditional themes indicate that there is still a debate to be had as to the kind of apocalypse—classic or Benjaminian—that best describes the apocalyptic overtones in *Magnolia*. However, reading the film as structured along the lines of classic apocalypse becomes further complicated when considered together with the film's critique of patriarchy and its byproducts, given that the apocalyptic genre has been critiqued for its frequent sexist images and its authorization of oppression.

Although, as noted earlier, the biblical apocalypse, the book of Revelation, may have been written as a resistant discourse, subsequent interpretations of it are far less positive. As critics of later apocalyptic images and texts have pointed out, images taken from the biblical apocalypse have grounded misogynist, colonial, and white-supremacist traditions (see Milhou 1999; Smolinski 1999; Quinby 1994; Pippin 1999; Keller 1996, 1997). Feminist scholars have also shown that the sexist imagery of the biblical apocalypse has given rise to later misogynist images that have bolstered various male homosocial and colonial visions (see Vander Stichele

2000; Carpenter 1995; Pippin 1992; 1999). The biblical Revelation's association of "a great whore" with "the beast" has reappeared as a common
trope in expressions of fear and anxiety over women's sexuality (see
Carpenter 1995; Vander Stichele 2000; Pippin 1992), over against which is
constructed "the 'master narrative' of individual male prophetic authority
and the erection of that authority on the necessary subordination of
women" (Carpenter 1995, 128). Further, Tina Pippin has shown how this
sexual anxiety is also racialized, as fear of black women's sexuality, in
"revampings" of the figure Jezebel (1999, 32). And as Catherine Keller has
so aptly argued, colonial politics motivated by visions of the apocalypse
have also conflated the land to be conquered with sexualized, dehumanized
women.[19] Given then that apocalypse tends to sexualize and demonize
women and people of color and to use that sexualization as a basis and
site for conquest, it is difficult to see quite how the genre can assist in a
critique of any kind of oppression, including patriarchy. It seems that
the history of the apocalyptic genre and its political uses would undercut
Magnolia's deployment of apocalyptic images to critique the patriarchal
relegation of women to the realm of sexual object and faithful domestic
support.

     Along similar lines, it might be asked whether the film's demand for
chronology and teleology undermines its potentially liberating movement,
by insisting on a kind of time that has been critiqued as particularly
Western and patriarchal. For instance, postcolonial theorist Homi
Bhabha—who cites Benjamin's apocalyptic "time of now" (1994, 4, 6)—
calls the demand for linear time-consciousness and originary realities the
"foundationalist epistemological positions of Western empiricism and historicism" (Bhabha 1994, 182). He suggests that both historicism and
empiricism are interconnected, ideologically constructed notions based on
belief in the ability to discern "reality" and represent it "coherently."
Moreover, for Bhabha, teleology, or "progress"—which, interestingly, Keller
suggests is a notion that represents the secularization of apocalyptic thought
(1996, 117, 165–66)—is, as it is for Benjamin, a red herring, masking all
kinds of evils done in its name. Along similar lines, feminist Lee Quinby
critiques apocalyptic thought as essentializing, universalizing, and hierarchicalizing; it is, as she puts it, a "technology of power/knowledge that
promotes homogenized forms of subjectivity, values of mastery and control,
and universalized Truth" (1994, xxiv). She argues that apocalypse demands
knowledge of "originary moments" (1994, xiv) and claims "absolute
knowledge of history" in its "promise of absolute knowledge . . . [and]
total control" (1994, 66). Quinby's argument suggests that apocalypse's
understanding of history is bound up with hierarchy and patriarchy.

     Both Bhabha's and Quinby's critiques of Western apocalyptic and ruling
discourses are contrary to the film's critique of patriarchy. Where *Magnolia*

would rupture the eternal present with the insertion of linear time and
actual history, Bhabha and Quinby would affiliate the demand for origins
and linear time with the Western, racist, patriarchal world; conversely, they
would align eternally circulating, repeating time with the possibility of
liberation through the production of difference. And it seems that perhaps
the film's critique of patriarchy through apocalypse does fall prey to its
demand for a return to the kinds of thing that have been critiqued in apocalyptic thought, such as transcendental salvation (e.g., frogs falling from the
sky, police officers to the rescue), originary truths (e.g., definitive traumatic
moments from which all dysfunction stems), and evolutionary time.
Perhaps the film seeks what Bhabha (after Benjamin) calls "the dead hand
of history that tells the beads of sequential time like a rosary, seeking to
establish serial, causal connections" (1994, 4).

To counter this kind of temporality, both Bhabha and Quinby focus on
an intersection of the present with the past. Bhabha theorizes the circulation
and repetition of language, peoples, and cultures as a means of disturbing
typical Western time and empirical practice. Here he uses Benjamin's
"present" to describe the postcolonial "non-synchronous time-space of . . .
cultural displacement and social discrimination—where political survivors
become the best historical witnesses" (1994, 8). Diasporic breaks in history
and tradition, he suggests, can also "locate an agency of empowerment" able
to intervene into oppressive situations (1994, 8–9). Quinby uses Foucault,
rather than Benjamin, to suggests a genealogical criticism that challenges
myths of origins and objective claims to truth (1994, xxiii). This, she suggests, focuses on historical specificities and subjugated knowledges (like
popular knowledge) in order to "establish a historical knowledge of struggles and to make use of this knowledge tactically today" (Michel Foucault,
cited in Quinby 1994, xiv). Like Bhabha and Benjamin, Quinby seems to
see the importance of reading the past and experience to rupture blindly
repeating tradition and to create an empowering "time of now."

Given the reading of *Magnolia* proposed here, the question is whether
or not the problematic aspects of apocalypse might be alleviated if the film
is read through cinema's potential to inaugurate a Benjaminian sort of messianic time. In other words, might *Magnolia*'s privileging of the medium of
film mitigate the negative effects of traditional apocalyptic thought? It may
be that two of the formal aspects of cinema already discussed (the temporality of deferral and the potential to blur aura and shock) suggest that perhaps a different kind of apocalypse is at work here. First, the blurring of the
line between aura and shock seems to engender the kind of messianic
temporality that Benjamin advocates. The continuous flow of patriarchal
televisual tradition is disrupted by the particular shock of the auratic
unconscious optics (symptomatic frogs and the static image of the past).

These auratic moments access experience and so, in a sense, intervene into tradition (the televisual) by enabling the characters to access their own personal experience. Second, as a medium characterized by deferral, film necessarily gives up on true origins and absolute knowledge. The original "scene" is inaccessible—as is the original traumatic scene—and can only be repeated differently. Because, as poststructural theorists like Derrida, Judith Butler, and Bhabha have been pointing out for some time, a repetition can never be identical to that which it repeats, it therefore also allows for minute, yet subversive, difference, or even for a cataclysmic repetition (as with the rain of frogs). Thus, the production of film, in general, with its infinitely repeated images and deferred scenarios, may also allegorize the possibility for empowerment opened up by repetition (and possibly also repetition compulsion).

But as Bhabha suggests, the true test of whether or not Benjamin's time of now has appeared is whether these apocalyptic impulses in *Magnolia* "transform the present into an expanded and ex-centric site of experience and empowerment" (1994, 4). While the characters within the film are empowered in some way, the more pertinent question may be whether or not *the viewer is empowered to access her own experience*, to confront the status quo. This returns to the question, posed by Sippi, of the film's ability to mediate discordant and raging emotions and to enable the viewer to set things right.

Since there are no easy points of identification for the viewer in the film (the characters are all larger than life in their irritating behaviors), the way into this question may be through a consideration of how the film formally positions the viewer at crucial moments (after the climax of the falling frogs) through shot/reverse-shot interpellation (or in theoretical terms, "suture"). Put simply, the viewer becomes aware, by means of a camera shot, not only of what or whom is visible, but at the same time, also of what is not visible, of an absent person whose point of view is shown. The viewer is placed in the position of looking through the eyes of this absent person. Then with the reverse shot, this absence is filled in by the image of what is missing: the absence is abolished "by someone (or something) placed within the same field" (Oudart 1978, 37). The viewer sees the person with whose eyes they have been looking. Thus identification is forced between the viewer and the reverse shot.[20] In considering this kind of formal positioning, my concern is not to say that viewers only identify in the ways that the film urges, but rather to think about what these attempts at positioning the viewer say about the apocalyptic and transformative nature of the film.[21]

Toward the end of the film, there are three point-of-view shot/reverse-shot sequences. It is important to note that these sequences occur after the story line involving African Americans has disappeared, so that the identifications and resistances that the film urges are as Anglo Americans of a certain class, which may limit their ability to push viewers beyond white middle-class norms. The first instance occurs as the frogs fall. Frank is at his father's bedside, where the camera holds both their faces in view as the frogs waken Earl for the last time. The first shot in the sequence is of Earl, seen as if through Frank's eyes. In the reverse shot, Frank fills in the absence, urging identification between Frank and the viewer. But the reverse shot is so protracted that it takes on the status of point-of-view shot itself, for which the reverse shot is Earl taking his last breath. The film thus sutures viewers into identifying with both Frank and Earl. This reminds viewers both of the regret that weighs upon Earl for abandoning his son and degrading his wife (as revealed in an earlier monologue), and of the possibility for change represented by Frank's struggle with his own past.

The second crucial sequence is between Stanley and his father. The first shot shows Stanley's father asleep on his bed. In the reverse shot, Stanley stands before him, saying, "You've got to be nicer to me, Dad." Here the film positions viewers to identify with a character who is actively resisting becoming what might be the inevitable response to his abuse (as figured by Donnie who appears in the next scene, covered in blood and crying, having been knocked off a telephone pole by a falling frog during a robbery escapade). This sequence between Stanley and his father is repeated. Stanley makes his demand twice. Both times the reply comes back, "Go to bed"— so that viewers are also urged to take on Stanley's persistence in the face of his father's indifference.

In the final sequence, a first shot shows Claudia in rehabilitation. It is a long shot, during which viewers hear and get glimpses of Jim, who comes in to tell her he loves her; but he is not shown in a reverse shot. Claudia looks at Jim, and at the moment one expects a reverse shot, she raises her eyes to the camera, smiles at the audience, and the film ends. There is, in fact, no reverse shot, and so viewers are left—in typical apocalyptic deferral—with an open-ended challenge in the face of the film. By this disruption of filmic convention, viewers are confronted with themselves and their own experiences.

The Sense of an Ending

The ending is ambiguous because just when it seems tempting to declare the film as exemplifying Benjamin's messianic time of now and free of traditionally sexist apocalyptic thought, this last long shot of Claudia looking back is joined by the Aimee Mann song, asking viewers to respond: "But can you save me? C'mon and save me . . . like Peter Pan or Superman, you will come to save me." At the very moment when the viewer is freed by the film to make a choice, to confront their own experience—and, significantly, not to be interpellated as a white, male, middle-class subject—the choice is flatly spelled out in the same superhero terms that were earlier critiqued as phallic, misogynist, and comical. The present, the "time of now"—for Claudia and for the audience—is bypassed by appealing to a time of (future) salvation.

However incongruous this ending might be, its ambiguity may also provide a critique of traditional apocalyptic thought. What is interesting here is that the reintroduction of the time and bearer of salvation is combined with the filmic structure of deferral, of which the final shot reminds. As noted, deferral is a characteristic shared by cinema, trauma, and traditional apocalyptic thought. However, in film and in trauma, the deferral is always of the origin (though here also of the ending), while in apocalyptic thought the deferral is of the ending. Yet if the deferral in film and in trauma serves to put into question the very possibility of the notion of absolute truth and origins, then the same thing can be said about apocalypse's deferral of the ending; for if the ending in traditional apocalyptic thought also serves in part to verify an origin (as, for example, with the notion of just deserts in which "sinners" deserve their punishment), then its continual deferral puts into question the essentializing, universalizing, and hierarchicalizing origin that it posits. Such a putting into question also necessarily destabilizes the claims of apocalypse to absolute knowledge and the oppression it can authorize.

In some ways then, it seems that Mark Olsen's assessment of *Magnolia* as "a film obviously in thrall to the process of movie-making, but . . . grappling with the fissure between the idealisations of the medium and the realisation of what it may lack" (2000, 28) is an assessment that could also be applied to its use of apocalypse. Perhaps the ambiguity of apocalypse in *Magnolia* is reflected by the ambiguity of the medium in which it is found. At the end of the day—and this would be the subject of another study—it may be that both *Magnolia's* and apocalypse's transformative potential can only be understood in terms of their relation to capital and the way they position their audiences with respect to capital. For as Benjamin puts it, "so long as the movie-makers' capital sets the fashion, as a rule no other revolutionary merit can be accredited to today's film than the promotion of a revolutionary criticism of traditional concepts of art" (1969 [1936], 231). At the very least, the film and its apocalyptic falling frogs, though fully embedded within the mainstream Hollywood film industry, envisions the shattering of the patriarchal, capitalistic world of television, and a working through of its traumas. What will remain ambiguous is whether *Magnolia* positions viewers to wait for a transcendental savior, or rather to make the task of resisting capitalist patriarchy their own.

Notes

INTRODUCTION

1. For discussions of the ways that film formally positions, or interpellates, viewers, see Christian Metz's classic formulation of the viewer's identification with the camera (1982 [1977], 49–52), and Daniel Dayan's description (1976) of suture through shot/reverse-shot sequences.

2. For discussions of biblical imagery in film, see Exum 1996; Forshey 1992; Aichele and Pippin 1997; Aichele 2000; Marconot 1996. A number of scholars seem particularly interested in the Christ story and Christ images as they appear in film (see Baugh 1997; Fraser 1998; Keil 1992; Gunning 1992; Gaudreault 1992; Raynauld 1992). Some exploration of biblical imagery in film has occurred in studies on religious imagery in film, or as part of discussions of film as the contemporary form of mythmaking (see B. B. Scott 1994; Beck 1995; Ostwalt 1995; Marsh and Ortiz 1998). For other analyses of religious themes and imagery in film, focusing less explicitly on the Bible, see May and Bird 1982; Miles 1996; Martin and Ostwalt 1995; Sanders 2002; May 1997.

3. For the use of biblical narratives to resist racist images and "to underscore African American claims to humanity and to full citizenship rights" in early race films, see Weisenfeld 2000.

4. For a similar argument about the influence of early Christian texts on culture, see Elizabeth Castelli's discussion of representations of the Columbine shootings (forthcoming 2004).

5. For excellent overviews of the development of cultural studies as a discipline and as it has found its way into biblical studies, see Exum and Moore 1997; Moore 1998a. For the range in cultural studies approaches to the Bible, see Bach 1994; Boer 1999; Exum 1996; Moore 1998b; Aichele 2000; Aichele and Pippin 1997; Pippin 1999; Moore 1996.

6. For a reflection on the psychical trace left by this kind of resistance, see Derrida 1998 [1996].

7. For feminist interventions on hysteria, see Gilman, King, Porter, Rousseau, and Showalter 1993; Showalter 1997; MacCannell 2000; Cixous 1980 [1975]; Modleski 1990. See Micale 1995 for commentary.

8. Connections have been made between some of these concepts. I hope to explore these connections more fully with respect to hysteria at a later date. For the connection between excess and sublime and between trauma and the sublime, see Freeman 1995, 109, 112, 127–28. For the connection between apocalypse and

the sublime, see Dellamora 1994, 16–17, 25; Derrida 1984 [1981], 12. Further, both Freeman (1995, 110–13) and Derrida (1984 [1981], 15–19) use Kant's reference to the veil of Isis in "On a Newly Emerged Noble Tone in Philosophy" to make their points about the sublime and apocalypse, respectively.

9. Freud observes that the hysteric identifies with the emotions of both a woman and a man (1959 [1908], 166). He calls this kind of split gender identification "bisexuality," but in contemporary terms, it could also be called transgenderism. For this kind of trangendered description of hysteria, see also Lacan 1985 [1975], 156.

CHAPTER 1

1. For over 2,000 stories of people shot and killed by police in the United States between 1990 and 1999, see Stolen Lives Project (1999). A number of these stories are extremely poignant. See also K. K. Russell 2000; Barr 2001. As I revised this essay, I received an e-mail from the October 22 Coalition Against Police Brutality documenting three deaths in one week: "April 16, 2002: Santiago Villanueva from Fort Washington—killed from police sitting on him while he suffered an epileptic seizure at his job in Bloomfield, NJ . . . . April 19, 2002: José Colon from Suffolk County, Long Island—gunned down as police prepared to raid a building for alleged drug activity. No drugs nor weapons were found on Colon. The police say the gun went off accidentally and praised the other police for not killing everyone else in the building. April 21, 2002: Ricardo Carlon from Staten Island—shot three times by a retired police officer who claimed Ricardo was trying to rob him." As I revised the essay, again, I took a flyer at a demonstration, issued by the October 22 Coalition, that stated that between September and July of 2002, twenty-eight people have been killed by law enforcement in New York City and its vicinity.

2. For Žižek, desire, and readings of other biblical texts, see Boer (1999, 2000).

3. Such an argument would require tracing the history of interpretation for Numbers 16, which would be an extremely interesting project but beyond the scope of this chapter. To a give a brief sampling, the story is mentioned in both Hebrew and Christian testaments of the Bible as a deterrent for disloyalty (Deut. 11:6; Ps. 106:16–18; Jude 11). In addition, James Scott, interpreting the Qumran scroll fragment 4Q423 5, argues that the story may have been used to condemn leaders within the Qumran community who spoke out against the Teacher of Righteousness. For other uses of the story in early Jewish and Christian writing, see J. M. Scott 2001, n. 36. It continued to be used in the Christian tradition to deter dissent; for example, Gregory of Nyssa, in his *Life of Moses*, relates Moses' conflict with the Levites to his own conflict with some of his followers (Olson 1996, 100).

4. For a range of material on the RCMP siege at Gustafsen Lake, including Ts'Peten Defenders' accounts of the events, mainstream media reports, and a record of court proceedings, see http://sisis.nativeweb.org/gustmain.html.

5. For a reading of the religious metaphors in Althusser's essay and the way they subordinate his notion of ideology to a notion of religious authority, see Butler 1997a, 106–31.

6. For a critique of Žižek's view of the *point de capiton*, see Butler 1993, 208–22. She questions whether his consideration of *points de capiton* allows for "the kind of variation and rearticulation required for an anti-essentialist radical democratic project" (1993, 211).

7. Milgrom uses this discrepancy over Korah's fate as a means of sorting out the various recensions of the text (1990, 414–19), suggesting that the "tent of Yahweh" (the tabernacle) becomes the "tents of Korah, Dathan and Abiram" in a late recension in order to associate Korah with Dathan and Abiram.

8. That land is an underlying issue in Numbers 16 is perhaps corroborated by, or carried on in, the Qumran tradition with the reference to Korah in what seems to be a farming manual or a wisdom book that makes extensive use of the farming metaphor; see Scott 2001.

9. Levine notes that archeological evidence for the Korahites' cultic skill is found at Arad. There, archeologists found an eighth-century-B.C.E. jar base that lists names of cultic personnel including the Korahites (1993, 429). Textual evidence for the Korahites' skill in cultic art is found in 1 Chronicles 6 and in the superscriptions on Psalms 42, 44–49, 84–85, 87–88 attributing them to the sons of Korah.

10. For an analysis of the relationship of schools to prisons, including comparison of architectural design, and footage of discrimination against lower-income youth of color by police, see Jim Davis and Juliana Fredman's video *Safety Orange*.

11. In the Diallo case, the officers were all acquitted (Fritsch 2000). Justice Joseph W. Teresi instructed the jury for four hours in favor of the defense (Waldman 2000). No disciplinary measures were taken against the officers by the police department (McFadden 2001).

12. Žižek uses Claude Lefort's discussion of democracy to argue the point that "lack" generates other struggles. Lefort argues that democracy can only operate if the locus of power remains empty. Žižek stresses "the distinction between the empty symbolic locus of power and the reality of those who, temporarily, exercise power" (Žižek 1993, 190; Lefort 1988 [1986], 228–30).

13. For an interesting reading of the land as the screen on which desire is played see Long 1999; Gunn (1999) also deals with this issue.

14. It might be said that the land is both the object and cause of colonial desire. On some level, each of the stories deals with resistance to colonization. The story of Korah, Abiram, and Dathan takes place on the verge of colonization, and is thought to deal, in part, with disputes surrounding entry into the land of Canaan. The events at Gustafsen Lake take place as a result of continued disputes over aboriginal land settlements and treaties in "Canada." And the events depicted in *Light it Up* can be seen as representative of a kind of domestic colonialism, one that insures white-middle-class privilege at "the socio-economic expense of a black underclass maintained by instruments and institutions of power" (Singh and Schmidt 2000, 37; see also Savitch 1978; Marable 1983; Jennings 1992).

15. For examples of feminized hysteria in Žižek's work, see 1989, 113; 1991, 65–66.
16. NYPD vehicles carry the logo, "Courtesy, Professionalism, Respect." The NYPD statement of values contains the following: "we pledge to . . . value human life, respect the dignity of each individual and render our services with courtesy and civility" (www.nyc.gov/html/nypd/html/mission.html).

CHAPTER 2

1. As Jennifer Glancy points out, the way in which "the trope of slavery under-write[s] the discourse of freedom and manhood" has, "in one version or another . . . dominated the European philosophical tradition since 1807 when Hegel published *Phenomenology of Spirit* with its pivotal dialectical moment between master and slave" (1996, 130).
2. Because Althusser is influenced by Hegel and Lacan (who was in turn influenced by a Kojèvian reading of Hegel), his formulation of ideology is situated within a broadly Hegelian framework, though turned on its head through his commitment to Marxism.
3. I am grateful to Ann Pellegrini and Mary-Jane McKitterick for pointing out the film's framing from the perspective of the young white girl. Yoast's daughter, who grows up to match the ideal standard of beauty for white women, may also recall the cult of womanhood in the South, and its ideals for white women (pious, virtuous, domestic, frail), against which stereotypes of black women (licentious, immoral, strong) were pitted (see Carby 1987). In some ways, the film reverses these stereotypes in portraying the little white girl as a tomboy and the little black girl (Coach Boone's daughter) as prim and proper. Nonetheless, it is the perspective of the grown, and altogether more staid, white woman that frames the narrative.
4. For discussions of French interpreters' readings of Hegel, see Butler 1987; Williams 1997, 366–80; Althusser 1997 [1945–51], 173–83.
5. Hegelian scholar Robert Williams argues, largely against Kojève, that mutual recognition is what Hegel is after, and that the master–slave dialectic is only one example of how recognition can be achieved (1997, 67).
6. There are definite Freudian and Lacanian overtones to the demand for sublimation in the film, whereby Boone acts as a sort of censoring super-ego. In the same scene in which he beats the fun out of football, he asserts, "I am the law," and in a later scene, he asks a player, "Who is your daddy?" Here the film mobilizes a popular expression that resonates with Hegelian concepts—via Lacan.
7. More recently, the story of Cain and Abel has been racialized for more positive purposes in South African liberation readings, along the lines of possession and dispossession. Itumeleng Mosala gives a provocative reading of the story, including a critique of Allan Boesak's sermon on that same text, in which he argues that the story is a ruling-class justification of the dispossession of peasants during the Davidic-Solomonic period, with Abel representing the ruling class and Cain the peasants (Mosala 1989, 34–36). For Mosala the text's ruling-class affiliation

makes untenable the analogy of murdered Abel to the oppressed in South Africa (so Boesak 1984, 137–45); rather, the dispossessed Cain holds a position more similar to that of many black South Africans. Though the ensuing discussions of Mosala's reading do not name race as a contributing factor (Gunn and Fewell 1993, 25–27, 31–32; Kabasele Mukenge 1990; McEntire 2000; West 1990), Mosala's context for reading, that is, black liberation in South Africa, necessarily makes it so. In a sense, Mosala's argument shows that the received biblical story is an imaginary ideological discourse that provokes misrecognition of race and class relations. Certainly its use in racist discourse seems to corroborate this view.

8. Indeed, given that Hegel begins thinking about mastery and slavery in his early theological writings, which contain his anti-Semitic interpretation that the Hebrew scriptures narrate Judaism as failed mastery, or slavishness (1948 [1775–79], 178), the master–slave dialectic may be a refracted interpretation of the Cain and Abel story at some level, though he does not refer specifically to it.

9. For a comparison of the Palestinian Targums of the Pentateuch, by means of Gen. 4:3–16, see Grelot 1959.

10. Cain's ambiguity within Genesis 4 also comes through in the tradition of literature on Abel and Cain. For instance, Quinones documents the very different traditions of Cain as citizen and Cain as monster (1991, 23–61).

11. As Butler describes the unhappy consciousness, "it involves splitting the psyche into two parts, a lordship and a bondage internal to a single consciousness, whereby the body is again dissimulated as an alterity, but where this alterity is not interior to the psyche itself. No longer subjected as an external instrument of labor, the body is still split off from consciousness. Reconstituted as an interior alien, the body is sustained through its disavowal as what consciousness must continue to disavow" (1997a, 42).

12. An explanation of just how scholarly reading of the Bible filters into popular culture is beyond the scope of this chapter, but the convergences serve as a cautionary tale to theologians and biblical scholars, myself included, who may tend to think that popular culture's use of the Bible is uninformed by scholarly debate.

13. See Bai and Tang 2002; N. Davis 2001; Nguyen 2002.

14. De Man notes that Hegel quotes the Lutheran Bible translation (1983, 153 n. 5). It is notable that Hegel's likening of humans to ephemeral flora in Ps. 90:6 is very similar to the language that appears in Isaiah 40:6–8, 24 prior to the segment that the film quotes (40:30–31). Indeed, the verses quoted in the film are indicative of the sublime sentiment running throughout Isaiah 40, with its insistence on the absolute dependence of humans on God, and their insignificance and inability without God. So in Hegel's terms, the biblical language borrowed by *Remember the Titans* is sublime. And perhaps *sublimity* is the affect evoked by the film's citation of Isaiah 40, though here the resistance that the sublime is said to inspire is not exactly what one might hope for.

15. De Man suggests that once Hegel gets to talking about what comes *after* the sublime art form (the comparative art form), the metaphor of the spatiality of exteriority might not be as appropriate as a temporal metaphor, because the

comparative art form is that which "projects into the future what belongs to the past of its own invention and repeats as if it were finding what it knew all along" (de Man 1983, 151). De Man goes so far as to align Hegel's discourse on the comparative art form with the slave because it moves away from an assessment of large, encompassing categories, such as genre, to analyze smaller, less important—therefore weaker—discontinuous categories, such as metaphor (1983, 152): "It is a discourse of the figure rather than of genre, of trope rather than of representation" (1983, 153). But, he concludes, this positioning of the enslaved discourse is symptomatic of its strength.

16. For a reading of African American culture and literature as functioning in the same way as the Kantian sublime, following Toni Morrison's writing on race as "the unspeakable," see Freeman 1995, 105–48.

CHAPTER 3

1. Technically, the 1991 war in Iraq was carried out by coalition forces, but as it was initiated and commanded by the United States, it is sometimes understood as a U.S. war. The colonial nature of the U.S. war in Iraq becomes clear in consideration of the U.S. refusal of diplomatic solution (see Chomsky 1991; Niva 1991). The colonial mentality of the U.S. armed forces personnel comes through in the comment made by a brigadier general, who described the operation in February 1991 thus, "We're deep in Indian country" (Niva 1991, 69; Elbaum 1991, 155).

2. For the background on the stakes in the Gulf War: see Ryan 1991 for a history of U.S. arms-dealing in the Middle East as a strategy to broker power, and Harak 1991 for a history of disputes over oil in the region.

3. For evidence of government censorship and the various interpretations and debates over government policies on media during the war in the Gulf, see H. Smith 1992. For analysis of the psychological effects of censorship, see Newhagen 1994a,b. For other analyses of the media during the war in the Gulf, see Denton 1993; Marks 1991; McLeod, Eveland, and Signorielli 1994; Zelizer 1992; and Pan, Ostman, Moy, and Reynolds 1994. In particular, analysts have noted the difference that live TV coverage made to news media during the time of the war, affecting the mechanisms of censorship (H. Smith 1992; Newhagen 1994a, b), the symbiotic success of media networks like CNN, and the formation of journalistic practice in live reporting (see Zelizer 1992). For instance, Zelizer points out that prior to the U.S. war in Iraq, CNN was considered a "second-rate news organization," a veritable "Chicken Noodle Network" (1992, 72). It rose to power, as it were, during the war, through its use of "the newest news-gathering technology, the satellite-fed communication" (1992, 71). In other words, CNN's success was dependent on war, and at the same time "gave the Gulf War story its form" (1992, 73). CNN failed to provide live reports of incidents such as the massacre of withdrawing Iraqi troops and the bombing of civilian targets.

4. Derrida notes that Kant uses Greek to "confer something approximating conceptual dignity" (1979, 18). He suggests that Kant, in designating the hors d'oeuvre, *parergon*, implicitly shows the importance of what is outside the work.

5. Derrida arrives at the *parergon*'s function of augmenting a lack through reading Kant's use of the term in *Religion within the Limits of Reason Alone* (1979, 20–22). Here Kant argues that "since reason is 'conscious of her inability to satisfy her moral need,' she has recourse to the *parergon*, to grace, to mysteries, miracles" (Derrida 1979 [1978], 21).

6. As Ulrich Luz explains, the Magi became kings in the Middle Ages on the basis of exegesis of Hebrew scriptures, such as Isa. 60:3, and Ps. 72:10–11, which medieval scholars considered to be prophesies of Christ (1990 [1985], 140). Interestingly, Luz argues that in the Middle Ages, "the Magi became figures with whom the believers identified" (1990 [1985], 141). Given this theological tradition it is perhaps not too surprising that in *Three Kings* the viewer is positioned to identify with the men who play the role of "kings."

7. Against the notion of Matthew's interpretation of Jesus as a second Moses, Albright and Mann argue that "Matthew's [Old Testament] quotations see Jesus as living, in himself, through the spiritual experience of a whole people, and not as an individual who becomes another Moses" (1971, 18). Patte suggests that the Moses tradition is present in the background but has been "completely displaced" in Matthew's text (1987, 41 n. 10).

8. For an examination of the way in which early white and black filmmakers treat African Americans' religious experience, see Weisenfeld 1996.

9. Though the film seems to have no compulsions about killing off the fourth "king," Conrad may serve as a sort of Christ figure in the tradition of the heroic bumpkin in the U.S. entertainment industry, alongside figures such as Sergeant York, Beetle Bailey, Forrest Gump, and Gomer Pyle.

10. For the use of the biblical exodus-conquest narrative as a motivator for the American colonization of aboriginal peoples, see L. Donaldson 1996. Donaldson notes that the nineteenth-century American preacher Nahum Gold called American Indians "red Canaanites" (1996, 11). The biblical story is, therefore, a well-ingrained part of the American colonial tradition.

11. Brown even goes so far as to say that the Balaam/Balak story is central to a pre-Matthean narrative that the text of Matthew cites: "I maintain that this pre-Matthean narrative based on Balak and Balaam was joined to a pre-Matthean narrative based on the birth of Moses. . . . The Matthean Herod [who tries to destroy Jesus] resembles both Pharaoh and Balak [both of whom try to destroy Moses]" (1977, 193). Harrington, following Brown, suggests that perhaps Balaam is a "biblical model for the Magi" (1991, 48–49).

12. For the development of fetish within the psychiatric tradition of Freud's day, see Nye 1993. For a good discussion of the gendering of fetish, see Grosz 1993. For a discussion of commodity fetish, media, the exchange of art, and ideology, see Baudrillard 1981 [1969–75]. For fetish as a resistant, feminist concept in filmmaking, see Mulvey 1996; for a more phallocentric reading of fetish in film, see Metz 1982 [1977], 69–78.

13. Obviously, gold has taken on a somewhat different function in contemporary economics. For a discussion of the relation of gold to dollars, see Henwood 1997.

14. This brings to mind the postcolonial critique of humanism. Postcolonialist critics have argued that the notion of one "humanity" effaces difference, erasing everyone—the woman, the slave, the colonized—under the sign of man (see Spivak 1993, 130–33). So gold, like the humanism for which it stands in, effaces the specificities of the labor that produces exchange-value. In its universalizing function, gold operates as Bhabha describes the fetish: it marks and facilitates the "disavowal of difference" (Bhabha 1994, 74).

15. Bush's "Just War" speech drew a good deal of analysis and commentary in the media, much of it negative. For commendation see the *Wall Street Journal* op-ed by Richard John Neuhaus (1991); for critique, see McCarthy 1991; Kenney 1992; Dart 1991.

16. Marks draws on an excellent essay by William Pietz (1993), which lays out the religious and colonial discourses informing Marx's work on commodity fetishism.

17. The connection of fetish to phallus is not surprising, since, as Christian Metz puts it, "the fetish always represents the penis, it is always a substitute for it, whether metaphorically (= it masks its absence) or metonymically (= it is contiguous with its empty place)" (1982 [1977], 71). Though many psychoanalyst theorists try to disassociate the phallus and the penis, to my mind they seem inextricable one from the other.

18. As Freud describes it, displacement in dream-work occurs when "elements which have a high psychical value [are stripped of] their intensity, and . . . elements of low psychical value [are given] new values" (Freud 1953 [1900], 307). So in relating the specific form of the gold to dream-work, I might say that the self-understanding of the United States as all-powerful, which has high psychical value, is displaced by the gold, which, in turn, is given new value.

19. As pointed out to me by Guy Austrian, after reading this chapter, "the colonial longing for gold recalls the search for gold in the Spanish conquest of the Americas, and the search for the phantasmic city of gold, El Dorado. The desire for gold in *Three Kings* transfers this colonial trope from the Americas to Iraq— interesting considering that oil, one of Iraq's prime exports, is also known as 'black gold' " (personal correspondence).

20. The notion of woman as central to the production and exchange of commodities brings to mind Elizabeth Cowie's reading of Claude Lévi-Strauss on woman as an exchangeable sign. Cowie notes Lévi-Strauss' observation that woman is the signifier of the highest value for some cultures. In this sense, woman plays a homologous role to Marx's description of gold, as the placemarker for the condition of possibility of exchange. Of interest with respect to my earlier argument regarding the relation of gold to humanism is her critique of Lévi-Strauss's humanist assumptions, which give woman a value (as human) prior to the structure in which she is exchanged.

21. Deleuze delineates two types of face (or close-up) shots: one in which the face is outlined and unified, and the other in which the face is fragmented by the

"intensive series that its parts successively traverse as far as paroxysm, each part taking on a kind of momentary independence" (1986 [1983], 88–89).

22. For an account of the buildup and execution of Clinton's "Operation Desert Fox," as well as international relations surrounding it, see Hiro 2001, 154–78. The connection between this attack and the Clinton impeachment vote resulting from the Monica Lewinsky scandal was no secret, in the United States or around the world. As Harun Kazaz (1998), writing for the *Turkish Daily News*, points out, on December 17, 1998, CNN simultaneously broadcast the debate over the impeachment vote and the bombing of Iraq, and the *Washington Post* ran an editorial that explicitly named Clinton's action as "the act of a desperate man."

23. It might be argued that the film tries to establish this kind of identification with Barlow's torturer, by having him compare his own suffering in losing his son to the suffering that Barlow would feel in losing his newborn daughter. But because the torturer viciously, inhumanly, pours oil down Barlow's throat, identification is effectively blocked, despite the fact that, as he points out, these torture tactics are learned in the United States.

CHAPTER 4

1. I read with the scribal correction (Qere) in the margin, in Mic. 1:10. The Masoretes corrected the written (Kethib) first-person singular form התפלשתי ("I roll") to the feminine singular imperative התפלשי ("roll"), in order to make it cohere with the feminine singular imperative, עברי ("pass by"), in the next line (Mic. 1:11a).

2. Hillers reads the pronominal suffix in Mic. 1:11 as feminine singular rather than masculine plural (לכם as לך) (1984, 26), and Wolff reads the feminine singular imperative as a masculine plural imperative (עברי as עברו) (1990 [1982], 44). For an extensive discussion of these kinds of textual ambiguities with respect to gender, as well as scholarly "correction" of them, see Runions 2001c.

3. The Syriac, Targum, and Vulgate read the feminine singular קבצה ("she gathered"), in Mic. 1:7, as if it were pointed as the masculine plural Pual (קבצו), in order to cohere with the masculine plural verbs at end of the line. McKane (1995) gives a number of scholarly views on who might actually be collecting the fees, ranging from the Baal cult to the wealthy temples of Samaria. I would point out that all of these proposed collectors of wages are conceived of as male-dominated (patriarchal) cultic institutes. (Against this, Bird's study of prostitution finds that the notion of a cultic prostitute cannot be found in the Hebrew Bible or in other ancient Semitic languages [1989, 76, 85–89].) Whether intentional or not, the effect is to erase (disavow) this behavior that tends to be considered a "male behavior" within discourses on gender—though this perception is perhaps slowly changing on the margins of society, as at least some sex trade workers begin to take charge of their work and to speak out about their experiences; see Bell 1993.

4. For both דוש and דקק, see Isa. 41:15. For דקק, see also 2 Chron. 34:4, 7; Dan. 2:34, 45; 7:7, 19. For דוש, see also Amos 1:3; Judg. 8:7; Jer. 3:11; Isa. 25:10; 28:27.

5. גדד signifies mourning in Deut. 14:1; 2 Kings 8:28; Jer. 16:6; 41:5; 47:5; 48:37.

6. The remnant is passively preserved in Gen. 45:7; Jer. 23:3; 31:7; Amos 5:15; Isa. 46:3; Zech. 8:12; passively led away in 2 Chron. 36:20; Jer. 41:16; 43:5; 44:12; and passively destroyed in 2 Kings 21:14; Isa. 14:30; Jer. 11:23; 15:9; 47:4; 50:26; Ezek. 9:8; 11:13; Ezra 9:14.Very occasionally the remnant "goes forth" into male territory (most notably in Zeph. 2:9, where the remnant plunders, but this is a rare exception; see also 2 Kings 19:31; Isa. 57:32; Jer. 44:28; Zeph. 3:13).

7. The vocatives, O heads of Jacob, ראשי יעקב, and, O heads of the house of Jacob, ראשי בית יעקב, do occur in Mic. 3:1 and 3:9, respectively.

8. See Runions 2001c for a more detailed exposition of these kinds of gendered interpretations of Micah.

9. This critique of the "myth of origins" is central to Bhabha's notion of hybridity—and his work as a whole. Here he takes up Derrida's notion of supplementarity. Like supplementarity, hybridity might be said to be "an indefinite process [that] has always already infiltrated presence [original culture], always already inscribed there the space of repetition and the splitting of the self" (Derrida 1974 [1967], 163). By differently repeating the "original culture," the "self" of colonial culture splits, revealing its requirement for difference and otherness in order to be established as superior. Bhabha builds the idea of repetition and the splitting of self (original culture) into his discussion of the production of hybridity: "the problem of cultural difference . . . is the problem of the not-one, the minus in the origin and repetition of cultural signs in a doubling that will not be sublated into a similitude" (Bhabha 1994, 245). In simpler terms, cultural "difference" doubles or repeats "original culture" in a way that forces a recognition of the normally disavowed and excluded components that make its "originality" possible.

10. As pointed out by Daniel Lang/Levitsky, in a conversation about this chapter, the imitated ideal in the category of Bangee Boy is neither race nor gender, but sexual orientation (i.e., it is an imitation of a straight, young, black man).

11. Examples of the stripping of a female figure as a Treaty Curse occur in Isa. 3:17–18; 47:1–4; Jer. 13:22, 26; Ezek. 16:37–38; 23:10, 29; Hos. 2:4–5, 11–12; Nah. 2:7–8; 3:5 (Magdalene 1995, 343–46).

12. I translate תחנך in Mic. 4:12 as a jussive, to accord with the jussive "let [our eyes] gaze" ותחז, that follows; but it too is ambiguous and could also be read, "you [masculine singular] will be desecrated."

13. For an alternate reading, in which the violence of Mic. 5:9–14 is read as punishment for the remnant's lionlike ravaging behavior, see Runions 2001c, 165, 230.

14. Quoting Venus Xtravaganza, *Paris Is Burning*.

CHAPTER 5

1. My choice of theory here and the kinds of arguments made are indebted to the readings and discussions that were part of the seminar "Psychoanalysis and Ethics," at Columbia University, spring 2001, co-taught by Ann Pellegrini and David Eng, in which I was fortunate to participate.

2. Shields notes that this is "the only text banned from use in the synagogue (*Meg.* 4:10; *b. Hag.* 131)" (1998, 5–6); so also Stiebert 2000, 268.

3. It seems from an interview in *Gay and Lesbian Review Worldwide* that perhaps Pierce views Brandon primarily as a woman crossing gender lines (rather than primarily as a man with the wrong genitals). Pierce says—and it is interesting to notice the use of pronouns and the order she chooses to give for name and surname here—"I really fell in love with this kid Teena Brandon, who one day put a sock in her pants and a cowboy hat on her head and reinvented herself into her fantasy of a boy and then went out and passed . . . ; and then after it all came crashing down, and Brandon found a deeper truer self" (2000b, 40). This deeper truer self that Pierce sees in Brandon, it would appear from the film, is a female, lesbian self.

4. Freud uses the word "introjection," but later theorists, including Butler, have called this "incorporation," following the distinction elaborated by Nicolas Abraham and Maria Torok (1980 [1972]). Introjection, Abraham and Torok suggest, is the process within mourning, in which the object is known to be lost, and can thus be spoken of and represented. Incorporation, on the other hand, is the establishment of the lost object in such a way that it cannot be acknowledged and cannot be represented; it is "anti-metaphorical" (1980 [1972], 9–10). Abraham and Torok call this a kind of encryption: "grief that cannot be expressed builds a secret vault [crypt] within the subject" (1980 [1972], 8; see also 1984 [1978], 4–5, 10–13). This crypt, Abraham suggests, can house either the subject's own secret, or a disavowed secret inherited from others (1988 [1978]).

5. For an interrogation of Butler on this point, see Prosser 1998, 27–44. Prosser takes issue with what he sees as Butler's "displacement of sex from material interiority into fantasized surface" (1998, 44). As I read it, his concern is with establishing the reasons why material sex might need to be changed in order to match up with the bodily ego (what Prosser calls interior perceptions of sex). Butler's emphasis on discursivity seems, to Prosser, to render sex abstract and imaginary, and therefore easily accommodated in whatever body one finds oneself. Prosser's insistence on the fact that transsexuals feel the materiality of their bodies as different from their bodily egos is part of an important critique of what he calls queer theory's appropriation of transsexuality (1998, 31)—the use of transsexualism as a deliteralized metaphor for "the essential inessentiality" (1998, 14). Such an appropriation refuses transsexuals' need either to change their bodies or to inhabit them differently.

6. For comment on the conflation of racism and misogyny in the derision of the Hittite woman, see Dempsey 1998, 62–63, 77.

7. Though Freud does not delineate the different functions of the super-ego in *The Ego and the Id* where the notion first appears, in later writings he distinguishes its various roles, of which the ego-ideal operates as the ideal standard by which the critical agency judges the ego; see Laplanche and Pontalis 1973 [1967], 144–45.

8. As an interesting counterpoint to my argument here, I might note that in the film, we witness Brandon—in response to this shaming revelation of his "lack" of manhood—step out of his body and look on, as the man he knows himself to be. This could be read as an instance of the by now rather banal psychoanalytic "truth" that the phallus stands in for lack. Or, alternatively, it could be read as Eve Sedgwick might read it, as a queer and liberating response of identity formation in response to shame (1993, 12–15). Such a reading might point to the role that shame plays in enforcing the loss of same-sex attachments, and therefore in shaping subsequent identifications.

9. Linda Day points out that the kind of language that Yahweh uses to address Jerusalem is typical of batterers who use insults like " 'dirty slut,' 'whore,' 'bitch,' 'stupid,' 'cunt,' 'slave,' 'dummy' . . . with great frequency" (2000, 220).

10. Shields argues that just as Jerusalem lives on in Ezekiel 16, in Ezekiel 23, Oholah and Oholibah live on in spite of being killed. She argues that this is because they are necessary "as warnings (*object* lessons) to other women . . . [and] as testaments to YHWH's power and identity" (2001, 149).

11. For a different kind of psychoanalytic reading, in which this rage is read as Ezekiel's rage against his own mother expressed in the metaphor of Yahweh's rage against Israel, see Halperin 1993, 160–67.

12. For elaboration on the point of objectification of the women in Ezekiel 16 and 23, see Shields (1998, 13; 2001, 146–49).

13. However, a related form occurs in Ezek. 36:13, in which the second-person feminine singular pronoun, אַתְּ, is spelled with a yod at the end, אתי, but is vocalized as usual.

14. Several reviewers open up the question of masculine identity and violence in *Boys Don't Cry*, without providing answers as to what, within heterosexual masculine identi-fication, gives rise to such rage (Moss and Zeavin 2000, Anderson 2000, Klawans 1999b).

15. Butler makes a related but differently focused argument in *Excitable Speech*, where she looks at how both social and psychic prohibitions on homosexuality are at once internalized and externalized (1997b, 119–26).

16. This same muted connection between the death drive, trauma, and incommensurable loss (melancholia) appears in Caruth's work. At one point she calls the death drive "the traumatic 'awakening' to life." She goes on to say, "Life itself, Freud says, is an awakening out of a 'death' *for which there is no preparation*" (1996, 65, emphasis mine). Likewise, her discussion of trauma as awakening is developed out of Freud's famous story of the grieving father who dreams of his dead (lost) son calling to him, "Father, father don't you see I'm burning?" (1996, 8–9).

17. Freud's description of melancholics' enjoyment of their suffering (1957 [1917], 251) is markedly like his description of the child's enjoyment of the game of loss and recovery.

18. Interestingly—in thinking about the connection between dreamwork and trauma—the film begins with what Pierce calls a "dream sequence" (Leigh 2000, 20), which incorporates moments from the car-chase scene.

19. For a more in-depth look at what role forms of address might play in forming readerly identification, see Runions 2001a, 158–61; 2002.

20. The film picks up and makes several uses of this phrase, "gender identity crisis," with which the real-life Brandon explained himself to the Falls City sheriff after his rape (as recorded on audio tape). This horrifying interrogation, in which the sheriff harasses and accuses Brandon, is aired in the documentary *The Brandon Teena Story*, directed by Susan Muska and Greta Olafsdottir (1998).

CHAPTER 6

1. The first draft of this essay, given at the annual meeting of the Canadian Society of Biblical Studies in Québec City, 2001, was very much inspired by the work of Adrienne Gibb and conversations with her, and also by the work of a former student, Linsey Rains, who wrote her undergraduate honors thesis on the film music in *Magnolia* and was good enough to let me read it. The revision of the paper was also done in conjunction with Adrienne Gibb, whose panel presentation on the relation between television, film, artwork, and memory in *Magnolia*, also given at the annual meeting of the Canadian Society of Biblical Studies in Québec City, 2001, was foundational. Gibb also contributed research and some initial drafting.

2. The bible-verse-bearing sign confirms what might be, for some, an obvious connection to Exodus in the film. This detail was pointed out in an online fan discussion of *Magnolia*. The number 82 also makes a repeated and pronounced appearance in the opening sequence, and then occasionally throughout the film.

3. As Rowland points out, there has been some dispute over the classification of the book of Revelation as apocalypse because of its "apparent lack of pseudo-nymity, its tightness of structure and its author's assertion that the book is prophecy" (1994, 546), though scholars such as J. J. Collins consider it as a variation of the genre of apocalypse (1979, 16).

4. The plague of frogs in Exodus 8 gets taken up again in Revelation 16. For an analysis of the way the writer of the Apocalypse modifies the plague theme of Exodus, see Mounce 1998, 291–305; Beale 1999, 88, 808–12.

5. Much of what readers of later texts call apocalypse, readers of early Jewish and Christian apocalypses would call apocalyptic eschatology and/or apocalypti-cism (J. J. Collins 1979, 3–4).

6. Readers of apocalypse have pointed out how the linear time of apocalyptic narratives has justified political positions and actions, for both dominant and resistant groups (see Pippin 1999; O'Leary 1994; Milhou 1999; Keller 1996;

Dellamora 1994). This diverse political use to which the apocalyptic tradition is put has caused Stephen O'Leary to make the helpful suggestion that apocalypses are primarily rhetorical, working "through the discursive reconstruction of temporality" to provide solutions to what he calls the problem of evil (1994, 14), but what might also be described as a sense of impending crisis or doom.

To understand how the connection between present crisis, cosmic origins, and preordained future might ground a political program, one has only to think about the American "war on terror." The American economic crisis in 2001–02 was marked by an apocalyptic fear of terrorism, which in turn authorized a future of U.S. imperialist bliss (made manifest in the "war on terrorism" in lands connected to oil supply), in a way that accords with U.S. notions of its national origins: set apart as a people chosen by God, mandated to conquer, etc.

7. For a longer meditation on apocalypse and deferral, see Derrida 1984 [1981].

8. For a reading of apocalyptic descriptions of raining frogs (as well as blood, worms, and snakes) in the Middle Ages, see Smoller 2000.

9. Kaja Silverman also reads Benjamin's artwork essay together with his Baudelaire essay to show that cinema might be auratic (1996, 93–104). Silverman is particularly interested in what she calls auratic "investiture" (the viewer invests the artwork with the ability to "look back" and therefore acknowledges it as subject too). This process, like the distance of the auratic artwork, enables the viewer to "identify at a distance from the self" (1996, 98). Thinking of cinema's auratic capacities fits with the kind of political cinema she envisions "challeng[ing] the very principle of an integral self, both because that principle is tantamount to an inexorable insistence upon sameness, and because of its hostile or colonizing relation to the realm of the other" (1996, 92).

10. For Benjamin, the inevitability of technological progress within capitalism is war. As he puts it in the artwork essay, "Only war makes it possible to mobilize all of today's technical resources while maintaining the property system" (1969 [1936], 241).

11. Developing a theory of experience is one of Benjamin's central concerns. Howard Caygill (1998) argues that Benjamin reworks the Kantian conception of experience as articulated in Kant's critical philosophy. Caygill characterizes Benjamin's concept of experience as chromatic, based on differentiation or that which is visible, rather than on linguistic signification, or, in Kantian terms, rather than as being aligned with understanding.

12. Benjamin warns that these concepts such as originality, uniqueness, authenticity, and genius that circulate around the auratic artwork can potentially be employed in the service of fascism; they are "concepts whose uncontrolled (and at present uncontrollable) application would lead to a processing of data in the Fascist sense" (1969 [1936], 218).

13. Laura Marks reads Deleuze's "optical image" as able to constitute the kind of shock that is able to "unroot a memory, to create of flow of experience" (1994, 258). That is, certain cinematic images that capture "any-instant whatever" (like Benjamin's "unconscious optic") are able "in severing cliches [classic images] from their context" not only to "make the hidden object visible . . . revealing what knowledge they constitute" (1994, 254), but also to

shock the viewer into involuntary memory and experience (1994, 258). In this way, she describes something like a rapprochement between aura and shock.

14. Spigel points out that television, like the architectural wall of windows or sliding doors popular in the 1940s and 1950s, served the suburban ideal of "separation from and integration into the outside world" (1997, 212). Likewise, the TV screen was popularly referred to as a "window on the world" (1997, 213). Interestingly, in *Magnolia*, Earl Partridge, television's patriarch of patriarchs, lies dying in a room walled with windows. Earl, as noted, is one of the few characters not introduced in the film by way of a TV screen. He owns the window onto the world.

15. For a discussion of television and capitalism, by way of Karl Marx's *Capital* and Jean-Paul Sartre's discussion of television in an appendix to his *Critique of Dialectical Reason*, see Dienst 1994, 45–58. *Magnolia* seems aptly to depict what Sartre calls the serial totalization that occurs in capitalism, exemplified by TV (Sartre 1991 [1985], 440–41). The serial unification represented by the operation of the TV frames in the film, linked to the fathers as these frames are, ultimately produces all of the characters' addictive and doomed compulsions.

16. As pointed out to me by Rick Delaney, the priority of the filmic (frogs) over television is also depicted in the reflection of the falling frogs on Claudia's turned-off TV screen.

17. Derrida's writing on Freud elaborates the connection between memory, supplement, writing, and deferral (1978 [1967]; 1987 [1980]). His discussion of memory as writing and trace in "Freud and the Scene of Writing" (1978 [1967]) resonates particularly with his suggestion in "Of an Apocalyptic Tone" that writing and apocalypse are similar in their structure: "if the [apocalyptic] dispatches always refer to other dispatches without decidable destination, the destination remaining to come . . . wouldn't the apocalyptic be a transcendental condition of all discourse, of all experience even, of every mark or every trace?" (1984 [1981], 27).

18. Interestingly, the precredit sequence consists of representations of historical film footage—of events taking place in 1911, 1961, and 1983—which self-reflexively refer to film's own history as a medium, once again registering a contrasting temporality to the eternal present of television.

19. Keller shows how Columbus' description of "paradise" is feminized, and that one of his strategic tactics for gaining the land was also to conquer the women (see Keller 1996, 1997). For a critique of Keller's attempt to connect indigenous forms of thought to Christian millennialism, see L. Donaldson 2002.

20. In psychoanalytic film theory, the shot/reverse-shot technique has been read as signifying an identification with lack. Film theorists termed this filling-in for lack "suture," after Jacques Lacan and Jacques-Alain Miller. Suture designates "the relation of the subject to the chain of its discourse" (Miller 1978, 25); that is, the way the subject fills in for what is lacking in the discourse of the Other, or the way the subject identifies with the lack in the other. For further explanation of this process, see Dayan 1976; for a critique, see Rothman 1976.

Here I am adapting the theory to talk about point-of-view shots and the shots that follow them.

21. In the late 1980s and early 1990s, film critics went beyond thinking that camera work and editing can control the viewer's ideological positioning and identification. For other discussions of identification, see Diawara 1988; Glendhill 1988; Hansen 2000 [1986]; Stacey 1994, 1999 [1991].

Works Consulted

ABC (Anarchist Black Cross, Montréal). 1997. *The Gustafsen Lake Crisis: Statements from Ts'Peten Defenders*. Montréal: McGill and Concordia Québec Public Interest Research Group.

Above the Law: Part 1, Deception at Gustafsen Lake. 1997. Prod. and dir. Mervyn Brown. Videotape. Vancouver, B.C.: Ts'Peten Defenders and Supporters.

Above the Law: Part 2, The Other Side. 1999. Prod. and dir. Mervyn Brown. Videotape. Vancouver, B.C.: Ts'Peten Defenders and Supporters.

Abraham, Nicolas. 1988 [1978]. "Notes on the Phantom: A Complement to Freud's Metapsychology." Trans. Nicholas Rand. In *The Trial(s) of Psychoanalysis*, ed. Françoise Meltzer, 75–80. Chicago: Chicago University Press.

Abraham, Nicolas and Maria Torok. 1980 [1972]. "Introjection—Incorporation: Mourning *or* Melancholia." In *Psychoanalysis in France*, ed. Serge Lebovici and Daniel Widlöcher, 3–16. New York: International Universities Press.

———. 1984 [1978]. "A Poetics of Pyschoanalysis: 'The Lost Object—Me.'" Trans. Nicholas Rand. *SubStance* 43:3–18.

Abu-Jamal, Mumia. 2001. *All Things Censored*. New York: Seven Stories.

Aichele, George. 1997. "Rewriting Superman." In *The Monstrous and the Unspeakable: The Bible as Fantastic Literature*, ed. George Aichele and Tina Pippin, 75–101. Playing the Texts 1. Sheffield: Sheffield Academic Press.

———. 2002. "Sitcom Mythology." In *Screening Scripture: Intertextual Connections Between Scripture and Film*, ed. George Aichele and Richard Walsh, 100–19. Harrisburg, PA: Trinity International Press.

———, ed. 2000. *Culture, Entertainment and the Bible*. Sheffield: Sheffield Academic Press.

Aichele, George, and Richard Walsh, eds. 2002. *Screening Scripture: Intertextual Connections between Scripture and Film*. Harrisburg, PA: Trinity International Press.

Aichele, George, and Tina Pippin, eds. 1997. *The Monstrous and the Unspeakable: The Bible as Fantastic Literature*. Playing the Texts 1. Sheffield: Sheffield Academic Press.

Albright, W. F., and C. S. Mann. 1971. *Matthew: Introduction, Translation, and Notes*. Anchor Bible. Garden City, NY: Doubleday.

Allen, Leslie C. 1976. *The Books of Joel, Obadiah, Jonah and Micah*. Grand Rapids, MI: Eerdmans.

Allison, Dale C. 1993. *The New Moses: A Matthean Typology*. Minneapolis: Fortress.

Althusser, Louis. 1984. "Ideological State Apparatuses (Notes toward an Investigation)." In *Essays on Ideology*, 1–60. London: Verso.

———. 1997 [1945–51]. *The Spectre of Hegel: Louis Althusser, Early Writings*. Trans. G. M. Goshgarian. London: Verso.

Anderson, Melissa. 2000. "*The Brandon Teena Story* and *Boys Don't Cry*." *Cineaste* 25, no. 2:54–56.

Anonymous. 2000. "Denzel Washington is Coach Who Unites Racially Divided Team and Community in *Remember the Titans*." *Jet* 98, no. 17:60–64.

Ansen, David. 1999. "Operation Desert Scam." Review of *Three Kings*. *Newsweek*, October 4, 64–65.

Aycock, D. Alan. 1983. "The Mark of Cain." In *Structuralist Interpretations of Biblical Myth*, ed. Edmund Leach and D. Alan Aycock, 120–27. Cambridge: Cambridge University Press.

Azevedo, Joaquim. 1999. "At the Door of Paradise: A Contextual Interpretation of Gen 4:7." *Biblische Notizen* 100:45–59.

Babington, Bruce, and Peter William Evans. 1993. *Biblical Epics: Sacred Narrative in the Hollywood Cinema*. Manchester: Manchester University Press.

Bach, Alice. 1996a. "Throw Them to the Lions, Sire: Transforming Biblical Narratives into Hollywood Spectaculars." *Semeia* 74:1–13.

———. 1998. "On the Road between Birmingham and Jerusalem." *Semeia* 82:297–305.

———, ed. 1994. *The Bible and Popular Culture*. Biblical Interpretation 2, no. 1. Leiden: Brill.

———, ed. 1996b. *Biblical Glamour and Hollywood Glitz*. Semeia 74. Atlanta: Scholars.

Bai, Jane, and Eric Tang. 2002. "The War at Home." *ColorLines* 5, no. 1 (spring): 28–29.

Baltzer, Klaus. 2001 [1999]. *Deutero-Isaiah: A Commentary on Isaiah 40–55*. Trans. Margaret Kohl. Hermeneia. Minneapolis: Fortress.

Barr, Heather. 2001. "Policing Madness: People with Mental Illness and the NYPD." In *Zero Intolerance: Quality of Life and the New Police Brutality in New York City*, ed. Andrea McArdle and Tanya Erzen, 50–84. New York: New York University Press.

Baudrillard, Jean 1981 [1969–75]. *For a Critique of the Political Economy of the Sign*. Trans. Charles Levin. St. Louis: Telos.

———. 1994 [1981]. *Simulacra and Simulation*. Trans. Sheila Faria Glaser. Ann Arbor: University of Michigan Press.

———. 1995 [1991]. *The Gulf War Did Not Take Place*. Trans. Paul Patton. Bloomington: Indiana University Press.

Baugh, Lloyd. 1997. *Imaging the Divine: Jesus and Christ-Figures in Film*. Kansas City: Sheed and Ward.

Beale, G. K. 1999. *The Book of Revelation: A Commentary on the Greek Text*. Grand Rapids, MI: Eerdmans; Carlisle: Paternoster.

Beck, Avent Childress. 1995. "The Christian Allegorical Structure of *Platoon*." In *Screening the Sacred: Religion, Myth and Ideology in Popular American Film*, ed. Joel W. Martin and Conrad E. Ostwalt, 44–54. Boulder, CO: Westview.

Bell, Shannon. 1995. *Whore Carnival*. New York: Autonomedia.

Benjamin, Walter. 1969 [1936]. "The Work of Art in the Age of Mechanical Reproduction." In *Illuminations*, ed. Hannah Arendt, trans. Harry Zohn, 217–52. New York: Schocken Books.

———. 1969 [1939]. "On Some Motifs in Baudelaire." In *Illuminations*, ed. Hannah Arendt, trans. Harry Zohn, 155–200. New York: Schocken Books.

———. 1969 [1940]. "Theses on the Philosophy of History." In *Illuminations*, ed. Hannah Arendt, trans. Harry Zohn, 253–64. New York: Schocken Books.

———. 1979 [1931]. "A Small History of Photography." In *One-Way Street: And Other Writings*, 240–57. Trans. Edmund Jephcott and Kingsley Shorter. London: Verso.

Bhabha, Homi K. 1990. "Introduction: Narrating the Nation." In *Nation and Narration*, ed. Homi K. Bhabha, 1–7. New York: Routledge.

———. 1994. *The Location of Culture*. New York: Routledge.

Bird, Phyllis. 1989. " 'To Play the Harlot': An Inquiry into the Old Testament Metaphor." In *Gender and Difference in Ancient Israel*, ed. Peggy L. Day, 75–94. Minneapolis: Fortress.

Blomberg, Craig L. 1991. "The Liberation of Illegitimacy: Women and Rulers in Matthew 1–2." *Biblical Theology Bulletin* 21 (winter): 145–50.

Bobo, Jacqueline, and Ellen Seiter. 1997. "Black Feminism and Media Criticism: *The Women of Brewster Place*." In *Feminist Television Criticism: A Reader*, ed. Charlotte Brunsdon, Julie D'Acci, and Lynn Spigel, 167–83. Oxford: Clarendon.

Boer, Roland. 1999. "David is a Thing." In *The Labour of Reading: Desire, Alienation, and Biblical Interpretation*, ed. Fiona Black, Roland Boer, and Erin Runions, 175–88. Semeia Studies 36. Atlanta: Scholars Press.

———. 1999. *Knockin' on Heaven's Door: The Bible and Popular Culture*. Biblical Limits. New York: Routledge.

———. 2000. "The Second Coming: Repetition and Insatiable Desire in the Song of Songs." *Biblical Interpretation* 8, no. 3:276–301.

———. 2002. "Non-Sense: *Total Recall*, Paul, and the Possibility of Psychosis." In *Screening Scripture: Intertextual Connections Between Scripture and Film*, ed. George Aichele and Richard Walsh, 120–54. Harrisburg, PA: Trinity International Press.

Boesak, Allan. 1984. *Black and Reformed: Apartheid, Liberation, and the Calvinist Tradition*. Maryknoll, NY: Orbis.

Bornstein, Kate. 1994. *Gender Outlaw: On Men, Women, and the Rest of Us*. New York: Routledge.

Bourke, Myles M. 1960. "The Literary Genus of Matthew 1–2." *Catholic Biblical Quarterly* 22, no. 2:160–75.

Brabban, Ralph J. 2002. "Alienation, Sex, and an Unsatisfactory Ending: Themes and Features of Stories Old and New." In *Screening Scripture: Intertextual Connections Between Scripture and Film*, ed. George Aichele and Richard Walsh, 58–76. Harrisburg, PA: Trinity International Press.

Breuer, Josef, and Sigmund Freud. 1955 [1893–95]. *Studies on Hysteria*. Vol. 2 of *The Standard Edition of the Complete Psychological Works of Sigmund Freud*. Trans. James Strachey. London: Hogarth.

Brooks, Xan. 2000. "Boys Don't Cry." Review of *Boys Don't Cry. Sight and Sound* 10 (April): 43–44.

Brown, Raymond E. 1977. *The Birth of the Messiah: A Commentary on the Infancy Narratives in Matthew and Luke*. Garden City, NY: Doubleday.

Browne, Julie. 1996. "The Labor of Doing Time." In *Criminal Injustice: Confronting the Prison Crisis*, ed. Elihu Rosenblatt, 61–72. Boston: South End Press.

Bruns, J. Edgar. 1961. "The Magi Episode in Matthew 2." *Catholic Biblical Quarterly* 23, no. 1:51–54.

Brunsdon, Charlotte, Julie D'Acci, and Lynn Spigel, eds. 1997. *Feminist Television Criticism: A Reader*. Oxford: Clarendon.

Buck-Morss, Susan. 1983. "Benjamin's *Passagen-Werk:* Redeeming Mass Culture for the Revolution." *New German Critique* 29 (spring/summer): 211–40.

———. 1992. "Aesthetics and Anaesthetics: Walter Benjamin's Artwork Essay Reconsidered." *October* 62 (fall): 3–41.

Budd, Philip J. 1984. *Numbers*. Word Biblical Commentary. Waco, TX: Word Books.

Bullough, Vern L., and Bonnie Bullough. 1993. *Cross-dressing, Sex, and Gender*. Philadelphia: University of Pennsylvania Press.

Burnett, Fred. 2002. "The Characterization of Martin Riggs in *Lethal Weapon 1*: An Archetypal Hero." In *Screening Scripture: Intertextual Connections Between Scripture and Film*, ed. George Aichele and Richard Walsh, 251–78. Harrisburg, PA: Trinity International Press.

Butler, Judith. 1987. *Subjects of Desire: Hegelian Reflections in Twentieth-Century France*. New York: Columbia University Press.

———. 1990. *Gender Trouble: Feminism and the Subversion of Identity*. New York: Routledge.

———. 1991. "Imitation and Gender Insubordination." In *Inside/Out: Lesbian Theories, Gay Theories*, ed. Diana Fuss, 13–31. New York: Routledge.

———. 1993. *Bodies That Matter: On the Discursive Limits of "Sex."* New York: Routledge.

———. 1997a. *The Psychic Life of Power: Theories in Subjection*. Stanford, CA: Stanford University Press.

———. 1997b. *Excitable Speech: A Politics of the Performative*. New York: Routledge.

Calloud, Jean. 1995. "Figure, Knowledge and Truth: Absence and Fulfillment in the Scriptures." *Semeia* 69/70:61–81.

Canadian Press. 1997. "Gustafsen Lake Not Land-Claims Issue, Crown Tells Jurors." *The Vancouver (B.C.) Sun*, May 1, B4 (http://sisis.nativeweb.org/court/may01cli.html).

Canby, Vincent. 1991. "Aching to be a Prima Donna, When You're a Man." Review of *Paris Is Burning. New York Times*, March 13, C13.

Carby, Hazel V. 1987. *Reconstructing Womanhood: The Emergence of the Afro-American Woman Novelist*. Oxford: Oxford University Press.

Carpenter, Mary Wilson. 1995. "Representing Apocalypse: Sexual Politics and the Violence of Revelation." In *Postmodern Apocalypse: Theory and Cultural Practice at the End*, ed. Richard Dellamora, 107–35. Philadelphia: University of Philadelphia Press.

Caruth, Cathy. 1996. *Unclaimed Experience: Trauma, Narrative, and History.* Baltimore: Johns Hopkins University Press.

———, ed. 1995. *Trauma: Explorations in Memory.* Baltimore: Johns Hopkins University Press.

Castelli, Elizabeth A. Forthcoming (2004). *Martyrdom and Memory: Early Christian Culture-making.* Religion and Gender. New York: Columbia University Press.

Caygill, Howard. 1998. *Walter Benjamin: The Colour of Experience.* New York: Routledge.

Cerf, Walter. 1977. "Speculative Philosophy and Intellectual Intuition: An Introduction to Hegel's *Essays.*" Foreword to *Faith and Knowledge,* by G. W. F. Hegel, xi–xxxvi. Albany: State University of New York Press.

Cernetig, Miro. 1997. "Judge Tough on Native Protesters: Gustafsen Standoff Hurt Democracy." *Toronto (Ont.) Globe and Mail,* July 31, A1 (http://sisis.nativeweb.org/court/jul31cli.html).

Chevillard-Maubuisson, Anne, and Alain Marchadour. 1993. "Caïn et Abel: Lecture et relectures." In *Le Temps de la lecture: Exégèse biblique et sémiotique: Recueil d'hommages pour Jean Delorme,* ed. Louis Panier, 267–88. Paris: Les Éditions du Cerf.

Chomsky, Noam. 1991. "After the Cold War: U.S. Middle East Policy." In *Beyond the Storm: A Gulf Crisis Reader,* ed. Phyllis Bennis and Michel Moushabeck, 75–87. New York: Olive Branch.

Churchill, Ward, and Jim Vander Wall. 1988. *Agents of Repression: The FBI's Secret Wars Against the Black Panther Party and the American Indian Movement.* Boston: South End.

Cixous, Hélène. 1980 [1975]. "The Laugh of the Medusa." In *The New French Feminisms: An Anthology,* ed. Elaine Marks and Isabelle de Courtivron, 245–64. Amherst: University of Massachusetts Press.

Coats, George W. 1968. *Rebellion in the Wilderness: The Murmuring Motif in the Wilderness.* Nashville: Abingdon.

Collins, Adela Yarbro. 1984. *Crisis and Catharsis: The Power of the Apocalypse.* Philadelphia: Westminster.

Collins, John J. 1979. "Introduction: Towards the Morphology of a Genre." *Semeia* 14:1–21.

Cooke, Miriam. 2001. *Women Claim Islam: Creating Islamic Feminism through Literature.* New York: Routledge.

Cooper, Michael. 1999. "Officers in Bronx Fire 41 Shots, and an Unarmed Man is Killed." *New York Times,* February 5, A1, B5.

Copher, Charles B. 1991. "The Black Presence in the Old Testament." In *Stony the Road We Trod: African American Biblical Interpretation,* ed. Cain Hope Felder, 146–64. Minneapolis: Fortress.

Corley, Derrick. 2000. "Derrick's View: Inmate Wages in New York State Prisons." *Fortune News* 35 (winter): 18.

Correctional Association. 2001. "Drop the Rock: The Time is Now to Repeal the Rockefeller Drug Laws." Leaflet for the Drop the Rock Campaign in New York City. Printed.

Cosandey, Roland, André Gaudreault, and Tom Gunning, eds. 1992. *Une invention du diable? Cinéma des premiers temps et religion*. Sainte-Foy: Les presses de l'Université Laval; Lausanne: Éditions payot Lausanne.

Cowie, Elizabeth. 2000 [1978]. "Woman as Sign." In *Feminism and Film*, ed. E. Ann Kaplan, 48–65. Oxford Readings in Feminism. Oxford: Oxford University Press.

Craigie, Peter C. 1985. *The Twelve Prophets*. Vol. 2. *Micah, Nahum, Habakkuk, Zephaniah, Haggai, Zechariah and Malachi*. Daily Study Bible. Philadelphia: Westminster.

Crisp, Quentin. 1991. "A Place Where Love Becomes a Chronic Invalid." *New York Times*, April 7, H20.

Darr, Katheryn Pfisterer. 1998. "Ezekiel." In *Women's Bible Commentary: Expanded Edition*, ed. Carol A. Newsom and Sharon H. Ringe, 183–90. Louisville: Westminster/John Knox.

Dart, John. 1991. "Churches' Response to Gulf War Emphasizes its Victims Mideast." *Los Angeles Times*, January 26, 12.

Dauphin, Gary. 1999. "School's Out and In Flames." Review of *Light it Up*. *Village Voice*, November 17–23, www.villagevoice.com/issues/9946/dauphin.php.

Davis, Angela. 1998. "Masked Racism: Reflections on the Prison Industrial Complex." *ColorLines* 1, no. 2 (fall): www.arc.org/C_Lines/CLArchive/story1_2_01.html.

Davis, Nicole. 2001. "The Slippery Slope of Racial Profiling." *ColorLines* (December Special Issue): 2–3.

Day, Linda. 2000. "Rhetoric and Domestic Violence in Ezekiel 16." *Biblical Interpretation* 8:205–30.

Day, Peggy L. 2000. "The Bitch Had it Coming to Her: Rhetoric and Interpretation in Ezekiel 16." *Biblical Interpretation* 8:231–55.

Dayan, Daniel. 1976. "The Tudor-code of Classical Cinema." In vol. 1 of *Movies and Method: An Anthology*, ed. Bill Nichols, 438–45. Berkeley: University of California Press.

de Man, Paul. 1983. "Hegel on the Sublime." In *Displacement: Derrida and After*, ed. Mark Krupnick, 139–53. Bloomington: Indiana University Press.

Deleuze, Gilles. 1986 [1983]. *Cinema 1: The Movement-Image*. Trans. Hugh Tomlinson and Barbara Habberjam. Minneapolis: University of Minnesota Press.

Dellamora, Richard. 1994. *Apocalyptic Overtures: Sexual Politics and the Sense of an Ending*. New Brunswick, NJ: Rutgers University Press.

Dempsey, Carol J. 1998. "The 'Whore' of Ezekiel 16: The Impact and Ramifications of Gender-Specific Metaphors in Light of Biblical Law and Divine Judgment." In *Gender and Law in the Hebrew Bible and the Ancient Near East*, ed. Victor H. Matthews, Bernard M. Levinson, and Tikva Frymer-Kensky, 58–78. Journal for the Study of the Old Testament Supplement Series 262. Sheffield: Sheffield Academic Press.

Denton, Robert E., ed. 1993. *The Media and the Persian Gulf War*. Westport, CT: Praeger.

Derrida, Jacques. 1974 [1967]. *Of Grammatology*. Trans. Gayatri Chakravorty Spivak. Baltimore: Johns Hopkins University Press.

———. 1978 [1967]. *Writing and Difference*. Trans. Alan Bass. Chicago: University of Chicago Press.

——. 1979 [1978]. "The Parergon." Trans. Craig Owens. *October* 9:3–11.

——. 1981 [1972]. *Dissemination*. Trans. Barbara Johnson. Chicago: University of Chicago Press.

——. 1984 [1981]. "Of an Apocalyptic Tone Recently Adopted in Philosophy." Trans. John P. Leavey. *Oxford Literary Review* 6, no. 2:3–37.

——. 1984. "My Chances/*Mes Chances*: A Rendezvous with Some Epicurean Stereophonies." In *Taking Chances: Derrida, Psychoanalysis, Literature*, ed. Joseph H. Smith and William Kerrigan, 1–32. Baltimore and London: Johns Hopkins University Press.

——. 1987 [1980]. *The Post Card: From Socrates to Freud and Beyond*. Trans. Alan Bass. Chicago: University of Chicago Press.

——. 1998 [1996]. *Resistances of Psychoanalysis*. Trans. Peggy Kamuf, Pascale-Anne Brault, and Michael Naas. Crossing Aesthetics. Stanford: Stanford University Press.

Diawara, Manthia. 1988. "Black Spectatorship: Problems of Identification and Resistance." *Screen* 29, no. 4 (autumn): 66–76.

Dick, Leslie. 2000. "Magnolia." Review of *Magnolia*. *Sight and Sound* (April): 56–57.

Dienst, Richard. 1994. *Still Life in Real Time: Theory after Television*. Durham, NC: Duke University Press.

DiGiglio-Bellemare, Mario. 2000. "*Magnolia* and the Signs of the Times: A Theological Reflection." *Journal of Religion and Film* 4, no. 2: www.unomaha.edu/~wwwjrf/magnolia.htm.

Doane, Mary Ann. 1987. *The Desire to Desire: The Woman's Film of the 1940s*. Bloomington: Indiana University Press.

Donaldson, Laura E. 1996. "Postcolonialism and Biblical Reading: An Introduction." *Semeia* 75:1–14.

——. 2002. "The Breast of Columbus: A Political Anatomy of Postcolonialism and Feminist Religious Discourse." In *Postcolonialism, Feminism and Religious Discourse*, ed. Laura E. Donaldson and Kwok Pui-Lan, 41–61. New York: Routledge.

Donaldson, Mara E. 1997. "Border Crossing: Fall and Fantasy in *Blade Runner* and *Thelma and Louise*." In *The Monstrous and the Unspeakable: The Bible as Fantastic Literature*, ed. George Aichele and Tina Pippin, 19–42. Playing the Texts 1. Sheffield: Sheffield Academic Press.

Dunne, John Gregory. 1997. "A Report at Large: The Humboldt Murders." *New Yorker*, January 13, 44–52.

Dyck, Carl. 2002. "Learning from *The Life of Brian*: Saviors for Seminars." In *Screening Scripture: Intertextual Connections Between Scripture and Film*, ed. George Aichele and Richard Walsh, 229–50. Harrisburg, PA: Trinity International Press.

Eagleton, Terry. 1994. "Ideology and its Vicissitudes in Western Marxism." In *Mapping Ideology*, ed. Slavoj Žižek, 179–226. London: Verso.

Ekins, Richard. 1997. *Male Femaling: A Grounded Theory Approach to Cross-dressing and Sex-changing*. New York: Routledge.

Ekins, Richard, and Dave King, eds. 1996. *Blending Genders: Social Aspects of Cross-dressing and Sex-changing*. New York: Routledge.

Elbaum, Max. 1991. "The Storm at Home: The U.S. Anti-War Movement." In *Beyond the Storm: A Gulf Crisis Reader*, ed. Phyllis Bennis and Michel Moushabeck, 142–59. New York: Olive Branch.

Eng, David L. 2001. *Racial Castration: Managing Masculinity in Asian America.* Durham, NC: Duke University Press.

Eng, David L., and Shinhee Han. 2000. "A Dialogue on Racial Melancholia." *Psychoanalytic Dialogues* 10:667–700.

Even-Shoshan, Abraham, ed. 1997. *A New Concordance of the Bible: Thesaurus of the Language of the Bible, Hebrew and Aramaic Roots, Words, Proper Names, Phrases, and Synonyms*, second ed. Jerusalem: Kiryat Sefer.

Exum, J. Cheryl. 1996. *Plotted, Shot and Painted: Cultural Representations of Biblical Women.* Journal for the Study of the Old Testament Supplement Series 215. Gender, Culture, Theory 3. Sheffield: Sheffield Academic Press.

———. 2000. "Desire Distorted and Exhibited: Lot and His Daughters in Psychoanalysis, Painting, and Film." In *"A Wise and Discerning Mind:" Essays in Honor of Burke O. Long*, ed. Saul Olyan and Robert C. Culley, 83–108. Providence, RI: Brown Judaic Studies.

———, ed. 1998. *The Bible and the Arts.* Biblical Interpretation 6. Leiden: Brill.

Exum, J. Cheryl, and Stephen Moore, eds. 1998. *Biblical Studies/Cultural Studies.* Journal for the Study of the Old Testament Supplement Series 266. Sheffield: Sheffield Academic Press.

Fanon, Frantz. 1967 [1952]. *Black Skin, White Masks.* Trans. Charles Lam Markmann. New York: Grove.

Farley, Christopher John. 2000. "That Old Black Magic." *Time* 156, no. 22 (November 27): 14.

Feinberg, Leslie. 1992. *Transgender Liberation: A Movement Whose Time Has Come.* New York: World View Forum.

Fiorenza, Elizabeth Schüssler. 1985. *The Book of Revelation: Justice and Judgment.* Philadelphia: Fortress.

Forshey, Gerald E. 1992. *American Religious and Biblical Spectaculars.* Media and Society Series. Westport, CT: Praeger.

France, R. T. 1981. "The Formula-Quotations of Matthew 2 and the Problem of Communication." *New Testament Studies* 27:233–51.

Francisco, Steven, and Amanda Devecka-Rinear. 2000. "Hostile Takeover." *Fortune News* 35 (winter): 12–13, www.fortunesociety.org.

Fraser, Peter. 1998. *Images of the Passion: The Sacramental Mode in Film.* Westport, CT: Praeger.

Freeman, Barbara Claire. 1995. *The Feminine Sublime: Gender and Excess in Women's Fiction.* Berkeley: University of California Press.

Freud, Sigmund. 1953 [1900]. *The Interpretation of Dreams.* In vols. 4–5 of *The Standard Edition of the Complete Psychological Works of Sigmund Freud*, trans. James Strachey. London: Hogarth.

———. 1953 [1905]a. *Fragment of an Analysis of a Case of Hysteria.* In vol. 7 of *The Standard Edition of the Complete Psychological Works of Sigmund Freud*, trans. James Strachey, 3–123. London: Hogarth.

———. 1953 [1905]b. *Three Essays on the Theory of Sexuality.* In vol. 7 of *The Standard Edition of the Complete Psychological Works of Sigmund Freud,* trans. James Strachey, 125–248. London: Hogarth.

———. 1955 [1920]. *Beyond the Pleasure Principle.* In vol. 18 of *The Standard Edition of the Complete Psychological Works of Sigmund Freud,* trans. James Strachey, 3–64. London: Hogarth.

———. 1955 [1921]. *Group Psychology and the Analysis of the Ego.* In vol. 18 of *The Standard Edition of the Complete Psychological Works of Sigmund Freud,* trans. James Strachey, 67–143. London: Hogarth.

———. 1957 [1917]. "Mourning and Melancholia." In vol. 14 of *The Standard Edition of the Complete Psychological Works of Sigmund Freud,* trans. James Strachey, 239–58. London: Hogarth.

———. 1959 [1908]. "'Civilized' Sexual Morality and Modern Nervous Illness." In vol. 9 of *The Standard Edition of the Complete Psychological Works of Sigmund Freud,* trans. James Strachey, 177–204. London: Hogarth.

———. 1959 [1908]. "Hysterical Phantasies and their Relation to Bisexuality." In vol. 9 of *The Standard Edition of the Complete Psychological Works of Sigmund Freud,* trans. James Strachey, 155–66. London: Hogarth.

———. 1959 [1909]. "Some General Remarks on Hysterical Attacks." In vol. 9 of *The Standard Edition of the Complete Psychological Works of Sigmund Freud,* trans. James Strachey, 229–34. London: Hogarth.

———. 1959 [1926]. *Inhibitions, Symptoms and Anxiety.* In vol. 20 of *The Standard Edition of the Complete Psychological Works of Sigmund Freud,* trans. James Strachey, 77–178. London: Hogarth.

———. 1961 [1923]. *The Ego and the Id.* In vol. 19 of *The Standard Edition of the Complete Psychological Works of Sigmund Freud,* trans. James Strachey, 3–63. London: Hogarth.

———. 1961 [1927]. "Fetishism." In vol. 21 of *The Standard Edition of the Complete Psychological Works of Sigmund Freud,* trans. James Strachey, 149–57. London: Hogarth.

———. 1961 [1930]. *Civilization and its Discontents.* In vol. 21 of *The Standard Edition of the Complete Psychological Works of Sigmund Freud,* trans. James Strachey, 57–146. London: Hogarth.

Friedberg, Anne. 1990. "A Denial of Difference: Theories of Cinematic Identification." In *Psychoanalysis and Cinema,* ed. E. Ann Kaplan, 36–45. New York: Routledge.

Fritsch, Jane. 2000. "4 Officers in Diallo Shootings are Acquitted of All Charges." *New York Times,* February 26, A1.

Frymer-Kensky, Tikva. 1992. *In the Wake of the Goddesses: Women, Culture and the Biblical Transformation of Pagan Myth.* New York: Fawcett Columbine.

Galambush, Julie. 1992. *Jerusalem in the Book of Ezekiel, the City as Yahweh's Wife.* Society of Biblical Studies Dissertation Series 130. Atlanta: Scholars.

Garber, Marjorie. 1992. *Vested Interests: Cross-dressing and Cultural Anxiety.* New York: Routledge.

Gaudreault, André. 1992. "La passion du Christ: une forme, un genre, un discours." In *Une invention du diable? Cinéma des premiers temps et religion*, ed. Roland Cosandey, André Gaudreault, and Tom Gunning, 91–101. Sainte-Foy: Les presses de l'Université Laval; Lausanne: Éditions payot Lausanne.

Gesenius, Wilhelm, and E. Kautzsch. 1910. *Gesenius' Hebrew Grammar as Edited and Enlarged by E. Kautzsch*. Rev. in Accordance with the Twenty-eighth German Edition (1909) by A. E. Cowley. Oxford: Clarendon.

Gilman, Sander L., Helen King, Roy Porter, G. S. Rousseau, and Elaine Showalter. 1993. *Hysteria Beyond Freud*. Berkeley: University of California Press.

Giltz, Michael. 2000. "Hilary's Journey." *The Advocate*, March 28, www.advocate.com/html/stories/808/808_cvr_hilary.asp.

Glancy, Jennifer. 1996. "The Mistress of the Gaze: Masculinity, Slavery, and Representation." *Semeia* 74:127–46.

Glendhill, Christine. 1988. "Pleasurable Negotiations." In *Female Spectators: Looking at Film and Television*, ed. E. Deidre Pribram, 64–89. London: Verso.

Gordon, Pamela, and Harold C. Washington. 1995. "Rape as a Military Metaphor in the Hebrew Bible." In *A Feminist Companion to the Latter Prophets*, ed. Athalya Brenner, 308–25. Sheffield: Sheffield Academic Press.

Gottwald, Norman K. 1991. "Social Class and Ideology in Isaiah 40–55." *Semeia* 59:43–57.

Greenberg, Moshe. 1983. *Ezekiel 1–20: A New Translation with Introduction and Commentary*. Anchor Bible 22. Garden City, NY: Doubleday.

Grelot, P. 1959. "Les Targums de pentateuque: Étude comparative d'après Genèse IV, 3–16." *Semitica* 9:59–88.

Grosz, Elizabeth. 1993. "Lesbian Fetishism?" In *Fetishism and Cultural Discourse*, ed. Emily Apter and William Pietz, 101–15. Ithaca, NY: Cornell University Press.

Gunn, David M. 1999. "Yearning for Jerusalem: Reading Myth on the Web." In *The Labour of Reading: Desire, Alienation, and Biblical Interpretation*, ed. Fiona Black, Roland Boer, and Erin Runions, 131–50. Semeia Studies 36. Atlanta: Scholars Press.

Gunn, David M., and Danna Nolan Fewell. 1993. *Narrative in the Hebrew Bible*. New York: Oxford University Press.

Gunning, Tom. 1992. "Passion Play as Palimpsest: The Nature of the Text in the History of Early Cinema." In *Une invention du diable? Cinéma des premiers temps et religion*, ed. Roland Cosandey, André Gaudreault, and Tom Gunning, 102–11. Sainte-Foy: Les presses de l'Université Laval; Lausanne: Éditions payot Lausanne.

Habermas, Jürgen. 1979. "Consciousness-Raising or Redemptive Criticism—The Contemporaneity of Walter Benjamin." *New German Critique* 17 (spring): 30–59.

Hagner, Donald A. 1993. *Matthew 1–13*. Word Biblical Commentary 33A. Dallas, TX: Word Books.

Hagstrom, David Gerald. 1988. *The Coherence of the Book of Micah: A Literary Analysis*. Society of Biblical Literature Dissertation Series 89. Atlanta: Scholars.

Halperin, David J. 1993. *Seeking Ezekiel: Text and Psychology*. University Park: Pennsylvania State University Press.

Hansen, Miriam. 1987. "Benjamin, Cinema and Experience: 'The Blue Flower in the Land of Technology.'" *New German Critique* 40 (winter): 179–224.

———. 1999. "Benjamin and Cinema: Not a One Way Street." *Critical Inquiry* 25 (winter): 306–41.

———. 2000. "Pleasure, Ambivalence, Identification: Valentino and Female Spectatorship." In *Feminism and Film*, ed. E. Ann Kaplan, 226–52. Oxford Readings in Feminism. Oxford: Oxford University Press.

Harak, G. Simon. 1991. "Hypertexting the War." *Cross Currents* 41 (winter): 506–19.

Harrington, Daniel J. 1991. *The Gospel of Matthew*. Sacra Pagina Series 1. Collegeville, MN: Liturgical Press.

Harry, Margot. 1987. *Attention, MOVE! This is America*. Chicago: Banner.

Hegel, G. W. F. 1948 [1775–79]. *Early Theological Writings*. Trans. T. M. Knox. Chicago: University of Chicago Press.

———. 1975 [1835]. *Aesthetics: Lectures on Fine Art*. Vol. 1. Trans. T. M. Knox. Oxford: Clarendon.

———. 1977 [1802–03]. *Faith and Knowledge*. Trans. Walter Cerf and H. S. Harris. Albany: State University of New York Press.

———. 1977 [1807]. *Phenomenology of Spirit*. Trans. A. V. Miller. Oxford: Oxford University Press.

Hentzi, Gary. 1991. "Paris Is Burning." Review of *Paris Is Burning. Film Quarterly* 45, no. 2:35–37.

Henwood, Doug. 1997. *Wall Street: How It Works and for Whom*. London: Verso.

Hillers, Delbert R. 1984. *Micah: A Commentary on the Book of the Prophet Micah*. Hermeneia. Philadelphia: Fortress.

Hiro, Dilip. 2001. *Neighbors, Not Friends: Iraq and Iran after the Gulf Wars*. London: Routledge.

Hoberman, J. 2000. "Burn, Blast, Bomb, Cut." Review of *Three Kings. Sight and Sound* 2:18–20.

hooks, bell. 1992. *Black Looks: Race and Representation*. Toronto: Between the Lines.

Hoover's, The Business Information Authority. 2002. www.hoovers.com.

Horsley, Richard A. 1989. *The Liberation of Christmas: The Infancy Narratives in Social Context*. New York: Crossroad.

Horwood, Holly. 1997a. "Mountie Regrets 'Smear' Remark." *Vancouver (B.C.) Province*, January 21, (http://sisis.nativeweb.org/court/jan2197.html).

———. 1997b. "Sgt. Cites Boss: 'Kill This Clark.'" *The Vancouver (B.C.) Province*, February 4, A4 (http://sisis.nativeweb.org/court/feb0497.html).

Hume, Mark. 1995. "Standoff at Gustafsen Lake Preceded by a Vision." *Vancouver (B.C.) Sun*, September 12 (http://sisis.nativeweb.org/gustlake/sep1295c.html).

Humphreys, Edith McEwan. 1995. *The Ladies and the Cities: Transformation and Apocalyptic Identity in Joseph and Aseneth, 4 Ezra, the Apocalypse and The Shepherd of Hermas*. Journal for the Study of the Pseudepigrapha Supplement Series 17. Sheffield: Sheffield Academic Press.

Ingebretsen, Edward J. 1996. *Maps of Heaven, Maps of Hell: Religious Terror as Memory from the Puritans to Stephen King*. Armonk, NY: M. E. Sharpe.

Isenberg, Noah. 1999. "Culture in Ruins: Walter Benjamin's Memories." In *Between Redemption and Doom: The Strains of German-Jewish Modernism*, 105–46. Lincoln: University of Nebraska Press.

Jennings, James, ed. 1992. *Race Politics and Economic Development: Community Perspectives*. London: Verso.

Jones, Kent. 2000. "P. T. Anderson's *Magnolia*." Review of *Magnolia*. *Film Comment* 36 (January/February): 39–40.

Kabasele Mukenge, André. 1999. "Relecture de Gn 4,1–16 dans le contexte Africain." In *Lectures et relectures de la Bible: Festschrift P.-M. Bogaert*, 421–41. Ed. J.-M. Auwers and A. Wénin. Leuven: Leuven University Press.

Kant, Immanuel. 2000 [1790]. *Critique of the Power of Judgment*. Ed. Paul Guyer. Trans. Paul Guyer and Eric Matthews. Cambridge: Cambridge University Press.

Kazaz, Harun. 1998. "Bombing of Iraq." *Turkish Daily News*, December 19, www.turkishdailynews.com/old_editions/12_19_98/harun.HTM.

Keenan, Thomas. 1993. "The Point is to (Ex)Change It: Reading *Capital*, Rhetorically." In *Fetishism and Cultural Discourse*, ed. Emily Apter and William Pietz, 152–85. Ithaca, NY: Cornell University Press.

Keener, Craig S. 1999. *A Commentary on the Gospel of Matthew*. Grand Rapids, MI: Eerdmans.

Keil, Charles. 1992. "*From the Manger to the Cross:* The New Testament Narrative and the Question of Stylistic Retardation." In *Une invention du diable? Cinéma des premiers temps et religion*, ed. Roland Cosandey, André Gaudreault, and Tom Gunning, 112–20. Sainte-Foy: Les presses de l'Université Laval; Lausanne: Éditions payot Lausanne.

Keller, Catherine. 1996. *Apocalypse Now and Then: A Feminist Guide to the End of the World*. Boston: Beacon.

———. 1997. "The Breast, the Apocalypse, and the Colonial Journey." In *The Year 2000: Essays on the End*, Charles B. Strozier and Michael Flynn, 42–58. New York: New York University Press.

Kelso, Julie. 2002. "Gazing at Impotence in Henry King's *David and Bathsheba*." In *Screening Scripture: Intertextual Connections Between Scripture and Film*, ed. George Aichele and Richard Walsh, 155–84. Harrisburg, PA: Trinity International Press.

Kenney, Michael. 1992. "What Happened in the Gulf, and Was It 'Just War?'" *Boston Globe*, March 17, 57.

Kenny, Glen. 2001. "Extreme Cinema: The 25 Most Dangerous Movies Ever Made." *Premiere* 14 (February): 92–97.

Kermode, Frank. 1967. *The Sense of an Ending: Studies in the Theory of Fiction*. Oxford: Oxford University Press.

Kerness, Bonnie. 2001. "Breeding Monsters." *Fortune News* 36 (summer): 9–12, www.fortunesociety.org.

Klawans, Stuart. 1999a. "Desert Storm 'n' Drang." Review of *Three Kings*. *Nation* 269, no. 13 (October 25): 42–44.

———. 1999b. "Rough and Tumble: *Fight Club, Boys Don't Cry, The City*." *Nation* 269, no. 15 (November 8): 32–36.

Kojève, Alexandre. 1969 [1947]. *Introduction to the Reading of Hegel: Lectures on The Phenomenology of Spirit, Assembled by Raymond Queneau*. Trans. James H. Nichols, Jr. Ithaca, NY: Cornell University Press.

Koosed, Jennifer L., and Tod Linafelt. 1996. "How the West Was Not One: Delilah Deconstructs the Western." *Semeia* 74:167–81.

Kreitzer, L. Joseph. 1994. *The Old Testament in Fiction and Film: On Reversing the Hermeneutical Flow*. Sheffield: Sheffield Academic Press.

Kroner, Richard. 1948. Introduction to *Early Theological Writings*, by G. W. F. Hegel. Chicago: University of Chicago Press.

Kugel, James. 1990. "Cain and Abel in Fact and Fable: Genesis 4:1–16." In *Hebrew Bible or Old Testament: Studying the Bible in Judaism and Christianity*, 167–90. Notre Dame, IN: University of Notre Dame Press.

Kuhn, Annette. 1985. *The Power of the Image*. London: Routledge and Kegan Paul.

Lacan, Jacques. 1977 [1966]. *Écrits: A Selection*. Trans. Alan Sheridan. New York: W. W. Norton.

———. 1978 [1973]. *The Seminar of Jacques Lacan*. Ed. Jacques-Alain Miller. Trans. Alan Sheridan. Bk. XI, *The Four Fundamental Concepts of Psychoanalysis*. New York: W. W. Norton.

———. 1985 [1975]. "A Love Letter." In *Feminine Sexuality: Jacques Lacan and the École Freudienne*, ed. Juliet Mitchell and Jacqueline Rose, 149–61. New York: W. W. Norton.

Laclau, Ernesto, and Chantal Mouffe. 1985. *Hegemony and Socialist Strategy: Toward a Radical Democratic Politics*. London: Verso.

Laplanche, J., and J.-B. Pontalis. 1973 [1967]. *The Language of Psycho-analysis*. Trans. Donald Nicholson-Smith. New York: W. W. Norton.

Lefort, Claude. 1988 [1986]. *Democracy and Political Theory*. Trans. David Macey. Cambridge: Polity Press.

Leigh, Danny. 2000. "Boy Wonder." Review of *Boys Don't Cry*. *Sight and Sound* 10 (March): 18–20.

Levine, Baruch A. 1993. *Numbers 1–20: A New Translation with Introduction and Commentary*. Anchor Bible. New York: Doubleday.

Lewins, Frank. 1995. *Transsexualism in Society*. South Melbourne: MacMillan Education Australia.

Leyland, Matthew. 2001. "Remember the Titans." Review of *Remember the Titans*. *Sight and Sound* 4:55.

Long, Burke O. 1999. "Reading the Land: Holy Land as Text of Witness." In *The Labour of Reading: Desire, Alienation, and Biblical Interpretation*, ed. Fiona Black, Roland Boer, and Erin Runions, 141–60. Semeia Studies 36. Atlanta: Scholars Press.

Lorber, Judith. 1994. *Paradoxes of Gender*. New Haven, CT: Yale University Press.

Lowe, Walter. 1999. "The Bitterness of Cain: (Post)modernity's Flight from Determinacy." In *Postmodern Philosophy and Christian Thought*, ed. Merold Westphal, 109–121. Bloomington: Indiana University Press.

Luz, Ulrich. 1990 [1985]. *Matthew 1–7: A Commentary*. Trans. Wilhelm C. Linss. Edinburgh: T & T Clark.

Lyotard, Jean-François. 1994 [1991]. *Lessons on the Analytic of the Sublime: (Kant's "Critique of Judgment," §§23–29)*. Trans. Elizabeth Rottenberg. Stanford, CA: Stanford University Press.

MacCannell, Juliet Flower. 2000. *The Hysteric's Guide to the Future Female Subject*. Minneapolis: University of Minnesota Press.

Magdalene, F. Rachel. 1995. "Ancient Near Eastern Treaty-Curses and the Ultimate Texts of Terror: A Study of the Language of Divine Sexual Abuse in the

Prophetic Corpus." In *A Feminist Companion to the Latter Prophets*, ed. Athalya Brenner, 326–53. Sheffield: Sheffield Academic Press.

Magonet, Jonathan. 1982. "The Korah Rebellion." *Journal for the Study of the Old Testament* 24:3–25.

Marable, Manning. 1983. *How Capitalism Underdeveloped Black America*. Boston: South End.

Marconot, Jean-Marie. 1996. *Le héros et l'héroïne bibliques dans la culture*. Actes du colloque de Montpellier les 22 et 23 novembre 1996. Montpellier: Université Paul-Valéry.

Marks, Laura U. 1991. "Tie a Yellow Ribbon Around Me: Masochism, Militarism, and the Gulf War on TV." *Camera Obscura: A Journal of Feminism, Culture, and Media* 27 (September): 55–74.

———. 1994. "A Deleuzian Politics of Hybrid Cinema." *Screen* 35, no. 3:244–64.

———. 2000. *The Skin of the Film: Intercultural Cinema, Embodiment, and the Senses*. Durham, NC: Duke University Press.

Marsh, Clive, and Gay Ortiz, eds. 1998. *Explorations in Theology and Film: Movies and Meaning*. Oxford: Blackwell.

Martin, Joel W., and Conrad E. Ostwalt, eds. 1995. *Screening the Sacred: Religion, Myth and Ideology in Popular American Film*. Boulder, CO: Westview.

Marx, Karl. 1977 [1867]. *Capital*. Vol. 1. Trans. Ben Fowkes. New York: Random House.

May, John R., ed. 1997. *New Image of Religious Film*. Kansas City: Sheed and Ward.

May, John R. and Michael Bird, eds. 1982. *Religion in Film*. Knoxville: University of Tennessee Press.

Mays, James Luther. 1976. *Micah: A Commentary*. Old Testament Library. Philadelphia: Westminster.

McCarthy, Colman. 1991. "Gung-Ho for God and Guns?" *Washington Post*, February 10, F2.

McEntire, Mark. 2000. "Cain and Abel in Africa: An Ethiopian Case Study in Competing Hermeneutics." In *The Bible In Africa: Transactions, Trajectories, and Trends*, ed. Gerald O. West and Musa W. Dube, 248–59. Leiden: Brill.

McFadden, Robert D. 2001. "Police Dept. Rejects Punishment for Officers in Diallo Shooting." *New York Times*, April 27, A1, B6.

McKane, William. 1995. "Micah 1, 2–7." Zeitschrift für die alttestamentliche Wissenschaft 107:420–34.

McLeod, Douglas M., William P. Eveland, Jr., and Nancy Signorielli. 1994. "Conflict and Public Opinion: Rallying Effects of the Persian Gulf War." *Journalism Quarterly* 71, no. 1 (spring): 20–31.

McNutt, Paula M. 1999. "In the Shadow of Cain." *Semeia* 87:45–64.

Mellinkoff, Ruth. 1981. *The Mark of Cain*. Berkeley: University of California Press.

Metz, Christian. 1982 [1977]. *The Imaginary Signifier: Psychoanalysis and Cinema*. Trans. Celia Britton, Annwyl Williams, Ben Brewster, and Alfred Guzzetti. Bloomington: Indiana University Press.

Micale, Mark S. 1995. *Approaching Hysteria: Disease and Its Interpretations*. Princeton, NJ: Princeton University Press.

Milbank, John. 1992. "'I Will Gasp and Pant': Deutero-Isaiah and the Birth of the Suffering Subject: A Response to Norman K. Gottwald, 'Social Class and Ideology in Isaiah 40–55.'" *Semeia* 59:61–71.

Miles, Margaret R. 1996. *Seeing and Believing: Religion and Values in the Movies.* Boston: Beacon.

Milgrom, Jacob. 1990. *Numbers: The Traditional Hebrew Text with the New JPS Translation Commentary.* Jewish Publication Society Torah Commentary. Philadelphia: The Jewish Publication Society.

Milhou, Alain. 1999. "Apocalypticism in Central and South American Colonialism." In *The Encyclopedia of Apocalypticism,* ed. Stephen J. Stein. Vol. 3, *Apocalypticism in the Modern Period and the Contemporary Age,* 3–35. New York: Continuum.

Miller, Jacques-Alain. 1978. "Suture (Elements of the Logic of the Signifier)." *Screen* 18, no. 4:24–34

Modleski, Tania. 1990. *Loving with a Vengeance: Mass-Produced Fantasies for Women.* New York: Routledge.

Monder, Eric. 1999. "Light it Up." Review of *Light it Up. Film Journal International,* www.filmjournal.com/PublSystem/objects/MovieCommon/_detail.cfm/StructID/57298389.

Moore, Stephen D. 1996. *God's Gym: Divine Male Bodies of the Bible.* New York: Routledge.

———. 1998a. "Between Birmingham and Jerusalem: Cultural Studies and Biblical Studies." *Semeia* 82:1–32.

———, ed. 1998b. *In Search of the Present: The Bible through Cultural Studies.* Semeia 82. Atlanta: Society of Biblical Literature.

Morris, Jan. 1974. *Conundrum.* New York: Harcourt Brace Jovanovich.

Mosala, Itumeleng J. 1989. *Biblical Hermeneutics and Black Theology in South Africa.* Grand Rapids, MI: Eerdmans.

Moss, Donald and Lynne Zeavin. 2000. "Film Review Essay: The Real Thing? Some Thoughts on *Boys Don't Cry.*" *International Journal of Psychoanalysis* 81:1227–30.

Mounce, Robert H. 1999. *The Book of Revelation.* Rev. ed. Grand Rapids, MI: Eerdmans.

Muhammad, Erika. 2000. "Independent Means." *Ms. Magazine* 10 (February/March): 75–77.

Mulvey, Laura. 1996. *Fetishism and Curiosity.* Bloomington: Indiana University Press.

Muska, Susan and Greta Olafsdottir. 1998. *The Brandon Teena Story.* Videorecording, 90 min. New York: Zeitgeist Films. Documentary.

Neuhaus, Richard John. 1991. "Just War and this War." *Wall Street Journal,* January 29, A18.

Newhagen, John E. 1994a. "The Relationship between Censorship and the Emotional and Critical Tone of Television News Coverage of the Persian Gulf War." *Journalism Quarterly* 71, no. 1 (spring): 32–42.

———. 1994b. "Effects of Televised Government Censorship Disclaimers on Memory and Thought Elaboration During the Gulf War." *Journal of Broadcasting and Electronic Media* 38, no. 3:339–49.

Nguyen, Tram. 2002. "Detained or Disappeared?" *ColorLines* 5, no. 2 (summer): 4–7.

Niva, Steve. 1991. "The Battle is Joined." In *Beyond the Storm: A Gulf Crisis Reader*, ed. Phyllis Bennis and Michel Moushabeck, 55–71. New York: Olive Branch.

Nolan, Brian M. 1992. "Rooting the Davidic Son of God of Matthew 1–2 in the Experience of the Evangelist's Attitude." *Estudios Bíblicos* 59:149–56.

Norris, Christopher. 1992. *Uncritical Theory: Postmodernism, Intellectuals, and the Gulf War*. Amherst: University of Massachusetts Press.

Noth, Martin. 1968. *Numbers: A Commentary*. Philadelphia: Westminster.

Nye, Robert A. 1993. "The Medical Origins of Sexual Fetishism." In *Fetishism and Cultural Discourse*, ed. Emily Apter and William Pietz, 13–30. Ithaca, NY: Cornell University Press.

O'Leary, Stephen. 1994. *Arguing the Apocalypse: A Theory of Millennial Rhetoric*. Oxford: Oxford University Press.

Ogilvie, Clare. 1997. "Up In Smoke and All On Video." *Vancouver (B.C.) Province*, January 31 (http://sisis.nativeweb.org/court/jan3197.html).

Olsen, Mark. 2000. "Singing in the Rain." Review of *Magnolia*. *Sight and Sound* (March): 26–28.

Olson, Dennis T. 1996. *Numbers*. Interpretation: A Bible Commentary for Teaching. Louisville: John Knox Press.

Ostwalt, Conrad E. 1995. "Hollywood and Armageddon: Apocalyptic Themes in Recent Cinematic Presentation." In *Screening the Sacred: Religion, Myth and Ideology in Popular American Film*, ed. Joel W. Martin and Conrad E. Ostwalt, 55–63. Boulder, CO: Westview.

Oudart, Jean-Pierre. 1978. "Cinema and Suture." *Screen* 18, no. 4:35–47.

Pan, Zhongdang, Ronald E. Ostman, Patricia Moy, and Paula Reynolds. 1994. "News Media Exposure and its Learning Effects during the Persian Gulf War." *Journalism Quarterly* 71, no. 1 (spring): 7–19.

Parenti, Christian. 1999. *Lockdown America: Police and Prisons in the Age of Crisis*. London: Verso.

Patte, Daniel. 1987. *The Gospel According to Matthew: A Structural Commentary on Matthew's Faith*. Philadelphia: Fortress.

Paul, Maarten J. 1996. "Genesis 4:17–24: A Case-Study in Eisegesis." *Tyndale Bulletin* 47, no. 1:143–62.

Pellegrini, Ann. 1997. *Performance Anxieties: Staging Psychoanalysis, Staging Race*. New York: Routledge.

Pesch, Rudolf. 1994. "'He Will Be Called a Nazorean': Messianic Exegesis in Matthew 1–2." In *The Gospels and the Scriptures of Israel*, ed. Stanley E. Porter, 129–78. Journal for the Study of the Old Testament Supplement Series 104. Studies in Scripture in Early Judaism and Christianity 3. Sheffield: Sheffield Academic Press.

Phelan, Peggy. 1993. "The Golden Apple: Jennie Livingston's *Paris Is Burning*." In *Unmarked: The Politics of Performance*, 93–111. New York: Routledge.

Pierce, Kimberly. 2000a. "Brandon Goes to Hollywood." *The Advocate*, March 28, www.advocate.com/html/stories/808/808_cvr_peirce.asp.

———. 2000b. "Putting Teena Brandon's Story on Film: An Interview by Francesca Miller." *Gay and Lesbian Review World Wide* 7 (fall): 39–40.

Pietz, William. 1993. "Fetishism and Materialism: The Limits of Theory in Marx." In *Fetishism and Cultural Discourse*, ed. Emily Apter and William Pietz, 119–51. Ithaca, NY: Cornell University Press.

Pippin, Tina. 1992. *Death and Desire: The Rhetoric of Gender in the Apocalypse of John*. Literary Currents in Biblical Interpretation. Louisville, KY: Westminster/ John Knox.

———. 1999. *Apocalyptic Bodies: The Biblical End of the World in Text and Image*. New York: Routledge.

———. 2002. "Of Gods and Demons: Blood Sacrifice and Eternal Life in *Dracula* and the Apocalypse of John." In *Screening Scripture: Intertextual Connections Between Scripture and Film*, ed. George Aichele and Richard Walsh, 24–41. Harrisburg, PA: Trinity International Press.

Prior, Michael. 1999. "The Bible and the Redeeming Idea of Colonialism." *Studies in World Christianity* 5:129–55.

Prison Activist Resource Center. 2002. www.prisonactivist.com.

Probyn, Elspeth. 1997. "New Traditionalism and Post-Feminism: TV Does the Home." In *Feminist Television Criticism: A Reader*, ed. Charlotte Brunsdon, Julie D'Acci, and Lynn Spigel, 126–37. Oxford: Clarendon.

Prosser, Jay. 1998. *Second Skins: The Body Narratives of Transsexuality*. New York: Columbia University Press.

Quinby, Lee. 1994. *Anti-Apocalypse: Exercises in Genealogical Criticism*. Minneapolis: University of Minnesota Press.

Quinones, Ricardo J. 1991. *The Changes of Cain: Violence and the Lost Brother in Cain and Abel Literature*. Princeton, NJ: Princeton University Press.

Rabinbach, Anson. 1985. "Between Enlightenment and Apocalypse: Benjamin, Bloch and Modern German Jewish Messianism." *New German Critique* 34 (winter): 78–124.

Rains, Linsey. 2000. "Narrative Functions and Agency of Nondiegetic Film Music in Contemporary Avant-Garde Cinema." Honors thesis, McGill University, Montréal.

Raynauld, Isabelle. 1992. "Les scénarios de la Passion selon Pathé (1902–1914)." In *Une invention du diable? Cinéma des premiers temps et religion*, ed. Roland Cosandey, André Gaudreault, and Tom Gunning, 131–41. Sainte-Foy: Les presses de l'Université Laval; Lausanne: Éditions payot Lausanne.

Roane, Kit R. 1999. "3 of the Officers Were Involved in Shootings in the Last 2 Years." *New York Times*, February 5, B5.

Rosario, Vernon A. 2000. "Transgenderism Comes of Age." *Gay and Lesbian Review Worldwide* 7 (fall): 31–33.

Rosenberg, Joel. 1998. "What the Bible and Old Movies Have in Common." *Biblical Interpretation* 6:266–91.

Rothman, William. 1976. "Against 'The System of Suture.'" In vol. 1 of *Movies and Method: An Anthology*, ed. Bill Nichols, 451–59. Berkeley: University of California Press.

Rowland, Christopher C. 1994. "Revelation." In *The New Interpreter's Bible.* Vol. 12. Nashville: Abingdon.

Rowlett, Lori L. 2000. "Disney's Pocahontas and Joshua's Rahab in Postcolonial Perspective." In *Culture, Entertainment and the Bible,* ed. George Aichele, 66–75. Sheffield: Sheffield Academic Press.

Runions, Erin. 2001a. "Called to Do Justice? A Bhabhian Reading of Micah 5 and 6:1–8." In *Postmodern Interpretations: A Reader,* ed. A. K. M. Adam, 153–64. St. Louis: Chalice.

———. 2001b. "Violence and the Economy of Desire in Ezekiel 16.1–45." In *A Feminist Companion to Daniel and the Prophets,* ed. Athalya Brenner, 156–69. Feminist Companion to the Bible, Second Series. Sheffield: Sheffield Academic Press.

———. 2001c. *Changing Subjects: Gender, Nation and Future in Micah.* Playing the Texts 7. London: Sheffield Academic Press.

Russell, David O. 1999. "Questions for David O. Russell: Love and Rockets: Interview with David O. Russell." By Lynn Hirschberg. *New York Times Magazine,* October 3, 6, 23.

Russell, Katheryn K. 2000. "What Did I Do to Be So Black and Blue?" In *Police Brutality: An Anthology,* ed. Jill Nelson, 135–48. New York: W. W. Norton.

Ryan, Sheila. 1991. "Countdown for a Decade: The U.S. Build-Up for War in the Gulf." In *Beyond the Storm: A Gulf Crisis Reader,* ed. Phyllis Bennis and Michel Moushabeck, 88–90. New York: Olive Branch.

Safety Orange. Prod. and dir. Jim Davis and Juliana Fredman. Videotape. New York.

Said, Edward W. 1988. "Michael Walzer's *Exodus and Revolution:* A Canaanite Reading." In *Blaming the Victims: Spurious Scholarship and the Palestinian Question,* ed. Edward W. Said and Christopher Hitchens, 161–78. London: Verso.

Sakenfeld, Katharine Doob. 1995. *Journeying with God: A Commentary on the Book of Numbers.* International Theological Commentary. Grand Rapids, MI: Eerdmans.

Sanchez, Romeo. 2001. "High Tech Dungeons." *Fortune News* 36 (summer): 20–21, www.fortunesociety.org.

Sanders, Theresa. 2002. *Celluloid Saints: Images of Sanctity in Film.* Macon, GA: Mercer University Press.

Sartre, Jean-Paul. 1991 [1985]. *Critique of Dialectical Reason.* Ed. Arlette Elkaïm-Sartre. Trans. Quintin Hoare. Vol. 2 (unfinished), *The Intelligibility of History.* London: Verso.

Savitch, H.V. 1978. "Black Cities/White Suburbs: Domestic Colonialism as an Interpretive Idea." In *Urban Black Politics,* ed. John R. Howard and Robert C. Smith, 118–34. The Annals of the American Academy of Political and Social Science 439. Philadelphia: American Academy of Political and Social Science.

Schickel, Richard. 1999. "Unconventional Warfare." Review of *Three Kings. Time* 154, no. 14 (October 4): 92–93.

———. 2000. "Fumbled: A Drama of Football and Race Undone by Clichés." Review of *Remember the Titans. Time* 156, no. 15 (October 9): 111.

Schiraldi, Vincent. 2000. "Trading Classrooms for Cellblocks." *Fortune News* 35 (winter): 10–11, www.fortunesociety.org.

Schor, Naomi. 1993. "Fetishism and its Ironies." In *Fetishism and Cultural Discourse*, ed. Emily Apter and William Pietz, 92–100. Ithaca, NY: Cornell University Press.

Scott, Bernard Brandon. 1994. *Hollywood Dreams and Biblical Stories*. Minneapolis: Fortress.

Scott, J. M. 2001. "Korah and Qumran." In *The Bible at Qumran: Text, Shape and Interpretation*, ed. P. W. Flint and Tae-Hun Kim, 182–202. Studies in the Dead Sea Scrolls and Related Literature. Grand Rapids, MI: Eerdmans.

Screech, M. A. 1978. "The Magi and the Star (Matthew 2)." *Histoire de l'exégèse au XVIe siècle: Textes du colloque international tenu à Genève en 1976*, ed. Olivier Fatio and Pierre Fraenkel, 385–409. Genève: Librairie Droz.

Sedgwick, Eve Kosofsky. 1993. "Queer Performativity: Henry James's *The Art of the Novel*." *GLQ: A Journal of Lesbian and Gay Studies* 1:1–16.

Segovia, Fernando F. 1995. "Cultural Studies and Contemporary Biblical Criticism: Ideological Criticism as a Mode of Discourse." In *Reading from this Place*. Vol. 2, *Social Location and Biblical Interpretation in Global Perspective*, ed. Fernando F. Segovia and Mary Ann Tolbert, 1–19. Minneapolis: Fortress.

———. 2000. *Decolonizing Biblical Studies: A View from the Margins*. Maryknoll, NY: Orbis.

Shakur, Assata. 1987. *Assata: An Autobiography*. Chicago: Lawrence Hill Books.

Sherwood, Yvonne. 1996. *The Prostitute and the Prophet: Hosea's Marriage in Literary-Theoretical Perspective*. Journal for the Study of the Old Testament Supplement Series 212. Gender, Culture, Theory 2. Sheffield: Sheffield Academic Press.

Shields, Mary E. 1998. "Multiple Exposures: Body Rhetoric and Gender Characterization in Ezekiel 16." *Journal of Feminist Studies in Religion* 14:5–18.

———. 2001. "Identity and Power/Gender and Violence in Ezekiel 23." In *Postmodern Interpretations: A Reader*, ed. A. K. M. Adam, 19–52. St. Louis: Chalice.

Showalter, Elaine. 1997. *Hystories: Hysterical Epidemics and Modern Culture*. New York: Columbia University Press.

Silverman, Kaja. 1996. *The Threshold of the Visible World*. New York: Routledge.

Singh, Amrijit, and Peter Schmidt. 2000. "On the Borders between U.S. Studies and Postcolonial Theory." In *Postcolonial Theory and the United States: Race, Ethnicity, and Literature*, ed. Amrijit Singh and Peter Schmidt, 1–69. Jackson: University Press of Mississippi.

Sippi, Diane. 2001. "Tomorrow is My Birthday: Placing Apocalypse in Millennial Cinema." *CineAction* 53:3–10.

Smith, Hedrick, ed. 1992. *The Media and the Gulf War*. Washington, D.C.: Seven Locks.

Smith, Paul. 1988. *Discerning the Subject*. Theory and History of Literature 55. Minneapolis: University of Minnesota Press.

Smolinski, Reiner. 1999. "Apocalypticism in Colonial North America." In *The Encyclopedia of Apocalypticism*, ed. Stephen J. Stein. Vol. 3, *Apocalypticism in the Modern Period and the Contemporary Age*, 36–71. New York: Continuum.

Smoller, Laura A. 2000. "Of Earthquakes, Hail, Frogs, and Geography: Plague and the Investigation of Apocalypse in the Later Middle Ages." In *Last Things: Death and the Apocalypse in the Middle Ages*, ed. Caroline Walker Bynum and Paul Freedman, 156–87. Philadelphia: University of Pennsylvania Press.

Snaith, N. H. 1967. *Leviticus and Numbers*. The Century Bible. London: Nelson.

Spigel, Lynn. 1997. "The Suburban Home Companion: Television and the Neighbourhood Ideal in Post-War America." In *Feminist Television Criticism: A Reader*, ed. Charlotte Brunsdon, Julie D'Acci, and Lynn Spigel, 211–34. Oxford: Clarendon.

Spivak, Gayatri. 1993. *Outside in the Teaching Machine*. London: Routledge.

Splitting the Sky Hill, John. 1998. Public Lecture. Montréal, Québec, February 14.

Squire, Corinne. 1997. "Empowering Women? The *Oprah Winfrey Show*." In *Feminist Television Criticism: A Reader*, ed. Charlotte Brunsdon, Julie D'Acci, and Lynn Spigel, 98–113. Oxford: Clarendon.

Stacey, Jackie. 1994. *Star Gazing: Hollywood Cinema and Female Spectatorship*. London: Routledge.

———. 1999 [1991]. "Feminine Fascinations: Forms of Identification in Star-Audience Relations." In *Feminist Film Theory: A Reader*, ed. Sue Thornham, 196–209. New York: New York University Press.

Staley, Jeffery L. 2002. "Meeting Patch Again for the First Time: Purity and Compassion in Marcus Borg, the Gospel of Mark, and *Patch Adams*." In *Screening Scripture: Intertextual Connections Between Scripture and Film*, ed. George Aichele and Richard Walsh, 213–28. Harrisburg, PA: Trinity International Press.

Stiebert, Johanna. 2000. "Shame and Prophecy: Approaches Past and Present." *Biblical Interpretation* 8:255–75.

Stolen Lives Project. 1999. *Stolen Lives: Killed by Law Enforcement*. New York: Stolen Lives Project.

Storey, John. 1996. *Cultural Studies and the Study of Popular Culture: Theories and Methods*. Edinburgh: Edinburgh University Press.

Studlar, Gaylyn. 1985. "Masochism and the Perverse Pleasures of the Cinema." In *Movies and Methods: An Anthology*, ed. Bill Nichols, 602–21. Vol. 2. Berkeley: University of California Press.

Taylor, Mark C. 1987. *Altarity*. Chicago: University of Chicago Press.

Thompson, Erica and Jan Susler. 1996. "Supermax Prisons: High-Tech Dungeons and Modern-Day Torture." In *Criminal Injustice: Confronting the Prison Crisis*, ed. Elihu Rosenblatt, 303–7. Boston: South End Press.

Travers, Peter. 1999. "Boys Don't Cry." Review of *Boys Don't Cry*. *Rolling Stone* 824 (October 28): 114.

———. 2000. "Remember the Titans." Review of *Remember the Titans*. *Rolling Stone* 852 (October 26): 122.

Tuleja, Tad. 1994. "Closing the Circle: Yellow Ribbons and the Redemption of the Past." *Journal of American Culture* 17, no. 1:23–33.

Turan, Kenneth. 1995. "Paris Is Burning." In *Flesh and Blood: The National Society of Film Critics on Sex, Violence and Censorship*, ed. Peter Keough, 122–25. San Francisco: Mercury House.

Tyler, Carole-Anne. 1991. "Boys Will be Girls: The Politics of Gay Drag." In *Inside/Out: Lesbian Theories, Gay Theories*, ed. Diana Fuss, 32–70. New York: Routledge.

Udovitch, Mim. 2000. "The Epic Obsessions of Paul Thomas Anderson." *Rolling Stone* 833 (February 3): 46–49, 69.

Valade, Claire. 2000. "Magnolia: Orageux en fin de journée." Review of *Magnolia*. *La Revue de séquences* 207 (Mars/Avril): 207–8.

van Wolde, Ellen. 1991. "The Story of Cain and Abel: A Narrative Study." *Journal for the Study of the Old Testament* 52:25–41.

Vander Stichele, Caroline. 2000. "Apocalypse, Art and Abjection: Images of the Great Whore." In *Culture, Entertainment and the Bible*, ed. George Aichele, 124–38. Sheffield: Sheffield Academic Press.

Veith, Ilza. 1965. *Hysteria: The History of a Disease*. Phoenix Books. Chicago: University of Chicago Press.

Via, Dan O. 1978. "Narrative World and Ethical Response: The Marvelous and Righteousness in Matthew 1–2." *Semeia* 12:123–45.

Waldman, Amy. 2000. "The Crucial Defense Element: the Judge's Instruction." *New York Times*, February 26, B6.

Warrior, Robert Allen. 1991. "A Native American Perspective: Canaanites, Cowboys, and Indians." In *Voices from the Margin: Interpreting the Bible in the Third World*, ed. R. S. Sugirtharajah, 287–95. Maryknoll, NY: Orbis.

Weems, Renita J. 1995. *Battered Love: Marriage, Sex and Violence in the Hebrew Prophets*. Minneapolis: Fortress.

Weinstein, Corey. 2001. "So Its Official, It's Torture . . . So What?" *Fortune News* 36 (summer): 14–16, www.fortunesociety.org.

Weisenfeld, Judith. 1996. "For Rent, 'Cabin in the Sky': Race, Religion, and Representational Quagmires in American Film." *Semeia* 74:147–67.

———. 2000. " 'For the Cause of Mankind': The Bible, Racial Uplift, and Early Race Movies." In *African Americans and the Bible: Sacred Texts and Social Textures*, ed. Vincent L. Wimbush, 728–42. New York: Continuum.

Wenham, Gordon J. 1981. *Numbers: An Introduction and Commentary*. Tyndale Old Testament Commentaries. Downers Grove, IL: Inter-Varsity Press.

West, Gerald. 1990. "Reading 'The Text' and Reading 'Behind the Text': The 'Cain and Abel' Story in a Context of Liberation." In *Bible in Three Dimensions: Essays in Celebration of Forty Years of Biblical Studies in the University of Sheffield*, ed. David J. A. Clines, Stephen E. Fowl, and Stanley E. Porter, 299–320. Journal for the Study of the Old Testament Supplement Series 87. Sheffield: Sheffield Academic Press.

Westermann, Claus. 1985 [1974]. *Genesis 1–11: A Commentary*. Trans. John J. Scullion. S. J. Minneapolis: Augsburg.

Wevers, John W. 1969. *Ezekiel*. The Century Bible. London: Thomas Nelson and Sons.

Whittle, Stephen. 1996. "Gender Fucking or Fucking Gender? Current Cultural Contributions to Theories of Gender Blending." In *Blending Genders: Social Aspects of Cross-dressing and Sex-changing*, ed. Richard Ekins and Dave King, 196–214. New York: Routledge.

Wiesel, Elie. 1998. "Cain and Abel." *Bible Review* (February): 20–21.

Williams, Robert R. 1997. *Hegel's Ethic of Recognition*. Berkeley: University of California Press.

Wolff, Hans Walter. 1990 [1982]. *Micah: A Commentary*. Trans. Gary Stansell. Minneapolis: Ausburg.

Wrathall, John. 2000. "Three Kings." Review of *Three Kings*. *Sight and Sound* 3:54–55.

Zelizer, Barbie. 1992. "CNN, the Gulf War, and Journalistic Practice." *Journal of Communications* 42, no. 1 (winter): 66–81.

Zimmerli, Walther. 1979 [1969]. *A Commentary on the Book of the Prophet Ezekiel*. Vol. 1, *Chapters 1–24*. Trans. Ronald E. Clements. Hermeneia. Philadelphia: Fortress.

Žižek, Slavoj. 1989. *The Sublime Object of Ideology*. Phronesis. London: Verso.

——. 1991. *Looking Awry: An Introduction to Jacques Lacan through Popular Culture*. October Books. Cambridge, MA: MIT Press.

——. 1993. *Tarrying with the Negative: Kant, Hegel and the Critique of Ideology*. Durham, NC: Duke University Press.

——. 1997. *The Abyss of Freedom/Ages of the Word: An Essay by Slavoj Žižek with the Text of Schelling's* Die Weltalter *(second draft, 1813) in English Translation by Judith Norman*. Ann Arbor: University of Michigan Press.

——, ed. 1994. *Mapping Ideology*. London: Verso.

INDEX